On the Book of Psalms

50 YEARS OF PUBLISHING
1945-1995

On the Book of Psalms

Exploring the Prayers of Ancient Israel

NAHUM M. SARNA

SCHOCKEN BOOKS   NEW YORK

Library of Congress Cataloging-in-Publication Data

Sarna, Nahum M.
    [Songs of the heart]
    On the book of Psalms : exploring the prayers of ancient
Israel / Nahum M. Sarna.
        p.   cm.
    Originally published: Songs of the heart. 1st ed. New York :
Schocken Books, © 1993.
    Includes bibliographical references and index.
    ISBN 0-8052-1023-7
    1. Bible.   O.T.   Psalms—Criticism, interpretation, etc.
I. Title.
BS1430.2.S235   1995
223'.206—dc20   94-30375

Book designed by Timothy O'Keeffe

Manufactured in the United States of America

9 8 7 6 5 4 3 2 1

First Paperback Edition

for

MARVIN AND JUNE FOX

(Proverbs 18:24)

Contents

PREFACE

In 1966 I was invited to join a committee of translators then being formed by the Jewish Publication Society to produce a new translation in modern English of the Ketuvim, the Hagiographa, the third section of the Hebrew Bible. My colleagues were Professors Moshe Greenberg and Jonas C. Greenfield, as well as Rabbis Saul Leeman, Martin Rozenberg, and David Shapiro. Dr. Chaim Potok was the secretary of the committee. This endeavor was part of the ongoing translation project started in 1955. Our initial efforts were concentrated on the Book of Psalms, and the fruits of our labors were published in 1972.

Serving on the translation committee turned out to be one of the great experiences of my life. Apart from the collegial cooperation and congenial atmosphere that unfailingly prevailed at our sessions, the pooling of knowledge and expertise, the interchange of ideas and interpretations, the careful analysis of text and context—all made for intellectual enrichment and scholarly refinement. Many of the insights to be found in this study doubtless owe their inspiration to the erudition, ideas, and observations of my colleagues. To each and all of my co-translators I express my profound gratitude. However, I take sole responsibility for errors and shortcomings.

In the course of writing this book, I have found myself under obligation to several other individuals. First and foremost, I have incurred an immeasurable debt of gratitude to my wife, who heroically typed the entire manuscript and made numerous improvements. Professor Marvin Fox, with his usual thoroughness, kindly offered valuable critical comments and suggestions. David Sarna, Jonathan Sarna, and Ruth Langer all contributed most helpful observations. Professor Marc Brettler and Dr. Aaron Katchen generously rendered assistance. I am also much obliged to the staff of the libraries of Brandeis University and the Boston Hebrew College. I am most grateful to the Jewish Publication Society for permission to make use of its new translation of the Book of Psalms. Occasionally, however, I have departed from it. Last, but by no means least, Ms. Bonny Fetterman, Senior Editor of Schocken Books, deserves special thanks for urging me to undertake the present study, and for her constant interest and encouragement.

On the Book of Psalms

INTRODUCTION

In the Law and the Prophets, God reaches out to man. The initiative is His. The message is His. He communicates, we receive. Our God-given free will allows us to be receptive, to be accepting, to turn a deaf ear, to reject. In the Psalms, human beings reach out to God. The initiative is human. The language is human. We make an effort to communicate. He receives; He chooses to respond or not, according to His inscrutable wisdom. He gives his assent or withholds it.

In the Psalms, the human soul extends itself beyond its confining, sheltering, impermanent house of clay. It strives for contact with the Ultimate Source of all life. It gropes for an experience of the divine Presence. The biblical psalms are essentially a record of the human quest for God. Hence, the variety of forms in which the ancient psalmists expressed themselves, reflective of the diverse and changing moods that possessed them as they do all human beings. In short, the psalms constitute a revealing portrayal of the human condition. No wonder that they infuse and inform the basic patterns of both Jewish and Christian worship, give character and essence to their respective liturgies, and govern the life of prayer and spiritual activity of the individual and the congregation.

*   *   *

"Said Rabbi Yudan in the name of Rabbi Judah, 'Whatever David says in his book pertains to himself, to all Israel, and to all times.' "[1]

What this astute observation about the Psalter conveys is that each psalm is multifaceted; it yields several levels of interpretation. It may be understood as a personal statement, as a manifestation of the soul-life of an individual, or it may be construed as an expression of the concerns and the life of faith of the entire community. Its composition, grounded in a radically different era, is a product of a social and cultural milieu wholly at variance with our own; nevertheless, the message and teachings it communicates are always meaningful and relevant. The genius of the Book of Psalms lies in this, that while it is time-bound in origin, it is ever fresh and timely, and hence timeless. It speaks to each reader in a great variety of moods.

There is another aspect of the psalms which evoked a subtle rabbinic comment, even if, at first glance, it appears to be somewhat artlessly formulated. Accepting the notion that a dream experience can be reflective of the inner life of the dreamer, the rabbis of the talmudic period said, "He who sees the Book of Psalms in a dream may hope for piety."[2] The plain implication is that the psalms possess intrinsic value, in that they fulfill a didactic function. They are meant to be internalized. Diligent recitation and study of them is propaedeutic to a higher level of spirituality and piety; and piety, in the biblical view, is not solely individualistic, certainly not egotistical, self-righteous, or sanctimonious. Importantly, it finds expression in the quality of interpersonal relationships.

It is a sad state of affairs that our twentieth century secularized society—to its own deprivation—no longer relates to those vast spiritual, moral, and intellectual treasures of the Psalter that our ancestors so reverently and fondly cherished. It hardly knows how to pray anymore. This situation is particularly distressing and disturbingly paradoxical when it arises among the descendants of the people that gave the world the Book of Psalms.

4

A Jew from Yemen once told me how he celebrated his bar mitzvah back in the land of his birth. The family was desperately poor; there were no parties, no gifts, no excitement, no speeches. The boy simply went to the synagogue on the designated Sabbath morning and read the appropriate portion of the Torah with the traditional blessings before and after. But what left an indelible impression on him, the experience that continues to move him deeply even forty years later, was staying up all the previous night with his grandfather, and together reciting the entire Book of Psalms.

Anatoly Sharansky spent nearly nine terrible years of deprivation and suffering as a "prisoner of Zion" in Soviet prisons and labor camps. His "crime" consisted of wanting to leave the hell of the "workers' paradise" in order to migrate to the land of Israel. By his own testimony, during all the years of enforced isolation, oppressive loneliness, appalling misery, agonizing suffering, and unutterable anguish, it was the copy of the Hebrew Psalter that he kept with him that sustained his spirit, gave him the strength to endure his bitter fate, and imparted the courage to persevere in hope.

While he was incarcerated, his wife, Avital, accepted on his behalf an honorary Doctorate of Humane Letters from Yeshiva University in New York. On that occasion, she told the audience, "Anatoly has been educated to his Jewishness in a lonely cell in Chistopol prison where, locked alone with the Psalms of David, he found expression for his innermost feelings in the outpourings of the king of Israel thousands of years ago." When he was finally released, and arrived in Jerusalem, he was carried to the Western Wall by his friends and admirers still clasping in his hands his beloved Book of Psalms.[3]

A sorry contrast is presented by the following incident reported in the Israeli press.[4] Zalman Aranne, who twice served as Israel's Minister of Education, once told that during World War I, he was wounded by cannon fire and lay helpless and unattended on the battlefield, drenched in blood. Believing that his life was ebbing away, and true to the old adage that there are no atheists in foxholes, he felt a strong urge to pray or recite a psalm. In his youth in the Ukraine he had received a traditional Jewish education, and he still remembered what he had learned in the formative period of his life. Yet, he could not bring himself to utter the words because, he said, he had for many years abandoned the practice of Judaism, and he thought that praying in those circumstances would be hypocritical. When he recounted this experience to Mordecai Bar-On, then Chief Education Officer in Israel's Defense Forces, the latter responded with an experience of his own. He had found himself in a similar situation when he served during one of the wars forced upon Israel by Arab aggression. He, too, had wanted to pray, but he needed no effort to suppress the urge, because he had not the slightest idea what to say.

Now let me tell of an experience of my own. For three months in 1989, I was privileged to serve as Scholar-in-Residence in the Greater Washington, D.C. area, sponsored by the local Foundation for Jewish Studies. Among the many courses I taught was one on the Book of Psalms. This was attended largely by people in government service. At the final session, a participant approached me and said, "I have not stepped into a synagogue these past thirty years. I have always regarded this religious stuff as mumbo jumbo. Having attended your weekly classes in the psalms, I have come to realize that the material does, indeed, contain profound ideas of lasting worth. Thank you."

I thought I would share some of these worthwhile ideas with a wider audience in this present-day biblically deprived generation.

MUSIC AND WORSHIP

Music, vocal and instrumental, played a significant role in the organized institutionalized worship of ancient Israel. It was an accepted constituent of religious self-expression. Nevertheless, Israel differed from other cultures of the ancient world in that biblical traditions did not ascribe a divine origin to music. The traditions of the Book of Genesis view musical instruments as a purely human and secular innovation. They look upon music as one of the pillars of civilized society.

In the seventh natural-born generation on earth, the children of Lamech are said to have pioneered three major advances in human culture: these are pastoral nomadism, musical instruments— stringed and wind, and the metalworking arts.[5] These three pursuits seem to have been characteristic of Semitic tribes, for they are vividly portrayed in splendid wall paintings at a site called Beni Hasan in Middle Egypt. (See illustration below.) Here, on the east bank of the Nile, about 150 miles (240 km.) south of Cairo, are tombs cut into rock cliffs. On the walls of one of them, belonging to a nobleman named Khnumhotep III, ruler of one of the nomes, or provinces,

into which ancient Egypt was divided, is depicted a group of thirty-seven west Semitic nomadic tribesmen from central Transjordan, led by their chief, named Absha. They had come down to Egypt around the year 1890 B.C.E. to trade their wares. What interests us is that two of the donkeys in the pictures carry skin bellows, a sure indication of metalworking, and one of the tribesmen holds a stringed lyre.[6] This scene calls to mind the aforementioned biblical narrative. That text also records the birth of a daughter, named Naamah, to Lamech. No accomplishment is ascribed to her, but since it is rare for daughters to be mentioned in the genealogies of the Book of Genesis, it may be assumed that she was the subject of some well-known legend. An ancient Jewish tradition fills in the gap; it holds her to have been a professional singer of religious music.[7] This is of interest for two reasons: the underlying root of the name Naamah, in Arabic and Syriac and in some Hebrew texts,[8] means "to sing"; and the account recognizes the great antiquity and high prestige of vocal and instrumental music, which it regards as one of the most noteworthy achievements of the human race.

Instrumental and vocal music were common in the temples and palaces of Mesopotamia. Fine examples of harps and lyres have been excavated in the Sumerian city of Ur dating from the middle of the third millennium B.C.E. From Assyrian and Egyptian sources it has become known that in pre-Israelite times Canaan was famed as a center of music. The Canaanite–Hebrew term for the lyre—*kinnor*—passed into Egyptian and other languages. In Cyprus, the name of the god of the zither, "Cinyras," was derived from the name of the instrument. The Greeks revered him as a musician.[9] At Ugarit, modern Ras Shamra on the Syrian coast, a tablet turned up on which is inscribed a hymn to a goddess. It is equipped with a notational system which has now been deciphered, and which reveals a musical scale consisting of seven notes.[10] Another tablet from the same site lists temple personnel, among whom are "singers" and "cymbalists."[11]

By the time the Israelites settled in Canaan, a well-established tradition of vocal and instrumental music as an important mode of religious expression had long existed there and everywhere else in the Near East. The same was true of sacrificial practices as a major element of worship. Israel adopted both entities, but the two were carefully separated.

Another item worth noting is that, according to the narratives of the Book of Genesis, the urge to worship God is something innate in human beings, for the very first such act is ascribed to the first natural-born human beings on earth, Cain and Abel.[12] Theirs is a spontaneous, unprescribed, unlearned exercise, and it consists solely of ritual acts performed in total silence. The vocal aspect of worship is attributed to another generation, that of Enosh: "It was then that men began to invoke the Lord by name."[13] It may be coincidental that this development is said to have occurred in the days of Enosh, whose name in Hebrew carries with it intimations of human frailty. The uncertainty and insecurity of life, its fleeting nature, the sense of utter dependence upon a Higher Being—it is such that stir the human instinct to reach out to God, that kindle the desire to offer petition or to express gratitude.

What is so significant about these Genesis narratives is the total separation of sacrifice from prayer; that is, the ritual act is differentiated from the ritual word. This is in line with later developments in the religion of Israel, in which sacrifice and prayer continued to be two distinct and discrete domains. The elaborate rules and regulations for the sacrificial rituals as laid down in the Torah are all but silent about accompanying prayer or music, while the headings to the psalms have nothing to say about any sacrificial association. The sacrificial ritual is the responsibility and prerogative of the priesthood; the recitative and musical components of the official worship are a Levitical franchise.[14]

This extraordinary dissociation of sacrifice from prayer is in striking contrast to the practice of Israel's contemporaries in the ancient Near East, where the two institutions were inextricably linked. There,

> Ritual activities and accompanying prayers are of like im-
> portance and constitute the religious act; to interpret the
> prayers without regard to the rituals in order to obtain in-
> sight into the religious concepts they may reflect distorts
> the testimony.[15]

Those rituals are carefully described in a section at the end of the
Mesopotamian prayer. The biblical psalms never feature such information. Furthermore, whereas sacrifice is traced back to the
Mosaic period, the institution of Psalmody is ascribed to David in
post-exilic biblical literature, those Scriptures that derive from after
the return of the exiled Jews from Babylon. This careful and consistent separation of the two components of worship, the assigning
of diverse histories to the sacrifices and liturgical components,[16] may
be explained as a conscious effort to distinguish Israel's mode of
worship from contemporary pagan patterns.[17]

THE TITLES

Unlike many biblical works, the Psalter itself contains no general
title or introductory phrase by which it would become known. Nor
is it called after its initial word or words, as are the books of the
Pentateuch in Hebrew. Our English title "Psalms" came to us via
the Latin *Liber Psalmorum*, which, in turn, was derived from the
Greek word for "a song sung to a stringed instrument." Another
name by which the book is known is the Psalter. This too was received
from the Latin, which inherited it from *psalterion*, the Greek word
for "a stringed instrument." Both words were Greek renderings of
the Hebrew *mizmor*, which occurs in the headings of many psalms.
This term never recurs in the Bible outside of Psalms and it came
to be used for liturgical singing accompanied by a musician. In the
course of time, the Hebrew term took on an extended meaning and
was used for each of the compositions of the book irrespective of

whether or not the word *mizmor* appears in its heading.[18] It is this term that underlies the Greek, Latin, and English titles of the book. These titles reflect musical terminology, and pertain to a technical detail, to an externality.[19] The title preserved and popularized among Jews ever since rabbinic times relates to content, to the emotion of the worshiper, to the devotional function. The Hebrew designation *Sefer Tehillim*, often shortened to *Tehillim*, means, "The Book of Songs of Praise."[20] True, many psalms cannot be so categorized. Yet the fact that the root *hll*, "to praise," both in verbal and nominal forms, appears predominantly in the Book of Psalms and that "Hallelujah" occurs nowhere else in the Bible, must have been decisive in calling the book *Tehillim*.[21] That title also recognizes that the disinterested praise of God expresses the very essence of the act of worship, and its highest expression.

THE HISTORIC IMPORTANCE OF THE PSALTER

A measure of the seminal importance that the Book of Psalms held in the religious consciousness of Israel is indicated by some citations from early texts. The Hebrew Bible is composed of three parts: the Law *(torah)*, the Prophets *(nevi'im)*, and the Writings *(ketuvim)*. The third section comprises diverse genres of literature and carries no specific name that might identify its contents. For this reason, it is particularly significant that ancient sources that mention the tripartite division specify the Psalter. The oldest so far is one of the very important texts from Qumran entitled *Miktsat Ma'aseh Ha-Torah* (4QMMT), deriving from about 152 B.C.E.[22] This is a letter from the founders of the sect that settled at that site and is apparently addressed to the Temple establishment. It refers to "the Book of Moses, the books of the Prophets, and David, and the deeds of each generation." The Second Book of Maccabees 2:13, composed sometime between 78 and 63 B.C.E., tells that Nehemiah, who was governor of Judea in the days of Persian hegemony, "founded a library and collected the books about the kings and the prophets and the books of David . . ."[23] The Hellenistic Jewish philosopher, Philo of Alexandria, who died around the year 50 C.E., mentions "the Law, the Prophets, and the Psalms . . ."[24] Although Josephus, the Jewish historian of the Second Temple, who died not long after 100 C.E., had a different arrangement of the books of the Holy Scriptures, he also singles out "hymns of God," which undoubtedly means the Book of Psalms.[25] The same distinctive prominence appears in the late first century C.E. New Testament Book of Luke (24:44), which speaks of "the Law of Moses, the Prophets, and the Psalms."

All this provides eloquent and incontrovertible testimony to the extraordinary status and high prestige that the Psalter acquired in the course of the Second Temple period, which came to an end around the year 70 C.E. Thereafter, when the sacrificial ritual could no longer be observed and became defunct, prayer and the study of the Torah took its place as the highest forms of spiritual activity. The psalms came to enjoy a position of the foremost rank in private prayer and public worship.

THE PROBLEM OF SURVIVAL

How did the psalms come to survive? No, I do not mean the canonized collection known as the Book of Psalms—I mean the one hundred and fifty individual compositions that make up the collection. The question is not as strange as it sounds. Given the fate of the bulk of the literary productions of the ancient world, it is indeed remarkable how much of the writings of Israel during the biblical period managed to defeat the ravages of time.

Consider this: The Greeks enjoyed a vast and enthusiastic constituency throughout east and west. By the fifth century B.C.E., Greek culture had already begun to expand the territorial confines of the

Greek people. In the fourth century B.C.E., the extensive conquests of Alexander the Great accelerated their penetration of the Mediterranean coastlands and the lands of the east as far as Persia and India. The Greek colonies and the spread of the Greek language ensured the wide diffusion of Greek civilization. Greek books were in great demand everywhere. The immense library of Alexandria, Egypt, was founded; there, resident scholars collected the manuscripts of the Greek classics, and carefully edited and preserved them. Later, when imperial Rome succeeded Greece as the intellectual center of the world, Greek language and literature continued to enjoy the greatest prestige. The appreciation and promotion of Greek culture was a mark of status.

But what fate did history have in store for the works of the great dramatists of fifth century B.C.E. Athens, that brilliant era characterized by a remarkable intellectual awakening which many scholars regard as having inaugurated a new era in the history of human culture?[26] Aeschylus, the first of the three greatest Attic tragedians, is said to have composed ninety plays; yet only seven have survived intact, and mere fragments of just over seventy more remain. Sophocles, the favorite dramatist of Athens, wrote over one hundred tragedies. Again, only seven have come down to us in complete form. Euripides, whose popularity on the stage was sustained for the next six hundred years, was reputed to have written at least seventy-five plays or, according to some, as many as ninety-two. The scholars of ancient Alexandria had access to sixty-seven, but only eighteen dramas certainly composed by him are extant in full.

Comedy fared no better than tragedy. Only eleven of a known corpus of at least forty-four comedies written by Aristophanes, the greatest of the writers of Greek Old Comedy, are still available. Menander, regarded as the outstanding dramatist of Greek New Comedy, composed more than one hundred plays, the titles of some eighty of which are currently known. His only surviving complete drama was first published in 1959.

If Greek literature, in the most favorable of circumstances, had to bow to the harsh imperatives of human history, what fate might have been expected for the literary compositions of ancient Israel?[27] This people in its day was demographically insignificant and relatively unimportant as compared with the great civilizations of Egypt and Mesopotamia. The trials and tribulations that commonly visited most ancient literatures were aggravated and augmented in the case of Israel by additional afflictions peculiar to itself. There were the general hazards incurred by the limitations of hand copying, which imposed severe restrictions on the number of copies in circulation, not to mention the perils inherent in the use of perishable organic writing materials such as papyrus, parchment, and leather, as well as fragile potsherds and waxed wooden tablets. Then there was the location of the Land of Israel and its strategic importance and vulnerability. The main international highway of the ancient Near East, which led from Egypt to the other great river valley civilization of Mesopotamia, traversed the land. This meant that it was frequently invaded, with the resultant devastation of its cities and towns. Archives and manuscript collections often succumbed to the periodic barbarities of warring nations.

There were still other factors at work in ancient Israel, more subtle and pacific, though no less powerful, that encouraged the disappearance of literature. One was the change of script. When the Aramaic mode of writing, still basically in use among Jews, eclipsed and displaced the paleo-Hebrew script of earlier times, many works not newly copied and transcribed by scribes would fall into disuse and were doomed to oblivion. Finally, the evolution of a fixed, completed canon of sacred literature indubitably contributed to the demise of many an excluded work. The Hebrew Bible, in fact, has preserved the names of some twenty compositions once well known, and now lost.[28]

If the chances of survival for ancient literature were so slim, it is legitimate to inquire how it came about that some one hundred and fifty psalms managed to resist the destructive agencies fashioned by nature and history. What counterforces operated to sponsor preservation and ensure immortalization? We shall respond to this question a little later.

THE PSALMS COLLECTIONS

We have just mentioned "one hundred and fifty psalms." Interestingly, the Greek translation made by the Jews of Alexandria, Egypt, perhaps as early as the third century B.C.E., has the same number even though it has different internal divisions in the case of some compositions. For instance, it combines our Psalms 9 and 10 into a single composition and it does the same for Psalms 114 and 115. On the other hand, our Psalms 116 and 147 are each divided into two. Moreover, the Greek Psalter contains an additional psalm not present in the standard Hebrew Bibles. In the important Greek Bible codices, or manuscript books, this extra psalm bears a special caption noting that it is "outside the number."[29] This phenomenon would appear to endow the number one hundred and fifty with some special significance.

However, before we jump to conclusions, we must also note that this number of psalms is by no means a hard and fast rule. We possess plenty of evidence for variant psalm divisions that yielded differing numberings. Thus we know of 146 psalms, of a widespread tradition about 147 psalms "corresponding to the life-span of the patriarch Jacob," of 149,151, and even 159 compositions.[30]

In addition to the number of psalms, we must also consider another phenomenon. Our printed Hebrew Bibles (likewise, the English translations) divide the Psalter into five "books" of unequal length, each sequentially labeled. The closing of these divisions is marked by a doxology, or formula expressing praise of God. Thus, Psalm 41:14 reads,

> Blessed is the Lord, God of Israel, from eternity to
> eternity.
> Amen and Amen.

Psalm 72:18–20 reads,

> Blessed is the Lord God, God of Israel, who alone does
> wonderful things.
> Blessed is His glorious name for ever; His glory fills the
> whole earth.
> Amen and Amen.
> End of the prayers of David son of Jesse.

Psalm 89:53 reads,

> Blessed is the Lord forever.
> Amen and Amen.

Psalm 106:48 reads,

> Blessed is the Lord, God of Israel, from eternity to
> eternity
> Let all the people say, "Amen and Amen;
> Hallelujah."

Psalm 150, which closes the fifth division, most likely is meant to serve as the doxology for the entire Book of Psalms.

If we examine these formulae in relation to the psalms to which they are attached, we observe at once that they are not really an integral part of the compositions; they give every appearance of being additions. [31] Moreover, the term "Amen" is a congregational response in a liturgical context. Certainly, the doxologies are very ancient, for they were already present in the Hebrew text that was used by the Alexandrian Jewish translators of the Psalter into Greek sometime before the second half of the second century B.C.E. [32] However, that version does not carry the headings "Book One," "Book Two," and so forth. [33]

That the Psalter comprised several entities is proven by the citation from the Second Book of Maccabees given above, which refers to "the books of David." The fivefold division itself was known in early Christian circles. The third century scholar Hippolytus of Rome and the Church father and biblical scholar Jerome (c. 347–

420 C.E.) both mention it.[34] The same appears in Jewish sources. A passage in the Talmud reports that Rabbi Simeon son of Rabbi Judah Ha-Nasi (early 3rd cent. C.E.) once claimed that he had taught Rabbi Ḥiyyah "two of the pentateuchal divisions of the Book of Psalms."[35] In the Middle Ages, an eleventh- or twelfth-century C.E. work by Mishael ben Uzziel on the Masoretes, the Palestinian Jewish scholars who specialized in recording the traditional spellings, vowel accents, and idiosyncratic features of the biblical Hebrew text, designates each "book" by the term "scroll" (Hebrew *megillah*).[36]

The pentateuchal division of the Psalter is very strange, considering that, unlike the Torah, this work is not so large as to require transcription onto several scrolls for ease of handling and convenience of study.[37] The rabbis of talmudic times interpreted the arrangement as corresponding to that of the Torah. As they phrased it, "Moses gave Israel five books of the Torah, and David gave Israel five books of the Psalms."[38] This parallel between the literary legacies of Moses and David is implicit in the Book of Chronicles, which correlates Moses' institution of the sacrificial system with David's inauguration of the Temple liturgy.[39] It is quite possible, therefore, that the fivefold division of the Psalter was intentionally created with that parallel in mind. Further support for this conclusion may be sought in the special character of the collection of Psalms 90 through 150, which constitute "books" four and five. These compositions are distinguished by certain outstanding features which differentiate them from those of "books" one through three. For instance, they are overwhemingly psalms of praise and thanksgiving, and lack the variety of genres found in the preceding collections; the term "Hallelujah" only occurs here. There are three times as many psalms without headings as in all the rest of the Psalter; those with headings contain none of the musical type; and the otherwise commonly used technical terms *selah* and "To the leader"[40] are very rare. Moreover, unlike the other instances, part of the doxology at the end of psalm 106 (which marks off "book" four) may well be an integral part of the psalm, as 1 Chronicles 16:36 indicates.

All this suggests that the cluster of psalms numbered 90–150 was originally a single collection and was at some time artificially split in two in a conscious effort to create five "books," in imitation of the Torah.[41]

If this conjecture is correct, it points to a likely solution to the varying enumerations of the psalms. They have been influenced by different customs relating to the serialized weekly readings of the Torah in public worship. Dividing the Pentateuch into fifty-four sections called *parashiyyot*, the Babylonian Jewish communities completed the entire reading in the course of a single year. But the synagogues in Palestine preferred a shorter Sabbath service, and they took three years, and in some cases three and one half years, to complete the cycle of readings.[42] The "triennial cycle," as it is called, persisted for a long time until the Babylonian custom finally became normative everywhere.[43] The Palestinian custom was not uniform, and the division of the Torah into weekly lections, called *sedarim*, varied from community to community.[44]

We now have proof that just as the Psalter was divided into five "books," so it was also subdivided into *sedarim* after the manner of the Torah.[45] What is lacking, however, is direct evidence for the public reading of a psalm in conjunction with the weekly Torah and prophetic selections. Perhaps that was reserved for private recitation. In fact, several attempts have been made to uncover connective themes and key terms or phrases linking a particular psalm to a specific weekly prophetic and/or Torah reading. While many of these suggestions are persuasive, they cannot be regarded as decisive.[46]

To return to the subject of the psalms collections: Whether or not the doxologies actually mark off an original division into books, it is clear that our Psalter is composed of what were once several smaller collections of psalms. Someone must have made a "Davidic" collection that was thought to be complete at the time, because Psalm 72, which closes the second book, plainly states (v. 20): "The prayers of David son of Jesse are ended." Then there must have been an "Asaphite" collection, because a number of contributions are attributed to Asaph, a Levite whom David is said to have appointed to be the choirmaster.[47] Another collection, now incorporated into books two and three, is credited to "The sons of Korah," the descendants of the Levite who rebelled against Moses and Aaron in the course of the wilderness wanderings, and whom "the earth swallowed up."[48] His sons, however, survived and one of their line was appointed by David to be among those in charge of song in the Temple.[49] Apart from these there is also a block of psalms, numbers 120–134, each headed by the title, "A Song of Ascents"—or so at least, that is how the English translations usually render the cryptic Hebrew title *shir ha-ma'alot*.[50]

DAVID AND THE PSALMS

We have referred to the "Davidic" collection, the largest in the Psalter. The headings of just fewer than half of all the psalms bear the name of the illustrious King David—seventy-three out of one hundred and fifty, to be exact. (The Greek version omits four of these designations,[51] but adds another thirteen.[52]) This still leaves seventy-seven psalms not attributed to David. Apart from the twelve Asaphite and eleven Korahite compositions, two bear the name of Solomon, and one each is accredited to Moses, Heman, and Ethan.[53] Forty-nine psalms are anonymous, or "orphan psalms."[54]

Why was the entire Psalter attributed to David? He was an intrepid warrior, a brilliant strategist, an empire builder, founder of Judah's only royal dynasty, a messianic symbol—but he is best known as the author of the Psalms. A talmudic statement expresses it thus: "David wrote the book of Psalms including in it the work of the elders, namely, Adam, Melchizedek, Abraham, Moses, Heman, Jeduthun, Asaph, and the three sons of Korah."[55] Another passage in the Talmud remarks, "All the praises which are stated in the Book of Psalms, David uttered each one of them."[56] The most all-embracing declaration is that cited above, to the effect that "David gave Israel five books of psalms." The ultimate expression of the association of David with Psalmody is to be found in the hyperbolic prose insert in the large Psalms scroll from Qumran by the Dead Sea. This says that David wrote 3600 hymns *(tehillim)* and 450 songs *(shir)*.[57]

That the entire Psalter should have come to be associated with the person of David is not really so surprising, given the traditions about his involvement in instrumental and choral music, as portrayed in the biblical prose texts. In his youth, he was known as one "skilled at playing the lyre."[58] He also had a mastery of various musical instruments, and is said to have himself invented some.[59] He composed dirges, and a song of thanksgiving.[60] He was, undeniably, a man of deep spirituality. He had the Ark of the Covenant brought to Jerusalem and permanently installed there, and so transformed the city into the religious center of Israel.[61] He is credited with having drafted plans to build the Temple,[62] and even though he himself was prevented from executing them, he made extensive preparations for his son to do so.[63] Further, he is said to have carefully arranged for the future Temple liturgy by organizing and assigning guilds of Temple singers and musicians.[64] Admittedly, no biblical text explicitly declares King David to be the author of the Psalter. As we have noted, only seventy-three psalms carry his name—and this in the form of *le-david*, a term that was interpreted to be an indication of authorship, as the last verse of Psalm 72 shows, although other possibilities exist.[65] Furthermore, a few headings directly connect the composition with an incident in the life of David.[66]

THE MUSICAL GUILDS

The traditions just cited that make David responsible for the institution of Temple singers and musicians are all post-exilic. They tell us that when the king transformed Jerusalem into a holy city and the spiritual center of Israel by installing there the Ark of the

Covenant, he appointed three individuals of the Levitical clans of Kohath, Gershon, and Merari—Heman, Asaph, and Ethan—to be in charge of the vocal and instrumental aspects of the service.[67] The question immediately arises as to how much credence can be placed in these reports. Are they inventions of the Chronicler? Do they actually reflect the reality of the Second Temple period retrojected onto Solomon's Temple?[68] In order to resolve these uncertainties, we must trace the histories of the clan-guilds, using that term in the sense of recognizable, cohesive groups of Temple personnel. The following data must be taken into account:

The Book of Ezra-Nehemiah lists the families who returned to the land of Israel from Babylon under the leadership of Zerubbabel following the edict of King Cyrus of Persia in 538 B.C.E. permitting the Jews to rebuild their Temple in Jerusalem. Only the Asaphite guild—with 147 members—is recorded among them.[69] Moreover, that is the only guild to have participated in the ceremony held to mark the laying of the foundation of the Second Temple.[70] In fact, no other guild is ever mentioned in Ezra-Nehemiah. Had Heman, Ethan, and the Korahites been active in the restoration period, what reason would the contemporary sources have had to suppress the fact? By the same token, why should the Chronicler (? 4th cent. B.C.E.) have invented these guilds if they never existed? It must also be taken into account that Books IV and V of the Psalter are certainly among the latest; yet no compositions therein are ascribed to any of the clan-guilds. We can also point to the discovery of the existence of the Korahites in the days of the First Temple, for they are mentioned on an inscribed bowl found in the excavations at Arad. They were active in the monotheistic Israelite cult center situated there.[71]

It can also be demonstrated that the data given in Chronicles are totally independent of the information that can be culled from the headings to the Psalms. The Chronicler portrays the Asaphites as the most important and prestigious of the clan-guilds,[72] while the Korahites are not included in the list of those appointed by David to participate in the Temple service. They are "guards of the threshold,"[73] "preparers of the wafers,"[74] and "gatekeepers."[75] Nevertheless, they contribute eleven psalms to the Psalter, to judge from the superscriptions, while the Asaphites can claim only one more. As far as the compiler of the collections of psalms was concerned, there was little to choose between the Korahites and the Asaphites. This shows that the Chronicler's account was not drawn from the headings to the psalms, nor were the latter influenced by the post-exilic historiography. They are independent of each other. The Chronicler did not invent the data he records. He did not retroject the reality of his day onto the days of the first Temple.

The same conclusion can be deduced in regard to Heman, to whom only one composition in the Psalter is attributed. Strangely, however, the Chronicler awards him great importance. He is said to have been the chief singer at the celebration held on the removal of the Ark to Jerusalem,[76] and Asaph was subordinate to him. He bears the official title of "Heman the Singer."[77] The great prestige he enjoyed is demonstrated by the twenty-one–generation genealogy given him by the Chronicler, in contrast to Asaph's fourteen generations.[78] Like Asaph, he is prominently featured in all the reports of public worship from the time of David down to the reign of Josiah. Strikingly, the Book of Ezra-Nehemiah ignores this guild, and, as noted, only a single psalm is attributed to him, and this not exclusively so. Once again, there is a serious discrepancy between the traditions about the first Temple and those about Second Temple times.

In sum, there is no reason to doubt the existence of musical guilds in Israel during the period of the first Temple, although not all of them operated in the Temple in Jerusalem. Some of them were attached to the provincial shrines that existed in Judah and Israel. Several of these cult sites enjoyed a great prestige, and certainly must have maintained a cadre of professional personnel.

THE SURVIVAL OF THE PSALMS

We are now in a position to respond to the question we raised earlier, how the one hundred and fifty psalms managed to overcome the ravages of time in the face of all odds. Some powerful factors were at work to save them from oblivion. One was the musical guilds. Each had its repertoire, recited, collected, and transmitted from generation to generation. The guilds were highly mobile. Its members could easily move either as a group or individually from one cult center to another when its home base was destroyed, bringing their repertoire with them.

Another determining factor was the liturgical tradition itself. That is to say, individual psalms belonged to or constituted standardized liturgies available for recitation or singing on different occasions. They were used when an Israelite felt the need to commune with God, whether to express adoration and praise; to offer thanksgiving; to confess sin and ask for forgiveness; to resort to petition and supplication in circumstances of peril, in a state of dire illness, or as the victim of false accusation or injustice. The Israelite might repair to the Temple or local shrine and there be given an appropriate psalm to recite or sing, or have recited or sung for him or her. Frequent repetition of these liturgies over the ages would have impressed upon them the stamp of familiarity in the minds of the worshipers. This practice would have been a powerful factor in the preservation of the psalms.

Chapter 1

PSALM ONE

The Moral Individual—
The Immoral Society

Happy is the one who has not followed the
    counsel of the wicked.
  or taken the path of sinners,
  or joined the company of the insolent;
  2rather, the Teaching of the LORD is his delight,
  and he studies that teaching day and night.
3He is like a tree planted beside streams of water,
  which yields its fruit in season,
  whose foliage never fades,
  and whatever it produces thrives.

4Not so the wicked;
  rather, they are like chaff that wind blows away.
5Therefore the wicked will not survive judgment,
  nor will sinners, in the assembly of the righteous.
6For the LORD cherishes the way of the righteous,
  but the way of the wicked is doomed.

Given the persistent tradition about King David's paramount role as a composer of psalms, it is extraordinary that the opening composition lacks the heading, "A Psalm of David." In fact, it has no superscription at all. It is what, in rabbinic parlance, is quaintly called "an orphan psalm."[1] Even more strangely, its vocabulary, style, and theme do not conform to the usual pattern of Psalmody. These have more in common with biblical Wisdom literature,[2] the books of Proverbs, Job, and Ecclesiastes, than with biblical poetry. Moreover, on the surface, Psalm 1 can hardly be termed "devotional" in the usual sense of the term, for it features no outpouring of the soul. One looks in vain for any invocation of God. Neither praise nor petition is present, neither lamentation nor jubilation. It is the human being, not God, who is the focus of attention.

Considering all these peculiarities, according this psalm pride of place is indeed puzzling. Why was the composition chosen to head the Book of Psalms? The selection must communicate an intention to make a statement, to inculcate at the outset certain fundamental ideas, and to promote some essential teachings. Not without excellent reason did the fourth century C.E. Palestinian teacher, Rabbi Yudan, pronounce Psalm 1 to be "the choicest of all psalms."[3]

First and foremost, there is its major theme: the ideal of the centrality of God's Teaching—in Hebrew *torah*—in the life of the individual and its indispensable role in the definition and attainment of righteousness. This alone would justify its preeminent position in the Psalter.

It will be recalled that the Torah and the Psalms are, in a very real sense, complementary. The former, revelation, is anthropotropic; it represents the divine outreach to humankind. The latter, worship, is theotropic; it epitomizes the human striving for contact with God.[4] The Decalogue, commonly known as the Ten Commandments, fittingly opens with "I am the Lord your God," and closes with "Your neighbor"—so the Book of Psalms appropriately symbolizes movement in the reverse direction by commencing with "Happy is the one," and ending with Hallelujah, "praise the Lord," marking the direction from humanity to God.

It will also be remembered that the fivefold division of the Book of Psalms may well have been influenced by the pentateuchal arrangement of the Torah,[5] and that the number of one hundred and fifty individual compositions has in all probability been conditioned by the original Palestinian triennial division of one hundred and fifty weekly Torah readings.[6] This conceptual association of Torah with Psalmody inevitably led the rabbis of the talmudic age to draw analogies between the deeds and words of the personalities with whom the authorship of the respective works was associated.[7] One felicitous example is that the initial word of Psalm 1, "happy" (in Hebrew *'ashrei*), is also the first word of Moses' final utterance just before his death: "Happy are you (in Hebrew *'ashreikha*) O Israel."[8]

If not by design, then by happy coincidence, the choice of Psalm 1 makes each major division of the standard Hebrew Bibles open with a reference to Torah.[9] The Former Prophets begin with the Book of Joshua, and chapter one contains the following:

> "You must be very strong and resolute to observe faithfully
> all the Teaching *(torah)* that My servant Moses enjoined
> upon you. Do not deviate from it to the right or to the
> left, that you may be successful wherever you go. Let not
> this Book of the Teaching *(torah)* cease from your lips, but
> recite it day and night, so that you may observe faithfully
> all that is written in it"(vv. 7, 8).

The Latter Prophets begin with the Book of Isaiah; its opening chapter calls upon Israel to

> "Hear the word of the Lord. . . .
> Give ear to our God's Teaching *(torah)*" (v. 10).

The final chapter of the prophetic division, the third in the Book of Malachi, likewise exhorts the people:

> "Be mindful of the Teaching *(torah)* of My servant
> Moses, whom I charged at Horeb with laws and
> rules for all Israel" (v. 22).

Since the Book of Psalms opens the third section of the Hebrew Bible, the *Ketuvim* (*Hagiographa*, or *Writings*, in English), it is to be expected that it, too, would commence with emphasis on *torah* and so a composition with the theme of Torah was selected for the purpose.

Of course, it is a superficial observation that our psalm is non-devotional, and that its place at the forefront of the book is therefore an oddity. The seeming incongruity of Psalm 1 in a collection of supplications and hymns arises solely from our limiting unduly the definition of "devotional," by restricting it to prayer and ritual. Such a notion obscures a fundamental principle that the psalmist wishes to highlight by according the theme of Torah a preeminent position in the Psalter. It is that the study of the sacred and revered text itself constitutes a pious act, a profoundly religious experience, and is an important mode of worship. [10] This seminal idea is emphasized and elaborated in Psalm 119, and it finds powerful expression in later Judaism.

There is another aspect of this psalm that needs to be stressed, especially in light of its wider application to the entire Book: the presupposition that the lives of human beings are ultimately governed by a divinely ordained, universal moral order. This affirmation, in fact, constitutes the ideological basis for any meaningful human appeal to God. To cry out for justice, for the righting of great wrongs, for the victory of the downtrodden righteous over the successful evildoers, would defy comprehension without prior conviction about the nature of God and His governance of the world. This, too, is expressed in our psalm, and it postulates a conception of God that springs from the teachings of the Torah.

Finally, as we shall see, the psalm implicitly proclaims unquestioned faith in the power of the individual to transform society, no matter how seemingly invulnerable be the forces of evil. This, too, derives from the Torah's teachings.

When the psalmist passionately and confidently declares "Happy is the one," he is describing an existing reality, not offering a cheering promise of a romanticized future. His is not "the religion of the sad soul," but the happiness of the religious one. The very first word is instructive. Although the English translations imply a verbal sentence underlying the original Hebrew text, this opening phrase contains no verb at all. The Hebrew *'ashrei*[11] is a noun in the construct state, that is, in the form it takes when joined to another noun on which it is dependent. Hence, the phrase is really an exclamation meaning, "O for the happiness of that person. . . !" It is the discriminating judgment of an observer who expresses wonderment and admiration over another's enviable state of being. More than this, *'ashrei* is in the plural, the inflectional form denoting intensity. This "plural of intensity," as it is called, communicates energetic focusing upon the basic idea inherent in the Hebrew root.[12] It is the highest form of happiness that the psalmist has in mind.

It is happiness, be it noted, not pleasure, that concerns the psalmist. Pleasure may be self-centered, a transient, agreeable sensation or emotion, an instinctive response to a particular stimulus that gratifies the senses; and it may be frivolous and illusory. By contrast, happiness is deep-rooted; it penetrates the very depths of one's being, and it is serious and enduring. In fact, it is this last quality which most distinguishes it from pleasure.

For this psalmist, the happy state of which he speaks is not a matter of natural disposition, nor does it stem simply from the cultivation of the proper mental attitudes. It proceeds necessarily from actions that are wholly controllable by the individual. Happiness results from the deliberate assumption of a commitment to a certain way of life, a course that is governed by God's Teaching *(torah)*.

The singular nature of this enduring condition of happiness is signified by the careful choice of the Hebrew term *'ashrei*. Unlike its kindred *barukh*, "blessed," it possesses no antonym; it always has a human being as its referent, never God; it cannot be conferred on another and so is never invoked in the bestowal of blessing; and without exception, it is employed to describe an existing situation, never one that is desired or promised. Moreover, the fact that *'ashrei* can be used with "nation,"[13] "people,"[14] and "land"[15] militates against an otherworldly interpretation of the happiness here described. The condition that the psalmist appraises has a decidedly this-worldly character.

"Happy is the one . . . " exclaims the psalmist, a phrase that looks straightforward enough in the English rendering. However, the Hebrew features a combination of words that is otherwise unexampled: *'ashrei ha-'ish*. This same sentiment is repeated several times in the Bible but with quite other Hebrew terms for the subject: *'adam*,[16] *gever*,[17] *'enosh*,[18]—all synonyms for "man," although to be sure, there are subtle shades of difference in meaning between them. Why then did our psalmist choose to depart from the conventional usages and employ *'ish?* It is hardly likely, given the context, that he wanted to put the emphasis on sexual distinction, and in any case, *'ish* is often used to designate the species "humankind," and may convey the sense of "people," "person(s)," irrespective of gender.[19] Two considerations that may have influenced our psalmist in his preference for *'ish* over other possible terms suggest themselves, one aesthetic, the other expressive.

Anyone who reads Hebrew will at once perceive the conscious artistry, the strong alliterative and assonantal pattern that characterizes the opening line. The first three words prominently feature the combination of the Hebrew consonants *'aleph* and *shin: 'ashrei ha-'ish 'asher;* in addition, the succession of the soothing sound *sh* is again repeated in the same line: *resha'im, moshav, yashav.* By enhancing the acoustic effect of the opening line in this manner, attention is immediately directed to the striking observation that the psalmist has made: the attainment of happiness is the sure consequence of the ideal life style he is about to describe and explain, and implicitly prescribe.

In addition to enriching the texture of the opening verse, the use of *'ish,* literally "man," is connotative, for the word appears in contexts that demand in high degree certain distinctive qualities.[20] It implies a desired standard of behavior that calls for resolution, courage, and stamina. These are the qualities demanded of one who would maintain moral integrity when surrounded by evil. And it is not unintentional that it is an individual, not a class, that is discussed, in sharp contrast to the "wicked"—in the plural—soon to be mentioned. It is the one against the many that is the focus of interest. Nor is it by chance, as we shall presently see, that here it is not the righteous versus the wicked, as so often in the Bible; but simply *'ish,* a person. How this person comes to join the ranks of the righteous is now detailed with the psalmist's listing of the aggregate of qualities that distinguish the one whose happiness he exclaims.

A commonsense rule frequently enunciated in the Bible, especially the Wisdom books,[21] is that an indispensable precondition for moral and spiritual self-improvement is the conscious withdrawal from social situations likely to produce deleterious effects. Hence, it is not surprising that our psalmist first registers virtues negatively formulated.[22] The person he has in view "has not walked in the counsel of the wicked."[23] That individual has resisted societal pressures to conform with prevailing mores. The wicked are many. By dint of their plurality and seeming success, it is they who set society's standards, who fix the patterns of behavior, and who wield the power to shape popular conceptions of right and wrong in accordance with their own perceived self-interests. Nevertheless, in an atmosphere of seductive depravity, our individual withstands the powerful allurements offered by the life style of the wicked. This person stands apart from the crowd.

References to "the wicked" abound in the Hebrew Bible. And no wonder, for the biblical writers, of necessity, rendered social judgment and criticism, given their particular worldview, their ideas about God and man and the relationships between them, their conception of human nature, their profound awareness of the existential human predicament, and their deep sense of human destiny. Their passionate moral concerns flowed from an unshakable faith in divinely decreed and hence universally and objectively valid norms of conduct.

Acutely conscious of the darker side of human nature and the variety of human corruption, the Hebrew Bible features several terms to designate those who practice it. The first one used in this psalm is the most severe. "The wicked," in Hebrew *resha'im* (singular *rasha'*), are time and again the focus of attention, especially in the books of Psalms and Proverbs, and in Isaiah and Ezekiel. *Rasha'*, together with its antonym *tsaddik*, apparently had a forensic context.[24] They meant, respectively, "the one [adjudged to be] in the wrong," "the one [adjudged to be] in the right." These terms came to be extended into the ethical, moral, and spiritual spheres of life.

"The wicked" are usually unidentified, but their defining unlovely characteristics can be culled from the several passages in Psalms and Proverbs in which the *resha'im* are explicitly mentioned. What an abhorrent portrait emerges. They are marked by arrogance, pride, and vainglorious bluster.[25] They are brazen-faced, insolent, derisive, and contemptuous of others.[26] They plot evil even in bed and scheme against the innocent.[27] They are enamored of injustice and deliberately pervert the administration of justice by means of bribery.[28] Lawlessness is their hallmark,[29] terror the instrument they wield against the lowly and disadvantaged of society, the widow, the stranger, and the orphan being their favored targets.[30] They even boast of their unbridled lusts.[31] They make an outward show of goodwill which conceals malice.[32] Their speech is deceitful and duplicitous, mendacious, fraudulent and treacherous.[33] They abuse another's friendship, repaying good with evil, love with hate.[34] They borrow and never pay back, although they amass wealth.[35] They abhor the person of integrity.[36] They cannot understand another's concern for the plight of the wretched of society, and should they feign compassion, it turns out to be cruelty.[37]

While the wicked are motivated by base desires, the actuating cause of these evil deeds is a false theology. A fallacious understanding of the nature of God convinces these reprobates that evil can be perpetrated with impunity.[38] They believe God to be wholly removed from the life of the world and altogether indifferent to human behavior.[39] Hence, the wicked neither put their trust in God nor fear Him. "Fear of God" is a phrase frequently cited in biblical texts in relation to situations that involve norms of moral and ethical behavior. The consciousness of a Higher Power, who makes moral demands on human beings and who calls people to account for violating them, constitutes the ultimate restraint on evil and the supreme incentive for good.[40] The wicked do not espouse philosophical atheism, but functional, or practical, atheism.[41] They believe in an otiose deity, withdrawn from the world, and morally neutral. They hypocritically offer sacrifices, a practice that is an abomination to God.[42]

So much for "the wicked" whose way of life the individual of our psalm has the moral fortitude to resist. Before moving to the second class of disreputable persons mentioned in verse one, it is worthwhile pointing to another aesthetic feature of the language. The association of the term *'ashrei* with the verb "to walk" and with the noun "way" is highly suggestive since it makes for a fine, if subtle, wordplay.[43] The common Semitic stem that underlies *'ashrei* yields both a verb meaning "to walk, advance," and a noun denoting "footstep."[44] The combination of words hints at a conception of happiness that is by no means a passive condition. It is a dynamic process, involving constant movement both away from one path and in the direction of another—a fixed path, which is about to be defined.

Less villainous than "the wicked" are "the sinners," who, for that reason, might possess greater drawing power for the ordinary person. In Hebrew, they are *hatta'im*. The primitive meaning of the stem of this word is "to miss, err, stray."[45] The *ḥote'*, "the sinner," is, therefore, one who strays from a path or misses the goal; a wayward person. In the religio-moral sphere, a *ḥote'* is one who strays from God's path or falls short of the standards God sets, not necessarily willfully, but as an inevitable byproduct of the human condition.[46] He is the least reprehensible of those guilty of moral failure. In fact, the *ḥote'* never attracts the interest of the psalmists. It is only the intensified form *hatta'*, and this solely in the plural, that occupies their attention.[47] This noun form is often used to indicate a line of work, an occupation or a profession: what one does repeatedly and regularly.[48] The sinners referred to are thus habitual moral blunderers; their sinning is a chronic condition. They are hardened sinners. Fellowship with them becomes a moral and spiritual danger,[49] and our psalmist observes that the person whose happiness he so admires "has not stood in the way" of such people.

Of course, this literal English translation of the Hebrew phrase does not convey to the reader what the psalmist intended. It is not that the estimable individual abstains from hindering or obstructing the ways of sinners; rather, the phrase means that "he does not linger" on their paths.[50] The idea is that he is not even attracted by their life style to the extent of hesitating whether or not to take their path. There is no uncertainty, no vacillation, only unequivocal rejection of their base practices.

Forming the third category in this cast of dishonorable characters are the "scoffers," in Hebrew *letsim* [sing. *lets*].[51] This term is also variously rendered in the English translations by "the scornful," "the mockers," "the cynics," all designations richly deserved by these people. Very frequently, the *letsim* are associated with the foolish,[52] the arrogant[53] and the wicked.[54] This should not be surprising because in the Bible, folly is less a condition of intellectual inadequacy than a lack of discrimination and judgment in the moral sphere— the inability or unwillingness to foresee or consider the consequences of one's actions. A close look at the passages that refer to the *lets*, overwhelmingly in the Book of Proverbs, shows that the one so described is outrageously and proudly insolent,[55] is a menace to the social order,[56] and is incorrigible, reacting abusively and hostilely to any reproof;[57] he is described as "an abomination to humankind."[58] Other derivations of the same Hebrew stem that underlies *lets* indicate that these types indulge in mocking poems and satires that deride the traditional values that society cherishes and taunt those who uphold them.[59]

Our psalmist speaks of "the seat/session of the scoffers."[60] This evokes a picture of the *letsim:* coteries of self-styled intellectuals seated in groups around the city-gate, declaiming their cynical and nihilistic teachings in the ears of bystanders—the curious, the idlers, and loiterers.[61] The city-gate in biblical times encompassed a large area where people could sit. One uncovered in the excavations at Tel Dan in northern Israel has a stone bench fifteen feet (4.6m) long around the wall of one of its towers. In the ancient Near East, the city-gate was a popular meeting place, and served as a civic center where the affairs of the community were conducted in full view of, and with the participation of, the citizenry. Here, justice would be dispensed, legal transactions arranged, and gossip exchanged and disseminated.[62] The decent individual, the *'ish* of whom the psalmist speaks, will have nothing to do with the *letsim*. He shuns their gatherings, entertaining though they may be.[63]

The essential preconditions for the formation and improvement of character, and for spiritual and moral elevation, have now been laid out. Their sum and substance is the disavowal of harmful though enticing social situations. And notice how the acts of distancing are expressed by means of a sequence of three verbs which convey increasing degrees of closeness: walking, standing, sitting.[64] The *'ish* can successfully wrestle with a true test of character—the ability to resist the powerful influence of peer pressure. "Steer clear of evil and do good" is the sage advice of another psalm,[65] and the same thought is implicit in the transition from verse 1 to the following verse. The virtuous life is unattainable solely by withdrawal from disreputable companionship. The achievement of a higher spiritual state demands positive action as well. So, in sharp antithesis to the previously mentioned villainous characters, the individual, the *'ish* of verse 1, concentrates spiritual and intellectual energies on God's Teaching *[torah]*.

Most English translations of verse 2a read, "Rather, the Teaching of the Lord is his delight," but this last word hardly does justice to the full range of meaning carried by the Hebrew noun *ḥefets*.[66] Apart from "desire," it can also be used for an "experience,[67] business,[68] goods,[69] and concern."[70] "Delight" and "concern," diligent, gratifying application, is what is here intended. This person is thoroughly absorbed in the sacred text entitled "the Lord's Teaching," in Hebrew, *torat YHVH*.

It is not possible to determine what exactly was comprehended by that phrase in this context. From the second half of the verse— "and he recites His *torah* day and night"—it seems certain that it must pertain to a fixed text that can be memorized. We shall soon discuss the word "recites"; for now, attention is focused on "the Lord's Teaching." Because the psalm is saturated with the vocabulary of Wisdom literature, that expression takes on special significance. It indicates that, by the time of the author, Hebrew Wisdom [*hokhmah*], originally secular, i.e., not particularly engaged in religious themes, had become identified with *torah*. This development is first registered in Deuteronomy 4:6,8, where Moses exhorts the people to observe faithfully God's laws and rules. This, he says "will be the proof of your wisdom and discernment to other peoples, who on hearing of all these laws will say, 'Surely that great nation is a wise and discerning people.' " And Moses asks, "What great nation has laws and rules as perfect as all this Teaching *(torah)* that I set before you this day?"

The impact of the Book of Deuteronomy is strongly evidenced in Israel for the first time in the days of King Josiah of Judah, in the wake of the far-reaching religious reforms he instituted in the year 622/1 B.C.E., as recorded in I Kings 22–24 and 2 Chronicles 34–35. From then on, Deuteronomy exerted a decisive influence on subsequent biblical literature. The oracles of the prophet Jeremiah, in particular, are replete with the distinctive orientation, themes, and phrases of that book. It is no coincidence, therefore, that Jeremiah, active in the days of King Josiah and in the aftermath of the reforms, is the one who gives evidence of the synonymousness of Wisdom and *torah*. Chastising the professional scribes, he asks, "How can you say 'we are wise and we possess the Teaching *(torah)* of the Lord?' . . . The wise shall be put to shame, shall be dismayed and caught; see, they reject the word of the Lord, so their widsom amounts to nothing."[71] The prophet accuses these scribes of misinterpreting the divine Teaching, but in so doing he takes for granted that the school of Wisdom has merged with that of Torah. The phrase "the Lord's Teaching" in our wisdom psalm clearly reflects this development.

Our text makes no mention of a "book" of the Torah. In fact, the word "book" never appears in any reference to Torah in the Psalter; nor is the definite article ever attached therein to *torah*.[72] Torah must here mean simply "teaching," "instruction." Nevertheless, as noted above, "the Lord's Teaching" must define a recognizable, established, and crystallized text that can be committed to memory and recited. This is so because the Hebrew verb, usually mistranslated "meditates," carries a decidedly oral nuance, as anyone who consults a concordance of the Hebrew Bible for the stem *h-g-h* will soon discover.[73] The verbal form is used for the moaning of a dove,[74] and the growl of a lion;[75] it takes as its subject the mouth,[76] the tongue,[77] and the palate.[78] The action of the verb obviously has an acoustical effect because the throat can be its instrument.[79] True, the Hebrew *lev*, "heart," also appears as the subject of the verb *h-g-h* but, as has been shown, the heart in the Bible can also be an organ of speech.[80] Moreover, the verb many times appears in a parallel relationship with another verb denoting sound.[81] Finally, there are three nouns from this stem, all of which are used in contexts which suggest sound or tonality.[82]

This understanding of the action of verse 2b as being recitative, not meditative, is reinforced by other biblical passages. A strikingly similar one is in God's address to Joshua upon his assumption of the leadership of Israel following Moses' death. It reads: "Let not this book of Teaching [*torah*] depart from your mouth, but recite [*vehagiyta*] it day and night" (Joshua 1:8). The mouth, of course, is here the organ of speech. This emphasis on the oral nature of the obligation is repeated several times.[83]

In short, what all this means is that the person described in our psalm is not one engaged in meditation and contemplation, such as is required in some mystical systems and traditions. Rather, this individual studies a sacred text which is the object of intense focus and concentration; and the method of study is reading aloud, rote learning, and constant oral repetition. These, in fact, formed the standard pattern of teaching and learning in the ancient world, neareastern and classical, and they continued well into the Middle Ages. Silent reading was extremely rare.[84] Not surprisingly, therefore, the Hebrew verb *k-r-'* can mean both "to read" and "to call, proclaim."

The same system existed in the ancient Egyptian schools. The instruction addressed to King Merikare, which derives from the ninth/tenth Dynasty (22nd–21st centuries B.C.E.), refers to a schoolmate as one with whom one "chanted the writings" in class.[85] Another Egyptian text which describes some of the duties of a schoolboy, this one from the New Kingdom (twentieth Dynasty, ca. 1185–1069 B.C.E.), advises him, "Write with your hand, read with your mouth."[86] In Ancient Mesopotamia, one of the verbs for "to call"— Akkadian *šasû*—also means "to shout, howl, call, read (aloud),"[87] and the same phenomenon obtains in Chinese writing in which the character for "to study" means "to read aloud."[88]

This inseparable association of reading with recitation—which meant that study was primarily an oral exercise—was a common feature of the cultural milieu of the ancient world, and Israel was no exception. As frequently in such cases, the shared component assumed in Israel a special distinctive quality. Study of the sacred text—*torah*—was not just an intellectual pursuit or matter of professional training, but a spiritual and moral discipline. It was the authoritative guide to right behavior. Constant repetition and review, "day and night," functioned to incorporate its values within the self so that they became a part of one's own being, consciously and subconsciously guiding one's actions. In other words, the principles embedded in the text decisively influenced the intellectual, moral, and social growth of the individual. This being so, it is easy to understand why in Israel knowledge of the sacred texts was an obligation on each individual, not an elitist enterprise, why study of Torah became a religious duty of the first rank, incumbent upon every member of the community of Israel, and why Jews have always displayed an enthusiastic reverence for learning. Furthermore, the study of Torah was not only an act of piety, but was also a fundamental mode of worship, both it and prayer being accorded in rabbinic literature the designation 'avodah, the standard term for the sacrificial system in the Temple in Jerusalem.[89]

In this connection, it is worth noting that the Jewish sectarians of Qumran in the Judean wilderness, in the days of the Second Temple, took the admonition to Joshua, cited above, very seriously. They seem to have reinterpreted it as though addressed to all Israel, or they took the corresponding passage in our psalm as prescriptive, not descriptive. Accordingly, in their "Manual of Discipline" that established the governing rules of their community, they made provision for one member in every subgroup of ten always to be studying the Torah, and they decreed that during each of the three watches into which the night was divided, one third of its personnel, in relays, would always be awake and engrossed in the sacred texts.[90]

Having sketched the distinctive and conspicuous characteristics and qualities of the one who is the focus of attention, the psalmist now proceeds to enlarge upon the advantages they bestow upon the individual and the benefits that redound to the general good. These judgments are voiced in vivid imagery:

> He is like a tree planted beside streams of water,
>> which yields its fruit in season,
>> whose foliage never fades,
>> and whatever it produces thrives.[91]

A close parallel to this passage is to be found in Jeremiah 17:7–8 concerning the one who has implicit trust in God,

> Blessed is the man who trusts in the Lord,
>> whose trust is the Lord alone.
> He is like a deep-rooted tree by the waterside,
>> putting forth its roots along the stream.
> It does not notice when the heat arrives;
>> its foliage is ever green.
> It has no care in a year of drought
>> it goes on yielding fruit.

Such arboreal imagery appears fairly frequently in the Bible, though generally not in so expansive a form as this. Amos tells of God having rid Canaan of its pre-Israelite inhabitants,[92]

"Who were as tall as the cedar,
    and as stout as the oak."
He "destroyed their fruit above
    and their roots below."

Jeremiah's enemies who plot against him say, "Let us destroy the tree with its sap in it."[93] The psalmist describes himself as "a thriving olive tree in God's House,"[94] and the righteous as flourishing "like a date-palm" and

growing tall like a cedar in Lebanon
deep-rooted in the House of the Lord,
flowering in the courts of our God.
They still yield fruit in old age,
    luxuriant and fresh.[95]

Similar figures of speech are employed several times in the Bible,[96] and they also occur in the literature of the ancient Near East. From the Ramesside period (13th–12th cents. B.C.E.) in Egypt comes the Instruction of Amenemope, in which a hotheaded man is compared to a tree grown outdoors, which suddenly loses its foliage, whereas the man who is truly self-controlled is like a tree grown in a garden: it flourishes, yields a double harvest, its fruit is sweet and its shade pleasant.[97] From Mesopotamia an encomium of King Shulgi of Ur (ca. 2095–2048 B.C.E.) has survived in which he is glorified as "a date palm planted by the waterditch" and "a cedar rooted by abundant water of pleasant shade."[98] From Phoenicia, an inscription on the sarcophagus of King Eshmun'azar (5th cent. B.C.E.) curses any who will disturb his casket, "Let them have no root below and no fruit above."[99] This closely resembles the aforecited Amos 2:9, as well as Isaiah 37:32 and Job 18:16.

Clearly, the picture of the ideal person given in Psalm 1 draws upon the standard conventional imagery of the ancient world, but it is embellished and amplified and so carefully phrased as to be no longer mere cliché, but a highly meaningful simile that constitutes

41

the heart of the entire composition. A detailed analysis of its imagistic elements is therefore warranted.

The tree symbolism by itself carries implications of the generative and regenerative processes. In addition, the tree is not a forest type but is specified as being fruit-laden. The power of the comparison is immediately apparent. The qualities of usefulness, serviceability, giving of oneself to others, are at once invoked. This individual nourishes and sustains society, enriching the lives of others.

Furthermore, the tree is "well-rooted," not simply "planted," as the English translations inadequately render it. The regular Hebrew natu'a, "planted," is studiously avoided. Instead, the rarer and more specialized technical term shatul is employed. The rabbinic sages long ago recognized that this means "well-rooted." The Midrash on the Book of Psalms comments, "[The text] does not say like a tree natu'a but like a tree shatul, in order to teach that even if all the world's winds were to blast it, they could not dislodge it."[100]

This tradition as to the true meaning of the Hebrew term is preserved in several other postbiblical texts,[101] and there is some additional biblical evidence that leads to the same conclusion.[102] The point is that our individual is resilient, stable, and steadfast because he is deeply rooted in the spiritual and ethical soil of the Torah. He possesses the strength of character and the fortitude to withstand the winds of adversity.

The tree, with its deep underground roots, is located in proximity to perennial streams, and so is protected from the vagaries of seasonal rainfall and the threat of drought such as obtains in the land of Israel. The picture is of a copious natural spring or gushing fountain which empties into a small reservoir from which water is gently channeled into water-ditches that nurture the fruit tree at all times.[103] In like manner, the ideal person's inner life is continuously fed and refreshed by the lifegiving waters of the Torah. In a morally and spiritually arid social climate, this individual can flourish and be a model of reliability like the fruit tree that yields its produce in its proper season.

Another outstanding feature of the tree is that, in contrast to most fruit trees, which are deciduous, this one is an evergreen. Its foliage provides perpetual shelter from the blazing sun. It is not unlikely that the leaves have another function as well. In the folk medicine of many peoples, leaves of trees are often considered to possess medicinal properties. They are used to make poultices for an assortment of bodily ailments and wounds, and in the preparation of diuretics and laxatives. The brew made by steeping them in water is believed to have a general tonic effect on the digestive tract. The prophet Ezekiel, in a literary image similar to that of this psalm, actually mentions the "leaves for healing" (47:12).[104] It is also to be noted that, whereas in Ezekiel 47:12 and in Jeremiah 17:8 the natural order of the process of growth is maintained—first the leaves, then the fruit—here it is reversed; the fruit precedes the leaves. This is because uppermost in the psalmist's mind is the matter of their utility, which he features in descending order of importance. The symbolism of the fruit and leaves may therefore be interpreted in terms of blessings and benefactions that our exemplary individual bestows liberally on fellow human beings, enhancing the quality of their lives, perhaps specifically by providing food, shelter, and medicines for those in need.

The final line of verse 3 is marvelously ambiguous. It rounds out the first part of the psalm, which begins with a description of a certain kind of person, and then moves on to portray a special kind of tree. The stanza appropriately closes with a sentence in which the subject of the two verbs may be either one or the other. We can safely assume that the dual possibility of association is a deliberate rhetorical device that allows for both meanings to be simultaneously apprehended.

The Hebrew may be translated, "Whatever he does prospers." This rendering is justified by the similarity of verse 2 to Joshua 1:8, which ends on the same note. The successor to Moses is told to recite God's Teachings day and night, and is assured that he will thereby be successful in his undertakings. Of Joseph in Potiphar's household, Genesis 39:2 records that the Lord was with him and

43

that "he was a successful man," and again that "the Lord lent success to everything he undertook" (v.3). In each of the above citations, the same Hebrew verb as is employed in our psalm verse is featured, and in the last, the same two verbs. These two, in fact, are combined in a host of biblical texts.

On the other hand, both verbs, 's-h and ts-l-ḥ, are also horticultural terms, so that their subject may be the fruit tree. The stem 's-h, "to make, produce," is frequently used in the Bible for the process of a tree yielding fruit, while Ezekiel 17:8–10, in a similar context to ours, twice uses ts-l-ḥ for a thriving vine, and that verb was still current in this sense in postbiblical Hebrew. Hence, the line in question may alternatively be translated, "Whatever it produces[105] thrives."[106] This rendering lays emphasis on the quality of the fruit, that is, on the excellence of the person's deeds rather than on the success of his undertakings.

In abrupt, polar antithesis to the foregoing, verse 4 succinctly describes the character and fate of the wicked in a consonance of form and content. The economy of words matches the image employed—in striking contrast to the preceding elaborate and detailed portrayal of the ideal individual.

> Not so the wicked;
> rather, they are like chaff that wind blows away.

The chaff, of course, is the outer covering of the kernel. Being very lightweight, it is easily separated from the grain in the winnowing process. In the land of Israel this was carried out between May and September. The farmer utilized the breezes that blow in from the Mediterranean Sea. He would toss the bunches of wheat with a fork into the wind so that the heavier grains would fall back onto the threshing floor while the wind carried off the chaff.[107]

In the Hebrew Bible, "chaff" is always used figuratively as a symbol of unsubstantiality and impermanence.[108] Appearance belies reality. As soon as they encounter the winds of adversity, the wicked, seemingly so powerful, are unmasked as useless and worthless persons, rootless nonentities lacking stability.

The psalmist now draws an inevitable, logical conclusion from this reality—logical, that is, within the framework of his world-view. Because the world is under God's governance, and because, therefore, there is inescapable accountability on the part of every human being, the fate of the wicked is ineluctable. Unfortunately, the precise connotation of verse 5 remains uncertain. The literal translation of the Hebrew is:

> Therefore, wicked people shall not stand up in
> judgment,
> Nor will hardened sinners, in the assembly of the
> righteous.

The lack of clarity derives from the different possibilities for understanding the Hebrew verb with its preposition *(yakum b-)*, as well as what is to be conveyed by "the judgment." Later exegesis, Jewish and Christian, understood the entire verse to refer to divine judgment of the individual in the hereafter;[109] but the Hebrew Bible contains no explicit reference to the judgment of the dead or to the destiny of the righteous and the wicked after death.

If the judgment is to be taken literally, then it must refer to the here and now. The psalmist may have in mind a human tribunal before which, he is convinced, the wicked will eventually be brought to account for their crimes. In that case, they will not prevail; justice will be done. Such an interpretation is perhaps supported by the Akkadian equivalent of the Hebrew phrase, making it a legal idiom. The verb *uzzuzu* "to stand up," is used in a juridical context in the sense of "to prevail, triumph in a lawsuit."[110]

Quite a different interpretation of the verse presents itself in the light of a usage of Hebrew *mishpat*, "judgment," to signify God's providence, His constant, watchful direction of human affairs. The idea is that reward and punishment are meted out by God in this life in response to virtue and wickedness so that the "judgment" is actually life's vicissitudes.[111] As internal and external affairs became more complex in ancient Israel, this simple belief came under increasing challenge. The suffering of the righteous and the prosperity of the wicked became more and more theologically problematic.[112] The doctrine of retribution espoused by Wisdom literature[113] clashed with the events of experience. The Book of Job is the supreme literary expression of this questioning. In our psalm, however, the pristine doctrine is taken for granted. At any rate, the conviction is that for want of rootage in the spiritual and moral soil of God's Teaching, the wicked lack the moral fiber to be able to withstand the shifting tides of fortune which the psalmist sees as the exercise of divine judgment.

The phrase "the assembly of the righteous" is particularly interesting, it being unique. Hebrew 'edah originally constituted a political institution vested with legislative and judicial powers. With the establishment of the monarchy in Israel, this organ of statecraft lost its raison d'être and disappeared.[114] The term then came to be used in the general sense of "coterie, gathering," as here in verse 5. This means that the social situation has undergone radical transformation. The individual of verse 1, who needed to shun the company of unwholesome characters, now has companionship. There is a fellowship of the righteous from which the hardened sinners are excluded. It is they who are condemned to self-centered isolation. The decent individual who has maintained his integrity in an immoral society has succeeded in changing the entire social order and he can do so because there is, after all, a divinely ordained moral law which must, in the end, prevail.[115]

The final verse of the psalm expresses this fundamental biblical credo in a different way:

> For the Lord cherishes (literally, "knows") the way of
> the righteous
> but the way of the wicked is doomed.

Without doubt, the two parts of the verse are meant to be contrastive, in antipodal relation one to the other. But how is "to know" the antonym of being doomed? The answer is that the Hebrew concept of knowledge belongs to a wholly different category from what is usually understood in western thought. In the latter, cognition largely involves intellectual apprehension. In Hebrew, however, as in other Semitic languages,[116] the verb "to know," *y-d-ʿ* possesses a rich semantic range within which the senses predominate. Emotional ties, empathy, intimacy, sexual experience, mutuality, and responsibility are all encompassed within the usages of the verbal stem.[117]

These specialized meanings have taken on added significance since the discovery of the use of the same verb "to know" in the technical language of ancient neareastern treaties and related texts.[118] There it is employed with reference to mutual legal recognition and obligations on the part of suzerain and vassal, and to the acceptance of binding treaty stipulations. When a superior monarch "knows" one who is subordinate to him it means that he places him under his protection and care. When the vassal "knows" his suzerain he is affirming his fealty and his acceptance of obligations.

It is now clear why a human being's ideal relationship to God should be phrased in terms of "knowledge," and why the Bible may often speak of God as "knowing" His select ones.[119] By declaring that "the Lord knows the way of the righteous," our psalmist is affirming that God maintains a special relationship with them. They are under His personal care and guidance, and He orders and sustains their pattern of life and their destiny.

The wicked, on the other hand, by their evil deeds, willfully distance themselves from God. Having severed the ties that bind God and human beings, they have forfeited divine protection.[120] Note how the psalmist employs a stative, intransitive verb, governed by "the way," to describe the fate of the wicked; the iniquitous path they have chosen to follow inexorably leads to their self-ruin. In contrast, he uses an active, transitive verb, with God as the subject, in relating the destiny of the righteous.

The moral individual has triumphed in an immoral society.

Chapter 2

P SALM E IGHT

Two Paradoxes:
God and Human Beings

¹For the leader; on the *gittith*. A psalm of David.

²O Lᴏʀᴅ, our Lord,
How majestic is Your Name throughout the earth,
You who have covered the heavens with Your
splendor!
³From the mouths of infants and sucklings
You have founded strength on account of Your foes,
to put an end to enemy and avenger.
⁴When I behold Your heavens, the work of Your fingers,
the moon and stars that You set in place,
⁵what is man that You are mindful of him,
mortal man that You take note of him,
⁶that You have made him little less than divine,
and adorned him with glory and majesty;
⁷You have made him master over Your handiwork,
laying the world at his feet,
⁸sheep and oxen, all of them,
and wild beasts, too;
⁹the birds of the heavens, the fish of the sea,
whatever travels the paths of the seas.
¹⁰O Lᴏʀᴅ, our Lord, how majestic is Your Name throughout the earth!

This is a philosophical psalm of a type unique in the Psalter.
The author reflects upon the nature of God and the nature of humankind. It was composed, as verse four suggests, under the over-
powering inspiration of a magnificent moonlit sky aglow with
sparkling stars. In a pensive mood, the psalmist muses upon a double
paradox. There is the seeming contradiction between God's tran-
scendence and His immanence: God is beyond the limits of human
cognition; yet He has chosen to make His presence indwell in the

life of humanity. Then there is the very real paradox that is the human situation: compared with God, men and women are but nullities; yet, they are endowed with surpassing power over the physical world.

Were the author a pagan, the splendrous sight he beholds would surely awaken deep-souled feelings of adoration of what to him would be animated objects of nature. To pagans, the celestial bodies and the varied phenomena of the universe were endowed with life, personalized and divinized. That the gods inhered in nature was one of the basic presuppositions of the polytheistic religions.

The strict and reiterated biblical injunctions against worship of the celestial bodies abundantly illustrate how attractive such beliefs were to the common people, even in Israel.[1] Israelite monotheism broke irreconcilably and uncompromisingly with this mode of thinking. To the Israelite, nature is not to be deified. There is no word for "Nature" in biblical Hebrew, and no conception of such an entity in biblical literature.

The theme of cosmogony, the attempt to explain the origin and order of the universe, plays a major role in ancient neareastern religions; but it assumes a minor function in the Bible. The pagan cosmogonies invariably are embedded in a mythological matrix; an absence of 'mythology,' in the usual sense of the term, is the outstanding characteristic of the biblical account of creation.[2] Nature is desacralized. The sun, moon, and stars are not regarded as living or acting forces, but as divinely created objects that are manifestations of the power and glory of the one, transcendent God of Creation.

This seminal concept finds clear expression in the psalm under discussion. The structural symmetry gives voice to it and provides a clue to the understanding of the composition. The opening seven Hebrew words—in English, "O Lord, how majestic is Your Name throughout the earth!"—are repeated exactly to form the closing sentence. This framing device, technically known as an inclusio, serves to place emphasis upon the essential, fundamental idea that is to be inculcated.[3]

The spontaneous response of the psalmist to the immeasurable grandeur of the nocturnal scene is adoration of its Creator, not of its constituents. That is why he begins by invoking YHVH—the sublime, mysterious, and potent divine name that is specific to the God of Israel, the God of revelation. There is an additional appellation. God is termed "our Lord," in Hebrew *'adoneinu*, literally, "our Master." Because this particular title for God is exceedingly rare in the Bible,[4] its use here must have special significance. Moreover, there must also be a definite reason for referring to *"our* Lord," while in verse 4 the psalmist speaks of himself in the first person singular.

Throughout the Bible, Hebrew *'adon* appears predominantly as a royal title. What it connotes when applied to God is spelled out in Psalm 135:5–12, where it means that He possesses absolute supremacy, omnipotence, sovereignty over nature, and mastery over history. In Psalm 147:5, the title "our Lord" specifies God's power and infinite wisdom, while in Nehemiah 10:30 it alludes to His being the source and sanction of law, and for that reason, He commands obedience.[5]

All these divine qualities are evoked by designating God as "Lord" at the beginning and end of this psalm. It heightens the consciousness both of the absolute superiority of God and, concomitantly, of the human being's feelings of absolute dependence on Him. Both perceptions are a prelude to the questions raised in verse five about the divine-human relationship. It should be noted that just as the English spelling carefully distinguishes the two applications of "lord"—human and divine—by the use of lower and upper case *l*, so Hebrew generally makes the same distinction, by varying the order of the words. When applied to God, the title (in the plural form) follows the divine name YHVH; otherwise it precedes the royal name.[6] The plural form of *'adon* is the "plural of majesty." In our psalm the first person plural suffix is appended because it is the universal Lord to whom the author addresses himself, and because the paradoxes he poses are of universal interest. He speaks on behalf of the entire community.[7]

Another expressive feature of our psalm is the artful use of the Hebrew interrogative *mah*, "what, how," in contrasting senses. In reference to the majesty of God, it functions as an exclamation signifying wonderment mingled with awe and admiration: "How majestic is Your Name throughout the earth!"[8] Applied to human beings, in verse 5, it is scornfully deprecatory:[9] "What is man!"

The quality of majesty is instinctively called to mind by the ideas of kingship and nobility, and Hebrew *'addir* is used as an adjective with the former, as a noun in connection with the latter.[10] It encompasses a wide range of properties, such as greatness, dominion, power, authority, and dignity—all those that are ideally associated with monarchy and aristocracy. Like so many other words that owe their currency to royal terminology, the Hebrew stem *'-d-r* is applied to God in the full richness of its manifold connotations, with the additional quality of holiness.[11]

It might be thought that the experience of God's overwhelming majesty, here glorified in an ecstatic outburst, would engender in the psalmist immediate reactions of reserve and reticence, a sense of God's inaccessibility and unapproachability. But this is not the case. He can still address God directly and intimately. It is "Your Name," "Your foes," "Your heavens," and so forth; not "His" in the third person. He speaks not *about* God, but *to* Him.

We may wonder why the psalmist refers to God's "Name." The answer requires an understanding of the concept of naming that prevailed in the ancient neareastern world of which Israel was a part.[12] The great Babylonian creation epic known as *Enuma Elish* describes primordial chaos as the time before names had been given to heaven and earth.[13] In like vein, an Egyptian text portrays the pre-creation state of the world as the time "when no name of anything had yet been named."[14] Not to have a name meant nonexistence.

The Egyptian *Book of the Dead* tells how the sun god created other gods by giving names to the parts of his body.[15] The name was thus thought to possess creative power. In the biblical account of creation, as told in the *Book of Genesis*, God carefully gives names to the cosmic phenomena connected with time and space.[16] These acts, while they do not initiate the creative processes, do finalize them. They also affirm divine sovereignty over time and space themselves, for the power to name carries with it dominion over that which receives the name. When God caused animal life to come into existence, he brought the living things to Adam "to see what he would call them; and whatsoever man called each living creature, that would be its name; and the man gave names to all the cattle and to the birds of the sky and to all the wild beasts."[17] This is another way of asserting that God bestowed on humankind mastery over the animal kingdom.[18]

Because the name was never simply a convenient means of identification, but was inextricably interwoven with existence, it was also regarded as being identical with its bearer. Hence the name was bound up with personality. It connoted all the attributes of character, the totality of the essential properties that define an individual.[19]

All this possesses special pertinence in relation to divine names. The name of God attests to the reality of His dynamic, active, potent presence. It bespeaks the nature of His Being as made manifest by His self-disclosure. No wonder it is the majesty of God's Name that the psalmist acclaims!

Associated with the idea of God's kingship is His radiance, or splendor, in Hebrew *hod*.[20] God's splendor, that is, the effulgent radiance that was thought to emanate from His Being, conveys pictorial imagery, and so the heavens present a more appropriate setting for it.[21] That Hebrew *hod* embraces the notion of light is apparent from Habakkuk 3:3–4, which describe a theophany, or manifestation of God:[22]

> His splendor (Hebrew *hodo*) covers the heavens;
> > the earth is filled with His radiance;[23]
> > there is brilliant light,
> > with His rays on every side.

Psalm 104:1–2 similarly connects *hod* with light:

> You are clothed with splendor (Hebrew *hod*) and glory,
> enveloped in light as in a robe.

In addition to these texts, several biblical passages poetically depict God as being suffused with light.[24] Particularly vivid is the description of Ezekiel, the prophet of the Babylonian exile, who, in the year 592 B.C.E., experienced a remarkable mystical vision of the divine Presence. In his altered state of consciousness, he witnessed "a glow as though of amber . . . like the appearance of fire . . . luminous all-around."[25] It will be remembered that when Moses descended from Mount Sinai after his forty-day encounter with God, "the skin of his face was radiant." The phenomenon expressed the reflected effulgence of the divine Presence.[26]

This aesthetic mode of apprehending the divine has always been widespread among the world's religions. Light was not only an attribute of numerous deities but was also applied to humans. In Mesopotamia, radiance was thought to be an inherent characteristic of both gods and kings. The Akkadian term *melammu* conveyed the idea of this supernatural, awe-inspiring quality.[27] Thus, in language similar to that reserved in the Hebrew Bible exclusively for God, Hammurabi declares: "The awe-inspiring sheen of my royalty covered heaven and earth."[28] In real life, this *melammu* might be symbolized by a golden head-mask.

In Egypt, the hieroglyphic sign for gold often appeared in the royal titulary, owing to the durable brightness of the metal. Its characteristic imperishable, lustrous quality symbolized the splendor that the pharaoh shared with the gods.[29] In Roman art, emperors are often depicted with a crown of rays. Again, the light emanating from the king's head was meant to reinforce the myth of his divine attributes.[30] A reflex of this symbol is the use of the nimbus, or halo, in Christian graphic and plastic art as a stylized representation of divinity or holiness.[31]

In Israel, the use of *hod* pertains both to God and to humans.[32]

Moses possesses *hod* with which he is to invest his successor, Joshua.[33] Jeremiah 22:18 informs us that the standard eulogy over a departed monarch included the phrase, "Ah, lord! (Hebrew *'adon*). Ah, his majesty! (Hebrew *hodoh*)." Several biblical texts demonstrate that kings were regarded as being endowed with *hod*.[34] What exactly was understood by this is unclear, but it is certain that it carried no connotation of divinity—the very notion would have been abhorrent in Israel. It must be remembered that the institution of the monarchy was a late development, and was initially resisted by the prophet Samuel as being sinful.[35] The king was subject to the law, and was reproved and denounced by prophets for its infraction.[36] Hence, it is most likely that the term *hod*, as applied to the human king, was simply conventional, formal usage—analogous to addressing a British monarch as "your/his majesty" however unimpressive his personality. It goes without saying that with respect to God, mention of His *hod* is a way of expressing a profound and vivid sense of the reality of His Being, the intense consciousness of His Presence. The psalmist declares that God's splendor is celebrated over the heavens.[37]

So far, the sense is clear. But now comes an enigmatic verse, part of which has become famous in English through the King James Version which reads:

> Out of the mouths of babes and sucklings
> hast Thou ordained strength
> because of Thine enemies
> that Thou mightest still the enemy and avenger.

Neither its meaning nor its connection with the preceding and following text is readily apparent.

One possibility is to join the initial words to the preceding verse, to read,

> You whose splendor is celebrated over the heavens
> from the mouths of babes and sucklings.

The reference might then be to the faculty of speech, which is unique to the human race.[38] To the psalmist, the incoherent and inarticulate babbling and gurgling of babes is, in reality, a celebration of God's splendor. And he adds,

> You established [Your] might on account of Your foes,
> to put an end to the vengeful enemy.

This verse would be figurative language for the idea that the miraculous, inborn capacity for speech constitutes irrefutable testimony to God's might and the conclusive answer to those who would deny His providence.

However, quite a different interpretation of verse 3b presents itself in light of investigation into the identity of God's "foes" elsewhere in the Bible. Numerous biblical passages show that popular legends about creation once circulated in Israel.[39] Expressed in mythological imagery, their deeper meaning is about the tension between order and chaos, symbolized respectively by God and the rebellious primordial waters. The references appear to be snippets of what was once an epic about the God of creation and mutinous forces of primeval chaos at the outset of the cosmogonic process. The rebels are variously termed Rahab, Leviathan, sea monster(s)/Dragon (Hebrew *tannin*, pl. *tanninim*); Sea (Hebrew *yam*, pl. *yammim*), River(s) (Hebrew *nahar*, pl. *neharim*); and Elusive Serpent (Hebrew *nahash bariah*). Isaiah tells that in primeval times, God's arm hacked Rahab in pieces, pierced Tannin, and dried up Yam, the waters of the great deep (Hebrew *tehom*).[40] Habakkuk refers to God's wrath at Neharim and His rage against Yam.[41] The Psalms depict God driving back Yam with His might, smashing the heads of the monsters on the waters, crushing the heads of Leviathan,[42] crushing Rahab so that he was like a corpse, and scattering His enemies with His powerful arm.[43] When God established the earth on its foundations, the waters fled at the blast, rushed away at the sound of His thunder. He set bounds that they may not pass so that they never again cover the earth.[44]

Similar echoes of this myth are found in Job, who asks God, "Am I Yam or Tannin that You have set a watch over me?"[45] In another passage, Job states that God does not restrain His anger; beneath Him, Rahab's helpers fall prostrate.[46] He stilled the sea, struck down Rahab, and pierced the Elusive Serpent.[47] When God finally answers Job out of the tempest, He asks him, "Where were you when I founded the earth . . . enclosed Yam behind doors . . . and said, you may come thus far, and no more; here, your surging waves are placed?"[48]

The rabbis of the talmudic period furnish more detailed accounts of these snippets of myth and locate them in a specific context. One legend has it that when God first decided to create the world, the suffusing primordial, chaotic waters refused to obey the divine command to gather into one area that the dry land might appear.[49] The sea kept on expanding; thereupon, He rebuked it, and it dried up.[50] Another version tells that God first ordered Rahab, "prince of the sea," to swallow the waters that covered the world so that dry land might appear. The angel, however, balked at the command, and was slain by God.[51] A third form of the myth features the world as completely overspread with water and God as giving the command to let the dry land be seen; but the waters would not obey the decree. God then smote Oceanus and killed him. When the other waters saw what happened, they retreated. God then set bounds to the sea.[52] Another variant has the primeval waters swelling up to cover the dry land that had appeared. God rebuked them and subdued them, and fixed the sand of the shore as their boundaries, not to be transgressed.[53]

As stated above, a convincing case has been made for believing that the foregoing biblical and rabbinic legends have their origin in an ancient, independent, popular Israelite epic, now lost. The adjective "independent" pertains to its distinctive Israelite character, although, admittedly, the surviving fragments indicate that it belongs to the genre of cosmological epic from Mesopotamia known as *Enuma Elish*, and also has close affinities with the Baal-Anath cycle of poetic narratives from Ugarit. This latter refers to the cuneiform alphabetic clay tablets found at Ras-Shamra–Ugarit on the North

Syrian coast, stemming from the second millennium B.C.E., which have shed considerable light on many texts in the Hebrew Bible.[54]

What is common to the different cultures is the portrayal of the conflict between order and chaos on a cosmic scale, the mental conversion of these abstract concepts into concrete objective entities, and the reduction of the opposing sides into divine or semi-divine beings. Finally, the personified disorder is represented by watery chaos transformed into sea-monsters. The fragments of the popular Israelite version of the conflict-myth share with the Mesopotamian *Enuma Elish* the association with the creation of the universe. They possess in common with the Ugaritic texts such names as Yam, Nahar, Leviathan, Prince Sea, Elusive Serpent, and Tannin, not to mention many verbal usages.

What fundamentally distinguishes the biblical references from the other neareastern examples is the Israelite, thoroughly monotheistic atmosphere: there is one supreme sovereign God; His foes are not divine beings; the motif of theogony, or birth of gods, is wholly absent; there are no titanic battles in which the outcome appears to be in doubt at one time or another; there is no mention of creation as a consequence of victory in combat; and there is an official, quite different, canonical Genesis creation narrative which expresses numerous polemical, anti-mythic elements. Above all, the fragments of the Israelite conflict-myth appear exclusively in poetic texts, and in the Psalms and Prophets they are cited as literary devices to dress historical events in mythological terms for didactic purposes.

To cite one or two examples of the latter: the prophet Isaiah poetically dubs Egypt "Rahab"—literally, "arrogance"—the female monster of chaos whom God smote and left prostrate.[55] The imagery is intended to reinforce the prophet's view that Egypt was impotent and that the policy of trying to ally Judah with her, advocated by many, was only a strategy for disaster. Ezekiel designates the contemporary pharaoh *tannin*, "the Dragon," to intimate a common fate.[56] The psalmist likewise invokes the conflict-myth in connection with the desired doom of invaders who had overrun the land, set fire to the sanctuary, and violated the Temple.[57]

To return to Psalm 8, verse 3b: our interest is in identifying the "foes" and "vengeful enemy," and there are reasons to believe that the reference may well be to those aforementioned, primordial opponents of God. In the first place, note that the succeeding verses refer to the creation of the universe. Another clue is Psalm 92:10,

> For lo, Your enemies, O Lord,
> For lo, Your enemies shall perish;
> All workers of iniquity shall be scattered.

It was long ago noted that there is a striking parallel between this verse and Ugaritic text III AB. A 8f.[58] In the great combat between Baal and Yam, the divine craftsman named Kothar-and-Hasis encourages Baal with these words:

> Lo, your enemy, O Baal,
> Lo, your enemy will you smite;
> Lo, you will cut off your foe.

It can be demonstrated that Psalm 92, the psalm for the Sabbath day, expresses a cosmogonic motif, so that the enemies there and the "enemy" here connect with the conflict-myth. Furthermore, Psalm 8 states (v. 3),

> You have established [Your] might . . .

Hebrew 'oz, "might," is an oft-extolled attribute of God,[59] asserted, in particular, in primordial times.[60] Thus, Isaiah 51:9 implores,

> Awake, awake, clothe yourself with might
> O arm of the Lord!
> Awake as in days of old,
> As in former ages!
> It was You that hacked Rahab in pieces,
> That pierced the Dragon.

The psalmist makes the same association. In Psalm 74:13–14 he declares,

> It was You who drove back the sea (Hebrew *yam*) with Your might, who smashed the heads of the monsters (Hebrew *tanninim*) in the waters; it was You who crushed the heads of the Leviathan.

Psalm 89:11 similarly exclaims,

> You crushed Rahab who became like a corpse; with Your mighty arm You scattered Your enemies.

To sum up: the first stanza of our psalm, verses 2–3, may be translated as follows:

> O Lord, our Lord,
> How majestic is Your Name throughout the earth,
> You whose splendor is celebrated over the heavens
> from the mouths of babes and sucklings.
> You established [Your] might on account of Your foes,
> to put an end to the vengeful enemy.[61]

The magnificent spectacle of the star-studded sky has prompted our psalmist to rhapsodize the majesty and splendor of God and to invoke His mighty deeds of yore. Now, his thoughts turn to questions of divine-human relationships.

> When I behold Your heavens, the work of Your fingers,
> the moon and the stars that You set in place . . .

The flow of the sentence is abruptly arrested, leaving the reader or audience to supply the missing words—a classic example of the rhetorical device technically known as "aposeopesis."[62] Apparently, the scene stirs feelings of "creature-consciousness" which, in turn, yield to a profound realization of the dual status of human beings. He asks,

> What is man that You are mindful of him,
> mortal man that You take note of him?

The deprecating, scornful import of the questions is intensified by the use of the Hebrew interrogative pronoun *mah*, that goes with an object, rather than *mi*, which refers to a person.[63] Moreover, the two Hebrew words used for the human race, *'enosh* and *ben 'adam*, are intentionally chosen because of their inflection of insignificance, being heavily charged with intimations of the impermanence and fleeting nature of human existence.

Although we have rendered *'enosh* by "man," no English word adequately conveys its true sense. The stem means "to be weak, frail."[64] It can describe a condition of desperate sickness, and in its noun form, *'enosh* lays emphasis on human vulnerability, on the essentially finite nature of human power.[65] Similar connotations adhere to the parallel term *ben 'adam* used in our psalm, which may be translated "an earthly being."[66] This preserves the wordplay of Genesis 2:7,

> the Lord God formed man (*'adam*)
> from the dust of the earth (*'adamah*)

It corresponds to the Latin pun, *homo* "man"—*humus* "earth, soil."

What the Psalmist wonders at is why God bothers with this puny creature, whose origin is dust and who is destined to return to the dust of the earth. As Genesis 3:19 expresses it,

> For dust you are, and to dust you shall return.

The same question is asked in another psalm (144:3–4):
> O Lord, what is man that You should care about him,
> mortal man, that You should think of him?
> Man is like a breath;
> his days are like a passing shadow.

By the very nature of the questions, it is clear that the psalmist's conception of God is not that of an otiose deity; that is, of a God who, having created the universe, has withdrawn from any active role in it, is remote and aloof, and has left humankind to its own devices. Far from being a passive God, He is intimately, directly, and benevolently involved in the lives of His creatures.

The two Hebrew verbs employed in parallelism[67] in verse 5, *z-kh-r* and *p-k-d*, are verbs of action. The first, often translated "to remember," conveys not the simple recall of things past, but connotes "to be mindful of," "to take note of." The second covers a wider semantic field, but also invokes the idea of concern, of being attentive to. Both verbs presuppose being moved to action, whether benevolently or punitively.[68] And therein lies the paradox that is inherent in the Israelite conception of God. He is of infinite magnitude, wholly transcending the world of nature, beyond the possibility of human comprehension. Nevertheless, He is a personal God who interacts with human beings, puny and insignificant though they be by comparison with Him.

The following verses focus attention on the contradictory aspect of being human. This earthly being possesses awesome potentialities:

> You have made him little less than divine,[69]
> and adorned him with glory and majesty.

The first thing to notice about these verses is that they are addressed directly to God. The psalmist recognizes that God is the sole source of human power, and that it was by His choice that the human race is so endowed. Then, there is the word here rendered "divine." The Hebrew is *'elohim*, the most common biblical term for God. But throughout the author speaks directly to God, so that in this instance *'elohim* is more likely to mean something else. In many texts, this word refers to angels because it is a term for supernatural beings in general. Just as a terrestrial monarch is accompanied by an entourage of attendants and ministers, so the divine Sovereign is pictured as surrounded by a celestial retinue, the angelic host.

In what way did God make men and women "a little less than the angels"? The phrasing implies that they possess certain qualities in common with angels but are inferior in one major respect. The answer must be sought in the traditions of Genesis 3, verses 5 and 22. There we are told that the serpent, in enticing Eve to eat of the forbidden fruit of the tree of knowledge, tells her, "God knows that as soon as you eat of it, your eyes will be opened and you will be like divine beings (Hebrew *'elohim*) who know good and bad." This characteristic of the angels appears again in 2 Samuel 14:17, "For my lord the king is like an angel of God, understanding . . . good and bad." Adam and Eve did eat of the fruit and, indeed, became like one of the divine retinue in that respect, as Genesis 3:22 describes; but they were expelled from Eden to ensure that they did not gain immortality. Herein lies the inferiority of humans to celestials: men and women are subject to the inevitability of death.

Despite their mortality, says the psalmist, God has endowed human beings with "glory and grandeur" (Hebrew *kavod, hadar*). Like *hod*, discussed above, these terms both belong to the vocabulary of kingship, divine and human.[70] Their governing Hebrew verb here means "adorn," a figurative usage derived from *'atarah*, a "coronet." In biblical times, this was worn as a sign of distinction and high rank, an emblem of nobility.[71] The psalmist's choice of words, both verb and nouns, bespeaks a transcendent vision of human dignity, the exaltation of each individual as a being of infinite worth. It is to this singular creature—at once pathetic and majestic—that God has handed over mastery of the physical world which is His own handiwork. This, of course, is the antithesis of the scornful exclamation of v. 5, "What is man?"

The text that focuses on this conception of human sovereignty may be literally translated as follows:

> You have given him mastery over the work of Your hands,
> You have placed all under his feet.[72]

The two parts of this binary verse correspond one to the other, the first expressing the basic thought straightforwardly, the second metaphorically. What is the origin and import of this imagery? The Bible and neareastern texts and art abundantly illustrate the reality behind it.

The Book of Joshua 10:24 relates that, following the Israelite leader's defeat and capture of five Canaanite kings, he ordered his army officers to come forward and place their feet on the necks of those vanquished monarchs. In the message that King Solomon sent to King Hiram of Tyre, soliciting his assistance in the building of the Temple in Jerusalem, he says that David, his father, was unable to carry out the project on account of the neighboring enemies "until the Lord had placed them under the soles of his feet" (1 Kings 5:17). Psalm 47:4 has,

> He put peoples under our control,
> nations, under our feet.

Psalm 110:1 expresses the same action in a somewhat different image: "I shall make your enemies your footstool."

The Babylonian creation story, *Enuma Elish*, tablet IV:104, tells that when Marduk had destroyed the monster Tiamat, "he threw down her carcass to stand upon it."[73] An inscription about the victory of the Sumerian king, Utu-khegal (2120-2114 B.C.E.) of Uruk, over King Tirigan states that he "set his foot upon his neck, and restored the kingship of Sumer unto his own hand."[74] This act signaled the end of two centuries of subjection to foreign kings. Another inscription, this from the Assyrian ruler Tukulti-Ninurta I (1242-1206 B.C.E.), referring to his victim, the Kassite king of Babylon, Kashtiliash IV, states how "his royal neck like a footstool I tread with my feet."[75] The same symbolic gesture is found in the Egyptian sphere. The pharaoh's version of the treaty of alliance between Ramses II and the Hittite king, Hattusilis, concluded in 1280 B.C.E., boasts that "all foreign countries are prostrate under his soles forever."[76] Lastly, far to the north of Egypt, in Asia Minor, a Phoenician

dedicatory inscription of King Azitawadda of Adana, found at Karatepe, and probably deriving from the eighth century B.C.E., similarly claims concerning his enemies, "I placed them under my
feet."[77] In addition to the literary sources, the scene of the conqueror
with his foot placed on the body or neck of his vanquished foe
appears as a motif in the art of the ancient Near East.[78]

The metaphorical use of this ancient and widespread gesture of
subjugation in verse 7 of our psalm lays added emphasis upon the
straightforward declaration of the initial parallel clause. Together,
they give powerful expression to the sentiment of verse 6 that the
human race, vis à vis the animal kingdom, possesses God-like qualities which place it in a unique relationship with God. Contrary to
the presuppositions of the ancient pagan religions which divinized
the forces of nature and which, as a consequence, believed that those
forces held humans in bondage, this psalmist proclaims the distinctively Israelite conviction that God, who created nature, has
given humanity the power to control it. These affirmations are res-
onant echoes of the Genesis Creation narratives which tell that when
God decided to create human beings, he ordained,

> They shall rule the fish of the sea,
> the birds of the sky, the cattle,
> the whole earth, and all the creeping things that creep
> on the earth (Gen. 1:26).

Having created male and female,

> God blessed them and God said to them,
> ". . . fill the earth and master it,
> and rule the fish of the sea, the birds of the sky, and all
> the living things that creep on earth" (Gen. 1:28).

These passages may not be misinterpreted as granting license for the
unbridled exploitation of nature's resources, for it must be remembered that humankind possesses no inherent right or power to use
them, other than as a privilege conferred by God. Moreover, the

sovereignty that people enjoy, according to the Bible, cannot be defined outside the biblical framework of kingship, which permits no unrestrained power. The rights and privileges of the monarch are curtailed and are to be exercised with responsibility. The violations of these restraints in the kingdoms of Judah and Israel inevitably aroused the denunciations of the prophets. Finally, the laws of land tenure must also be taken into account in considering the full meaning of the biblical concept of human sovereignty over the physical world. Leviticus 25:23 restricts the right of permanent alienation of land, the absolute transference of title and possession, for the reason that

> all the earth is Mine;
> you are but strangers resident with Me.

Human beings are looked upon as God's tenants. What Genesis 1:26, 28 and Psalm 8:7–9 enunciate is the principle of stewardship, not proprietorship. Verses 8–9 specify the generalized statement of verse 7. The order is domesticated cattle, small[79] and large,[80] the beasts of the field,[81] birds,[82] fish,[83] and "what traverses the paths of the seas."[84] This latter may well be a poetic rephrasing of "the great sea monsters" of Genesis 1:21.

It might have been thought that just as exhilaration over the spectacular night-time scene had prompted adoration of God, so review of the immense power of human beings would yield to exaltation of man. But this is not the case. Any tendency toward human arrogance is checked by the sobering reality of the opening and closing affirmation,

> O Lord, our Lord, how majestic is Your Name through-
> out the earth!

Chapter 3

PSALM NINETEEN

*The Excellence of Torah:
An Anti-pagan Polemic*

For the leader. A psalm of David.

²The heavens declare the glory of God,
    His handiwork the sky proclaims.
³Day to day makes utterance,
    night to night speaks out.
⁴There is no utterance,
    there are no words,
    whose sound goes unheard.
⁵Their voice carries throughout the earth,
    their words to the end of the world.
He placed in them a tent for the sun,
    ⁶who is like a groom coming forth from the chamber,
    like a hero, eager to run his course.
⁷His rising-place is at one end of heaven,
    and his circuit reaches the other;
    nothing escapes His sun.

⁸The Teaching of the LORD is perfect,
    reviving the spirit;
    the decrees of the LORD are enduring,
    making the simple wise;
⁹The precepts of the LORD are just,
    rejoicing the heart;
    the instruction of the LORD is lucid,
    making the eyes light up.
¹⁰The fear of the LORD is pure,
    abiding forever;
    the judgments of the LORD are true,
    righteous altogether,
    ¹¹more desirable than gold,
    than much fine gold;

sweeter than honey,
than drippings of the comb.
¹²Your servant pays them heed;
in obeying them there is much reward.
¹³Who can be aware of errors?
Clear me of unperceived guilt,
¹⁴and from arrogant men keep Your servant;
let them not dominate me;
then shall I be blameless
and clear of grave offense.
¹⁵May the words of my mouth
and the utterance of my heart
be acceptable to You,
O Lord, my rock and my redeemer.

In biblical times, Israel had to engage in unremitting and intense struggle for its soul, not just for its physical survival. The age-old, traditional, highly conservative civilizations of the region perennially exerted a corrosive influence upon the people. The territory in which Israel settled stood at the crossroads of the world forming the land bridge between the continents of Africa and Asia. This turbulent part of the globe was the arena of unceasing contention between the great powers. As a result, it was always strategically exposed, ever subject to the seductive, if destructive, incursions of a variety of peoples and cultures.

Biblical literature exhibits an acute sensitivity to this situation. It does so directly, through its repeated denunciations of polytheism and its accompanying phenomena, and also by educational legislation. These overt measures attempted to isolate the people and insulate them from the baleful pressures of the alien cultures. The Bible also employs more subtle means to combat the menace. It engages in tacit polemic against the basic ideas and concepts that animated the pagan religions. Such is the case with the Creation and Flood narratives in the Book of Genesis.[1] Often the technique is to use the very terminology and phraseology of pagan myth or liturgy, empty them of their objectionable content, and transform them to make them compatible with the monotheistic religion of Israel.

While the cults of the Canaanite god Baal and the mother goddess Ashtoreth posed the greatest threat to the integrity of Israelite religion, there was a period when astral deities in general, and sun worship in particular, seem to have been especially popular.

There is evidence of the existence of an indigenous sun cult in Canaan even in pre-Israelite times; witness such place-names as Beth-shemesh, "Temple of the Sun," which belonged to several sites; Ir-shemesh, meaning "City of the Sun"; Ein-shemesh, "Spring of the Sun"; Har-heres, "Mountain of the Sun"; and Ma'aleh-heres, "The Ascent of the Sun," using another Hebrew term for the luminary.[2]

The Decalogue forbids making and worshiping a sculptured image or likeness of "what is in the heavens above."[3] More specific are Moses' admonitions in his farewell address in the Book of Deuteronomy. He warns, "When you look up to the sky and behold the sun, the moon, and the stars, the whole heavenly host, you must not be lured into bowing down to them or serving them."[4] The same book enacts legislation designating such practices as a capital offense.[5] The Book of Kings informs us that King Manasseh of Judah (687/6 B.C.E.–642 B.C.E.), who was a vassal of Assyria, paganized Jerusalem, worshipped astral deities, and even built altars for them within the Temple precincts.[6]

In reaction to all of this, Manasseh's grandson, King Josiah (640 B.C.E.–609 B.C.E.), instituted far-reaching religious reforms in the course of which he rid Judea of "objects made for all the host of heaven" and suppressed the idolatrous priests who had officiated at the provincial shrines where the people had been bringing offerings to "the sun, the moon, and the constellations." He abolished "the horses that the kings of Judah had dedicated to the sun at the entrance" of the Temple, and "burned the sun-chariots."[7] These probably were associated with a mythology in which the sun's journey across the sky was effectuated by means of a horsedrawn chariot.

All of these drastic measures are said to have come about as a result of the chance find of a "book of the Torah" during the renovation of the Temple undertaken by King Josiah. This book was read to the king, who was so deeply moved by its contents that he instituted a thoroughgoing religious reformation. This resulted both in the drastic measures described above and in a formal national ceremony of the renewal of the ancient covenant between God and Israel. Henceforth, the religion of Israel became book-centered—a revolutionary development in the history of religion. In the course of time, the study and exposition of Torah became pivotal in the religious life and spiritual experience of the people of Israel, and has remained so in Judaism to this day.

Yet, popular acceptance of this ideal apparently did not occur at once. Notwithstanding the radical measures taken by King Josiah, the astral cults persisted; the prophet Zephaniah, whose ministry occurred in Josiah's day, mentions "those who bow down on the roofs to the host of heaven."[8] His contemporary, the prophet Jeremiah, testifies that in the towns of Judah and streets of Jerusalem, the entire family was engaged in the worship of the "Queen of Heaven," doubtless the appellation of the goddess Ishtar. He says the people loved to serve and follow the sun, moon, and all the host of heaven, and brought offerings to them on the roofs of their houses.[9] The prophet of the Babylonian exile, Ezekiel, probably recalling the days of King Manasseh, tells that in the inner court of the Temple, between the portico and the altar, about twenty-five men, their backs to the Temple and their faces to the east, were bowing low to the rising sun.[10] This scene had a curious resonance in Second Temple times. The Mishnah, tractate Sukkah 5:4, reports that in the course of the water-drawing ceremony during the festival of Tabernacles, when the procession reached the gate that led out to the east, the worshipers turned from east to west in order to face the Temple, and proclaimed: "Our fathers who were in this place had their backs to the Temple of the Lord, their faces turned eastward, and they worshiped the sun toward the east, but as for us, our eyes are turned to the Lord."

There is no evidence to support a claim that sun worship in Judah was dictated by Assyrian imperialism.[11] However, it is beyond cavil that its popularity reached its height during the period of Assyrian domination of the West. There is good reason to conclude that Psalm 19 in its present form was composed following the reforms of Josiah in the year 622/1 B.C.E., and that it is a tacit polemic against the cult of the sun worshipers.[12]

Anyone who reads the psalm is immediately struck by the abrupt and puzzling change of theme that occurs beginning with verse 8. At a first reading, it would seem that two discrete hymns have somehow been conjoined under a single heading. Indeed, many modern scholars so hold, seeing that the first section (verses 2–7) features a cosmic motif in which all natural phenomena rhapsodize their Maker, while the second part (verses 8–11) celebrates the excellence of Torah.[13] There are also considerable divergences in form and style between the two hymns. As a matter of fact, biblical texts and ancient sources do testify to differences in the divisions and combinations of other psalm units. For instance, our two distinct psalms 1 and 2 at one time were taken by some to be a single composition, as were our psalms now numbered 9 and 10 and 42 and 43; while our psalm 108 is made up of Ps. 57:8–2 and 60:7–14. In the Greek version of the Jews of Alexandria, our Hebrew Psalms 114 and 115 appear as one unified psalm, while Psalm 147 is split into two. Nevertheless, a persuasive case may be made for the unity of Psalm 19 in its present form. But before we deal with that, attention must be directed to some other pertinent issues.

The singularities mentioned above are compounded by the extraordinary mythological personification of the heavens, of day and night, and especially of the sun. As we shall see, this provides the key to the interpretation of the psalm as a whole. Also, if we compare

Psalm 19 with Psalms 1 and 8, we notice both close similarities and important contrasts. Psalm 19 shares with Psalm 8 the appreciation of God's glory as manifested in cosmic phenomena, and it has in common with Psalm 1 the transcendent significance of Torah. However, it is the majestic spectacle of the morning's rising sun, not the sparkling stars at night, as in Psalm 8, that stirs the author's poetic spirit; and it is Torah itself, not the student of Torah, as in Psalm 8, that energizes his talents. Whereas in Psalm 8 our poet stresses the divine endowment of humankind with mastery over nature, here, the theme is God's gift of Torah, by which men and women may gain mastery over themselves. Also, it is not the inconsequence or greatness of human beings that interests our psalmist, but the recognition of their inherent imperfection and their need of divine help in striving for self-improvement. This is the content of the third section, verses 12–15.

Medieval Jewish Bible commentators, like their modern counterparts, grappled with the problem of the unity of the psalm. Saadiah (882–942 C.E.) regarded the section devoted to Torah as the content of the communications mentioned in verses 2–5. Rashi (1040–1105) perceptively points to the use of some solar expressions employed in relation to Torah, specifically in verses 8–9. Abraham ibn Ezra (1089–1164) also recognized solar language among the attributes of Torah, and added that both cosmic phenomena and Torah testify to the glory of God. David Kimḥi (1160?–1235?) similarly reasons that the heavens and their constituents are vital to the preservation and welfare of humanity, and the same is true of Torah, thus providing a thematic connection between the two parts.

In addition to the aforementioned, further points of contact between the disparate sections can be suggested. The light radiated from the sun may be intentionally, if inferentially, correlated with the spiritual enlightenment imparted by Torah. As Proverbs 6:23 expresses it, "For the commandment is a lamp, the Teaching (*torah*) is a light." There may also be the notion that cosmic phenomena and Torah are twin sources for the knowledge of God. Moreover, it is hardly likely to be mere coincidence that the nature hymn refers to God as 'el, and the Torah hymn employs the tetragrammaton YHVH—no less than seven times.[14] 'El is the oldest and the most conventional term for "God" in the Semitic languages.[15] In some pantheons it was used as a proper name for the chief god. On account of its generalized character, it is more appropriate that it be used for the deity in the hymn that deals with aspects of the cosmos, whereas YHVH, the appellation of God specific to Israel, befits the hymn devoted to Torah, God's revelation to His people.

There is one further, quite compelling reason for accepting the entire psalm as a unity and for believing that there is a generic connection between its two sections. As we have pointed out, the worship of the sun as a god was widespread throughout the ancient Near East and elsewhere.[16] Also accepted was the notion that darkness was associated with evil and with the foul deeds perpetrated during the night hours. Conversely, light was considered to be the natural adversary of the dark; and so the sun, as the source and dispenser of light, became associated with the principle of the good and the lawful. Whatever the name under which the sun god was venerated, it was everywhere taken to be the guardian of law and justice. The hymns devoted to that deity portray him as both the god of light and the god of justice, the two motifs intermingling and succeeding one another smoothly and naturally. By analogy, the apparent lack of logical thought sequence in Psalm 19 may be a reflex of a well-established liturgical pattern in the ancient Near East.

The anti-pagan polemic begins with the opening lines of the psalm, which state that the cosmic phenomena rhapsodize God, their Maker. They express at once the fundamental conception of Israelite thought: that God wholly transcends nature, which itself testifies to His glory and greatness. This is in striking contrast to the basic assumptions of neareastern religions that the phenomena of nature themselves constitute manifestations of the deity. Verses 2 and 3 read as follows:

> The heavens declare the glory of God,
>> His handiwork the sky proclaims.
> Day to day makes utterance,
>> night to night speaks out.

The first thing to notice is the initial chiastic arrangement, that is, the subject-verb-object followed by the reverse order in the parallel clause. This is a literary device by which two "simultaneously occurring aspects of the same situation" can be presented as a single picture.[17] The next two lines present sequence, not simultaneity, and so are not chiastic.

Although we have just used the term "verb," and in English translation that is what the first two lines would indicate, this terminology is not quite accurate. The Hebrew employs two participles, a grammatical form that partakes of the character of both noun and verb, expressing the subject in the continuous uninterrupted exercise of the activity.[18] The temporal dimension is lacking; what is being stressed is not so much time duration as timelessness and eternity. The heavens and sky can never cease from their telling and proclaiming, because the subject of their declamation must inherently endure for all time, in that it flows from the unchanging One to whom the very concept of time, with its intrinsic limitations, is wholly inapplicable.

Our poet describes the celestial regions by two terms: "heavens" and "sky," in Hebrew *shamayim* and *rakia'*. The former is the general, common, biblical word for the expansive space above the surface of the earth. But the heavens are conceived in the Bible as being multilayered, which is why we encounter a phrase like "the highest heaven."[19] The "abode" of God was popularly thought to be in heaven,[20] and therefore one of His appellations is "the God of heaven."[21] This region is distinct from "sky," which is the lower level, that part of the celestial sphere visible to an observer here on earth.[22] That is where the sun, moon, and other astronomical phenomena are situated.[23] The psalmist has very carefully selected his vocabulary. Because God is imagined to reside in or above the heavens, it is the heavens that relate His glory; since the observable celestial bodies are located in the sky, the sky proclaims His "handi-work," that is, His creation.

The poetic notion of nature's constituents extolling their Maker is not unique to this composition. The same idea is expressed in Psalm 148:1–6, in which all heavenly beings and objects are called upon to rhapsodize God:

> Hallelujah.
> Praise the Lord from the heavens;
>> praise Him in the heights.
> Praise Him, all His angels,
>> praise Him, all His hosts.
> Praise Him, O sun and moon;
>> praise Him, all bright stars.
> Praise Him, O highest heavens,
>> and you waters above the heavens.
> Let them praise the Name of the Lord;
>> for He it is who gave a command, and they were
>> created.
> He established them for all eternity,
>> He set an order, never to change.

Another example of this type of animation is found in Job 38:7, where we are told that at the creation of the world,

> The morning stars chanted in unison,
> and all divine beings shouted for joy.

We are dealing, of course, with figurative language. Human feelings and emotional reactions to the timeless magnificence of the celestial scene heighten consciousness of its Creator, and quicken the impulse to celebrate His handiwork and give vocal expression to the inward, spiritual experience it arouses. The poet projects this situation onto the heavens and the heavenly bodies, which are now all personified.

This kind of personification, with similar imagery, though in an entirely different context, has a history in the ancient Near East. It can be found in Ugaritic literature. In the epic known as Baal and Anath, the god sends a message of love to the goddess that includes the following:

> I have a word which I would tell,
> a matter I would recite to you,
> a word of the trees and a whisper of the stones,
> discourse of heaven with earth,
> of the deeps with the stars,
> of thunderbolts the heavens do not know,
> a word which men do not know,
> and which the earthly mass do not comprehend. [24]

There is some resemblance, too, to the theory of the "music of the spheres" advanced by the Greek mathematician and philosopher Pythagoras (ca. 580 B.C.E.–ca. 497 B.C.E.) and his school. They believed that the planets revolved in circular orbits and, as they did so, produced a variety of sounds whose frequencies differed according to variations in speed of the individual planets and their distance from the center. The resultant "music" was inaudible to human beings because it was beyond the threshold of human hearing. [25] Unlike our psalm, this was put forward as "scientific" theory to account for some aspects of the physical world. The "music" supposedly generated by the planets was not in exaltation of God and had no spiritual implication. In like manner, a "scientific" explanation is given for the inability of humans to receive the "music." The afore-cited Ugaritic passage is somewhat closer to the tenor of the psalm in that the language of the inanimate objects mentioned is unintelligible to outsiders. Psalm 19 continues:

> There is no speech,
> There are no words,
> Their voices are unheard.

That is to say, the heavens, and day and night, as it were, recount God's glory in their own special way, in a language that is neither perceptible to the ear nor understandable to human beings on earth. Nevertheless, says the poet (verse 5),

> Their voice[26] carries throughout the earth,
> their words to the end of the world.

The entire universe resounds with doxology, the praise of God.

At this point, in order to forge the transition from the glorification of God to the glorification of His Torah, the psalmist injects a stanza devoted to the movement of the sun across the sky. How the latter bears upon the former becomes apparent upon close study of the extraordinary imagery and phraseology employed (verses 5–7):

> He placed in them a tent for the sun;
> who is like a groom coming forth from the
> chamber,
> like a hero, eager[27] to run his course.
> His rising-place is at one end of heaven,
> and his circuit reaches the other;
> nothing escapes His sun.

In this passage, our psalmist leaves no doubt that the sun is under God's control. It is God who placed a tent for it in the sky; it is "His sun."[28] The tent undoubtedly is where the sun was thought to rest from its tiring activity of the day, traversing the expanse of the heaven. An ancient Mesopotamian prayer to the gods of the night explains sunset and darkness in terms of Shamash, the sun god, betaking himself to his chamber.[29] A Sumerian simile uses the comparison "like the sun coming forth from its sleeping chamber."[30] Moreover, in Mesopotamian mythology, Shamash has a consort named Aya who is frequently given the epithet "bride."[31] This is why our psalmist figuratively describes the sunrise as the emergence of a bridegroom from his chamber. The author of our psalm obviously is familiar with the pagan mythology, and his use of it implies an assumption that the allusions would be widely understood. Incidentally, there is a clever wordplay involved in calling the sun's chamber "a tent," for the consonants of the Hebrew word for "tent" also form the stem of a verb denoting "to shine,"[32] so providing two levels of meaning.

The other simile enlisted to describe the emergence of the morning sun invokes the image of a youthful hero or warrior, all set and ready to go. This, too, draws upon common neareastern literary usage, also reflected in pictorial representation. In Mesopotamia the epithet "hero/warrior" is frequently attached to Shamash, the sun god, who was also a warrior god; further, the "sun god militant" appears on cylinder seals, as does his portrayal as a runner.[33] One of his epithets is, "He who traverses the way of heaven and earth." A Hittite hymn to the male sun god Istanu carries the line, "You stride through the four eternal corners."[34] In Egypt, the morning sun is hailed as "the valiant one" because its daily rising was seen as a victory over the forces of evil.[35] The sun god is also described as "runner, racer, courser," and as "the great runner swift of step." He is explicitly said to "race a course" each day. The same figure is implied in the Bible in Ecclesiastes 1:5: The sun rises and the sun sets, and comes panting back to its place where it rises [again].

The first hymn closes with mention of the universal, inescapable effect upon the earth of the sun's presence in the sky, most likely referring to the heat and light that it generates for the benefit of humankind. This idea of the ubiquitous penetration of the sun's rays is also stressed in the neareastern hymns of adoration addressed to the sun god. His votaries declare that he sees everything, that his fierce rays illuminate the entire earth; every land is filled with his beauty, and his intense brightness reaches down even to the abyss.[36] Our Israelite psalmist is careful to nullify belief in the sun as an independent agency. By means of two simple devices, he neutralizes any possibility of deifying it: he uses a synonym instead of the usual word for "sun" that was employed in verse 5—Hebrew *hammah* in place of *shemesh*—to avoid confusion with the Mesopotamian sun god who was named Shamash; and then he attaches the possessive suffix to the word in order to accentuate its subordination and God's proprietorship.

It was pointed out above that the sun god, in addition to his cosmic role as the source of heat and light, was also worshiped as the god of right and justice.[37] This association flowed from the identification of light with the principle of the good, and from the notion that his lofty height enabled him to observe the doings of all creatures on earth. The ancient texts that relate to the deified sun give frequent expression to these beliefs. Thus, in Elam, modern Khuzistan in southwestern Iran, north of the Persian Gulf, the sun god, named Nahhunte, was also the god of law, truth, and justice.[38] Among the Hittites, the sun god was conceived to be the god of right and justice who daily sits in judgment over all living creatures.[39] In Mesopotamia, Shamash, the sun god, represented the principle of cosmic justice. He supervised the moral order, and among the epithets applied to him were "judge of heaven and earth" and "the judge of the gods and of mankind." In the mythology, he and his consort Aya produced a daughter, Kittu, and a son, Mesharu, names that respectively mean "truth" and "justice/equity"—abstractions personified and deified. It is no wonder that Shamash was regarded as the inspiration for legislation, and that his name was invoked in the Mesopotamian law collections.[40]

The earliest extant example of this comes from King Ur-Nammu (2112–2095 B.C.E.), founder of the Sumerian Third Dynasty at the city of Ur, situated west of the Euphrates River in southern Iraq. The prologue to his legislative record claims that he operates "in accordance with the true word of Utu," the Sumerian sun god.[41] Another collection, that of Lipit-Ishtar (ca. 1870 B.C.E.) of the city of Isin in central lower Mesopotamia, calls upon the sun god to punish whoever damages the stele on which it was inscribed.[42] King Hammurabi of Babylon (ca. 1728–1686 B.C.E.) mentions Shamash repeatedly in both the prologue and epilogue to his great collection of laws. In addition, the bas-relief that adorns the upper part of the front of the stele shows a god whom many scholars identify with Shamash investing the king with the symbols of sovereignty; that is, authorizing him to promulgate his laws.[43] Lastly, Ammisaduqa, the tenth ruler of the Hammurabi Dynasty in Babylon (1646–1626 B.C.E.), issued an edict imposing social and economic reform. The text of the proclamation, substantially preserved, likens the king to Shamash in that "he rose forth in steadfastness over his country, and instituted justice for all the people."[44]

So much for the legal documents. The same twofold function of the sun god, the physical and the judicio-moral, is featured in liturgical texts. The great hymn to Shamash, which was popular in the times of the Assyrian King Ashurbanipal (668–627 B.C.E.), hails the god as the one who illuminates the world and dispels darkness, who enforces justice and morality, and punishes evildoing.[45]

In Egyptian religion, the principle of order and stability was expressed by the word *ma'at*, which can be used variously for "truth," "justice," "righteousness," and "order." This principle was personified and deified, with Ma'at becoming the name of a goddess. It is germane to our topic that she was represented as the daughter and confidante of the sun god Re.[46] It is also not without interest that among the Greeks, the god Apollo, whose forename was Phoebus, which means "pure," "bright," "radiant," was connected with the sun; he was considered to be the supervisor of everything to do with law and order and deemed to be the source and interpreter of legislation.[47]

In light of this widespread tradition, it should occasion no surprise that our biblical psalm proceeds from concern with the solar to preoccupation with Torah. Nor, in view of its anti-sun cult polemical nature, is it to be wondered that most of the epithets applied to the Torah occur as attributes of the sun god in the ancient near-eastern literature.

The sun's outpourings of light and heat are vital to the support of life on earth; but the psalmist knows full well that mere physical existence is not the same as living. The quality of life is ultimately determined by obedience to God's Teaching, for which six different terms are used. Each noun is attached to the name YHVH, "Lord," to indicate that the norms of behavior implied by these expressions are divine imperatives, and thus possess eternal validity. Moreover, the supreme inspiration for them and for the authority behind them is YHVH, Israel's God of revelation, not any sun god.

The first line of the second hymn (verse 8) reads: "The Teaching (*torah*) of the Lord is perfect, reviving the spirit."[48] The Hebrew word rendered here "perfect" can also mean "complete," "unblemished," "unimpaired," "possessing integrity." Torah, God's Teaching to His people, is an unerring ethical guide along the path of life, all-embracing in scope, a comprehensive system that nourishes existence. Superficially, this parallels Egyptian hymns to the sun god in which his perfection and generative, lifegiving powers are stressed.[49] So, too, in Mesopotamian texts, Shamash is "one who gives life," "who revives the dead."[50] According to Babylonian lore, that god passes through the underworld during the night and brings light, food, and drink to the dead. The aforementioned Hittite hymn to the sun god, Istanu, likewise describes him as "lifegiving."[51]

Our psalmist tacitly dismisses all this by redefining the terminology. He shifts from material and physical attributes to the world of spiritual and moral values. It is the way of Torah that leads to the life that strives for perfection that is life-sustaining; that buoys the flagging spirit and enables the victim of misfortune firmly to endure life's trials and tribulations.

> The decrees of the Lord are enduring,
> making the simple wise.

The indissoluble relationship between God and His people, forged at Sinai, is expressed in the Bible in terms of a covenant, or pact solemnly contracted between the two parties. This is the central, pervasive idea of the religion of Israel. Its stipulations have ever since regulated the people's way of life and determined its weal and woe.

The usual Hebrew word for the covenant is *brit*; here, our text uses instead an ancient Semitic term for a pact sealed by an oath that fell into disuse in Hebrew (*'edut*). [52] It is used specifically for the two Tablets of Stone on which the Decalogue, the core of the covenant obligations, was incised. [53] It is also occasionally employed, as in the present instance, as a synonym of Torah, or divine teaching in general. [54] Because this ancient Hebrew word for "covenant" (*'edut*) became obsolete and was replaced by *b'rith*, the early translators of the Bible into Aramaic, Greek, and Latin were unaware of its original meaning. They rendered it "testimony" on account of its similarity in sound and written form to the word for "witness" (*'ed*).

God's covenant, or pact, is said to impart wisdom to the naive. In parallel with "Torah," it is clearly envisioned as literature that is to be studied and internalized so as to become part of one's inner being and mental structure. The Hebrew term that we have translated as "simple" (*peti*) is used frequently in the Book of Proverbs to describe one who is wholly inexperienced in the ways of the world, whose moral consciousness is undeveloped, and who, through the vice of ignorance, lacks the critical ability to weigh ethical issues and to make prudent decisions. He is not a person stricken with inherent incapacity, and his ready credulity can be cured by serious immersion in the written record of God's covenant, with the demands it makes on human behavior. These latter are the subject of the following verse (9):

> The precepts of the Lord are just,
>> rejoicing the heart;
>> the instruction of the Lord is lucid,
>> making the eyes light up.

This couplet and the preceding one are mutually complementary. Verse 8 employs two nouns which, as noted, suggest formal study which might be a mere theoretical and academic exercise. The present verse therefore translates theory into action. The terms "precepts" and "command" call for performance, for deeds, not simply contemplation and catechism.

It is striking that each of the descriptive terms and phrases used in verse 9 is redolent of the language of the sun god texts. Thus, it is hardly coincidental that in declaring the Torah to be "just," our psalm uses the identical locution to that which underlies similar designations in the neareastern solar compositions. Popular epithets of the Mesopotamian god Shamash are "the one who directs aright" and "the lord of truth and right."[55] Furthermore, as we noted, the male offspring of that god was the mythological personification of "right."

In like manner, in stating that the Lord's Torah gladdens the heart, the poet once again echoes the idea expressed in Egyptian hymns that the sun god, as he joyfully embarks on his daily journey across the sky, brings joy to the world. In a hymn addressed to the sun god Re, the worshiper declares, "When you rise on the horizon of heaven, a cry of joy goes forth to you from all the people . . . In every place every heart swells with joy at your rising."[56]

Furthermore, the association with the sun is enhanced subtly by a double entendre embedded in the Hebrew word used for "gladdening," or "rejoicing the heart." The same term appears in several biblical passages in the sense of "to shine, beam."[57] In addition, the word we have translated "radiant," which describes the Lord's command, is specifically used in the Song of Songs (6:10) as descriptive of the sun. It is also used as a cliché in legal documents from Ugarit.[58] Incidentally, the last phrase of the verse, which literally means "lighting up the eyes," does not refer to intellectual enlightenment, but rather to revitalization of physical vigor. Torpidity deprives the eyes of their luster, so that brightness of the eye indicates possession of vital energy.[59]

The third couplet in this series of affirmations in praise of God's revelation reads:

> The fear of the Lord is pure,
> > abiding forever;

> the judgments of the Lord are true,
> righteous altogether.

Here, a difficulty arises. In each other instance (vv. 8–10), the compound phrase expresses something that originates with God. Not one is a human quality, but rather a divine gift bestowed on human beings. In this case, however, "fear of God" would seem to refer to an individual's relationship to the deity. The phrase usually implies the consciousness of the existence of an omnipotent God who imposes certain norms of moral and ethical conduct on His earthbound subjects. As such, it often acts as a restraint on evildoing or an incentive for good in situations in which neither legal sanction nor reward is enforceable. For instance, Genesis 20:1–11 tells that when Abraham ventured into the royal city of Gerar in the western Negev, he feared for his life and for the honor of his wife because he thought, "Surely there is no fear of God in this place." On the other hand, when Joseph, the all-powerful Egyptian bureaucrat, wanted to reassure his skeptical brothers that he was a man of his word, he told them, "I fear God"—as Genesis 42:18 reports. Clearly, this meaning of the expression is inappropriate to the context of Psalm 19.

Another sense in which "fear of the Lord" is used in the Bible— an extension of the preceding—is as something that can be taught and learned. For instance, Isaiah (29:13) denounces the shallow, mechanical performance of ritual acts devoid of inward feeling and devotion of the heart. He uses words that, translated literally, read:

> Because this people has approached [Me] with its
> mouth,
> and honored Me with its lips,
> but has kept its heart far from Me,
> and their fear of Me has been
> a commandment of men, learned by rote . . .

Here, "fear of God" means religious practice, or religion in general. Another passage is Psalm 34:12:

> Come, O sons, listen to Me;
> I will teach you fear of the Lord.

The succeeding verses of Psalm 34 elucidate the content of the teaching:

> Guard your tongue from evil,
>> your lips from deceitful speech.
> Shun evil and do good,
>> seek amity and pursue it.

Most instructive for clarifying this second meaning of "fear of the Lord" is the narrative in 2 Kings 17:25–28. This tells how the Assyrian king, having deported the northern tribes of Israel to distant localities within his empire, settled alien peoples in their stead in the former territory of the kingdom of Israel. These pagan colonists were afflicted by a plague of lions, which was interpreted as punishment for neglecting the worship of the "God of the land." Thereupon, the Assyrian king summoned one of the exiled Israelite priests and dispatched him to Bethel in order to teach the new settlers the practices of the "God of the land." So he came and taught them "how they should fear the Lord."[60]

These passages show that "fear of the Lord" can be synonymous with right religious conduct. That is to say, it can describe the entire religious relationship which, in the Bible, is governed by divinely imposed norms and commitments, not by an individual's feeling or emotional attitude nor by natural piety or popular perceptions of right and wrong.

Our verse once again employs characterizations familiar from neareastern sun god texts. A Meṣopotamian hymn to Shamash from Neo-Babylonian times carries the line, "By your pure word which is unchanging . . ."[61] The notion of the purity of the sun gave rise to the standard cliché in legal documents from Ugarit in the Akkadian language, "pure as the sun." The sun as a symbol of eternity appears as a figure of speech in Psalm 72:5, "Let them revere You as long as the sun exists," and in Psalm 89:37, "His line shall continue forever, his throne as the sun before Me." In Ugaritic texts we find the divine title "the sun of eternity,"[62] and a Phoenician inscription from Karatepe in Asiatic Turkey features the same epithet.[63] Not only is the sun a figure of permanence, but his word, too, is said to be eternal. The great Mesopotamian hymn to Shamash has, "Your manifest utterance cannot be changed."[64] This same idea is echoed in a Babylonian proverb, "Like Shamash, the king's word is sure, his command unequaled, and his utterance cannot be altered."[65] Egyptian hymns refer to Re as one "whose utterances are permanent," "whose ordinances stand fast and are not destroyed."[66]

The psalmist continues his glorification of Torah by proclaiming that God's "judgments are true, altogether just." That this reflects the same literary background is evidenced by Psalm 37:6, which portrays justice and judgments shining forth like the rising sun and the full light of noon. The prophet Hosea (6:5) employs similar imagery when he compares the rendering of judgments to the light of sunrise. Another prophet, Micah (7:9), has the people confess its faith that God will "give judgment for him" and "will bring him into the light" and that Israel "will see His justice." Malachi (3:20), the last of the prophetic corpus of the Hebrew Bible, is even more explicit in his use of the solar imagery. He assures the reconstituted Jewish community in Jerusalem after the Babylonian exile that "the sun of righteousness will arise" for those who fear God.

The psalmist crowns the hymn to the Torah in all its varied identities with a climactic conclusion. God's words are

> more desirable than gold,
> than much fine gold;
> sweeter than honey,
> than drippings of the comb.

The first part of this judgment closely resembles a statement made by Socrates, according to the testimony of the *Memorabilia* of Xenophon (ca. 428–354 B.C.E.). In a conversation on the subject of virtue (by which was meant efficiency in the conduct of life) that the great sage held with Euthydemus, a member of the class of itinerant professional savants known as Sophists, Socrates stated,

> By Hera, I do admire you for valuing the treasures of wisdom above gold and silver. For you are evidently of the opinion that, while gold and silver cannot make men better, the thoughts of the wise enrich their possessors with virtue. [67]

In the Wisdom literature of the Bible, an oft-repeated sentiment is that knowledge and wisdom are far superior to and more desired than gold and silver, the most prized material possessions. [68] Once Wisdom had become identified with Torah, [69] the characteristic phraseology of the former was transferred to the latter. In the present instance, silver is, exceptionally, not mentioned, only gold, and one might wonder whether here too the influence of the sun god literature is not at work.

The Egyptian god Re is known as the "golden sun disk" and supposedly says of himself, "my skin is of pure gold." [70] An Egyptian hymn to the sun goes further, declaring, "fine gold does not match your radiance." [71] In Mesopotamian texts the name of the sun god Shamash is used as a synonym for gold, and gold sun disks are used as a type of ornament, the color of its metal symbolizing the celestial object. Incidentally, it is of interest that alchemists and metallurgists in the Middle Ages believed that gold ore grew in the earth under the influence of the sun. [72]

The parallelism of honey with gold in verse 11 of our psalm may be occasioned by its dark golden color. Honey was the earliest and the prime sweetener for food and beverages in the ancient world. "What is sweeter than honey?" exclaimed the Philistines to Samson. [73] The biblical Hebrew term for it covers both bee's honey and the thick, intensely sweet syrup made from dates and grape juice. The celebrated designation of the land of Israel is of one "flowing with milk and honey." The latter is one of the seven characteristic products of the land, as specified in Deuteronomy 8, verse 8. Because all the other items listed are the yield of the soil, it is hardly likely that bee's honey is intended. Further, there is no evidence for apiculture in the land of Israel in biblical times, and references to bee's honey point to the wild variety.[74]

The substance is evoked figuratively as a symbol of things pleasant and gratifying, and is particularly employed in relation to wisdom and speech. Proverbs 24, verses 13–14, advise,

> My son, eat honey, for it is good;
>> let its sweet drops be on your palate.
> Know, such is wisdom for your soul . . .

The same book (16:24) states,

> Pleasant words are like a honeycomb,
>> sweet to the palate and a cure for the body.

The "sweetness" of God's word is a property mentioned several times in the Bible. The outstanding example is to be found in Ezekiel 2:8–3:3. There it is related that, in a vision, the prophet was handed a scroll on which were inscribed lamentations, dirges, and woes— predictions of unmitigated disaster. He was ordered to eat it, that is, to absorb the divine word into his inner being. When he obeyed, he found that it tasted "as sweet as honey." This simile is illuminated by Jeremiah 15, verse 16. In a moment of bitterness and dejection, he discloses that he "devoured" the proffered word of God. It became to him a source of delight and joy, because it made him alive to his privileged position of experiencing intimate communion with God, and of being the recipient of His revelation. Psalm 119, which is wholly devoted to extolling the Torah, carries the line (v. 103),

> How desirable is Your word to my palate,
>> sweeter than honey.

Here, the psalmist expresses the satisfaction he derives from being engaged in the word of God. Our Psalm 19 makes the same observation.

"Sweetness" as a description of the divine word is paralleled in

Egyptian and Hittite sun god texts. A hymn to Amon-Re calls the god "possessor of sweetness," and says to him, "The sweetness of thee is in the northern sky."[75] A Hittite hymn declares that the sun god Istanu's "message is sweet to everyone."[76]

The numerous parallels between the descriptive terminology employed in praise of Torah in our psalm and the conventional language of the neareastern sun god liturgies demonstrate that the latter were well-known in Israel. They would have gained wide currency during the period of King Manasseh, when the popular astral and solar cults enjoyed official royal patronage in Judah, as outlined earlier in this chapter. Those who remained faithful to the true monotheistic religion of Israel fiercely opposed this gross paganization of the national culture. A central feature of the opposition was the emphasis upon and exaltation of the Torah, of which this psalm is an example. In a very real sense, therefore, Psalm 19 is a polemic. The frame of reference for the epithets and metaphors attached to the Torah is the characteristic terminology of the solar cults. Cleverly, the appropriated vocabulary has been emptied of its pagan content and has taken on new life. It is not YHVH, God of Israel, versus the sun god, but His Torah that is the focus of contrast. And since the Torah of which the psalmist speaks is the divinely ordained guide for human living, the exercise of righteousness and the striving for perfection have been removed from the metaphysical to the human plane. By implication, the descriptive has been transmuted into the prescriptive. This understanding provides the nexus of thought with the third section of the psalm, the concluding four verses of which are of a specifically personal nature.

> Your servant pays them heed;[77]
> in obeying them there is much reward.

The psalmist defines himself as God's servant, which is the biblical way of saying that he willingly surrenders himself to the demands of God's will as revealed in the Torah he has just extolled. What is unclear is whether the "reward" that he believes to be the concomitant of obeying God's Torah is thought of as being material or spiritual.

Although the psalmist is careful and conscientious in the discharge of the obligations the Torah imposes, there is nothing sanctimonious or self-righteous about his piety. With Ecclesiastes 7, verse 20, he is acutely aware that "there is no righteous person on earth who does [only] good and never sins." It is taken for granted that the psalmist, who heaps lavish praise upon the Torah, would not be guilty of deliberate violation of its precepts. But he is concerned about sins of which he may be unaware. Hence, he asks, "Who can be aware of errors?" and pleads, "Clear me of unperceived guilt."

The priestly legislation of the Torah registers two main categories of sin: a wrongful action performed in the full consciousness of its illicit nature, and an infraction unintentionally committed either due to ignorance of the law or because of a mistaken assumption about the nature of the offense.[78] Only in the case of the second category does the Torah prescribe expiation by means of sacrifice once the reality of the situation becomes apparent. There are also sins committed inadvertently of which a person may never become aware. They are known, however, to God, a verity that is presupposed by the request to be "cleared." The interrogative of the first clause of verse 13 therefore really becomes a rhetorical question.[79]

The import of the second clause is more complex. The Hebrew term behind the phrase "to clear" belongs to juridical terminology, indicative of the seriousness with which even unperceived sin is regarded. It implies an underlying conception of sin as self-acting. It automatically creates an interruption in the relationship between God and the individual offender, causing a suspension of the intimacy that prevails between them. Since, by the very nature of the situation, no expiatory process can exist, the psalmist prays for divine grace.

He has still another source of concern, this more worrisome:

> and from arrogant men[80] keep Your servant;
> let them not dominate me.

Human beings possess a natural proclivity for sin. [81] More dangerous, because more insidious, are pressures from without—the malign, erosive influence of evil men who climb to power. What the author has in mind can be determined from other biblical texts that refer to the "arrogant men." Their pride is the haughtiness of tyrants; they perpetrate evil without fear of retribution; they are scoffers, and ruthless people. [82] Significantly and revealingly, over half the biblical references are to be found in Psalm 119, whose one hundred and seventy-six verses are devoted to the Torah and the psalmist's strivings to follow its teachings. This cluster tells us that the "arrogant men" stray from God's commandments, taunt, and make false accusations against the one who holds fast to his principles, wronging him without provocation and trying to entrap him. [83] Their purpose obviously is to sway the psalmist from the right path in life and persuade him to abandon his fealty to the Torah. He is fully alive to the dangers, and he prays for divine help in resisting the pressures. He declares,

> then shall I be blameless,
> and clear of grave offense.

The final verse is a prayer for divine approval of the psalmist's endeavors. Although it is intensely personal, the form in which it is expressed imparts to it a deeper level of meaning, which has far wider application. It gives voice to a profoundly innovative concept.

> May the words of my mouth,
> and the utterance of my heart, [84]
> be acceptable to You,
> O Lord, my rock and my redeemer.

In asking that his words gain acceptance before God, the psalmist employs terminology characteristic of the priestly legislation concerning sacrificial ritual. The Book of Leviticus repeatedly uses this very phrase in formulating the intent of the worshiper in bringing an offering to the altar. If the prescribed norms are not adhered to, the sacrifice is said to be unacceptable, and the harmony in the relationship between the devotee and God that it is intended to promote remains disturbed.[85] By drawing upon the formulaic phraseology of the sacrificial cult, the psalmist very subtly intimates that the utterances of the heart in spiritual, prayerful communion with God perform the same function as does sacrifice. This conviction is reiterated explicitly in a later psalm (141:2), where the psalmist pleads that his prayer might be as favorably received as the incense-offering, his outspread hands as acceptable as the evening meal-offering.

Once the sacrificial setting of the key term of the petition in verse 15 is recognized, the question may be raised as to whether any other phrase might not similarly take on fresh meaning. Is it nothing more than coincidence that the hymn in praise of the Torah begins with the descriptive phrase, "The Torah of the Lord is perfect"? The query is valid because the Hebrew adjective really means "without blemish," and is also characteristic of the Torah legislation pertaining to sacrifice. The worshiper is cautioned repeatedly that to be "acceptable," the animal brought for sacrifice must be "unblemished."[86] This is an indispensable requirement. In designating the Torah by this technical term, the psalmist appears to imply the idea that Torah study is an act of worship, a mode of intercourse of the soul with God. This topic was discussed above in our exposition of Psalm 1.

The psalmist addresses God as his "rock and deliverer." Both terms are frequently used divine appellations. The adamantine quality of rock made it a symbol of firmness. Rocky heights gave a defender an advantage over a would-be assailant stationed below, and its clefts afforded shelter. For these reasons, a rock became a symbol of permanence, stability, defense, and refuge; and hence an appropriate epithet of God when called upon to exercise those qualities.[87] The psalmist has need of them because he feels himself in danger from "arrogant men."

For the same reason, he also refers to God as "my redeemer." This translation is by no means incorrect, provided that it is understood in its original etymological sense as derived from the Latin, and is not confused with its later Christian theological usage in the sense of salvation from sin and perdition. The English "redemption, redeem," can be traced back to the Latin *red-emere*, "to buy back," and this is probably, though not certainly, the original meaning of the root *ga'al*, which is peculiar to the Hebrew language and so far has no known cognate in other Semitic languages. This word is never used in connection with salvation from sin. It has an interesting history rooted in ancient Israelite family law. In early times, the extended family constituted the basic societal group. It provided emotional, psychological, and physical security to its individual members. Its cohesion and solidarity depended on fostering an acute sense of mutual responsibility and instilling the common duty to protect one another. Hence, the next of kin assumed special obligations. He had to "buy back" a kinsman who had fallen into slavery or been taken prisoner, and to repurchase his kinsman's property if it had become forfeited due to poverty. It also devolved upon him to "redeem," that is, to avenge, the blood of a kinsman that had been shed.

As a consequence of the responsibilities with which the *go'el* was charged, the Hebrew verbal and nominal forms gradually acquired extended meaning, no longer necessarily juridical. They came to be associated with the general concepts of protection, deliverance, and liberation, a development which readily permitted them to be applied to God, as in the last line of our psalm and many times in the Bible, especially in the prophecies of the Isaiah who was active during the Babylonian exile.

Chapter 4

PSALMS FIFTEEN AND
TWENTY-FOUR

Morality and Worship

PSALM FIFTEEN

A psalm of David.

LORD, who may sojourn in Your tent,
who may dwell on Your holy mountain?
²He who lives without blame,
who does what is right,
and in his heart acknowledges the truth;
³who has had no slander upon his tongue;
who has never done harm to his fellow,
or borne reproach for [his acts toward] his
neighbor;
⁴for whom a contemptible man is
abhorrent,
but who honors those who fear the LORD;
who stands by his oath even to his own hurt,
and does not retract.
⁵who has never lent money at interest,
or accepted a bribe against the innocent.
The man who acts thus shall never be shaken.

PSALM TWENTY-FOUR

Of David. A psalm.

The earth is the LORD's and all that it holds,
the world and its inhabitants.
²For He founded it upon the ocean,
set it on the nether-streams.

³Who may ascend the mountain of the LORD?
Who may stand in His holy place?—

⁴He who has clean hands and a pure heart,
who has not taken a false oath by My life
or sworn deceitfully.
⁵He shall carry away a blessing from the LORD,
a just reward from God, his deliverer.
⁶Such is the circle of those who turn to Him,
Jacob, who seek Your presence.

⁷O gates, lift up your heads!
Up high, you everlasting doors,
so the King of glory may come in!
⁸Who is the King of glory?—
the LORD, mighty and valiant,
the LORD, valiant in battle.
⁹O gates, lift up your heads!
Lift them up, you everlasting doors,
so the King of glory may come in!

¹⁰Who is the King of glory?—
the LORD of hosts,
He is the King of glory!

Modern scholars have entitled these two psalms "Liturgies of Entrance."[1] The reason for this designation is that their central theme is the proper understanding of the nature and meaning of the divine-human encounter within the sacred precincts of the Temple. It is suggested that they reflect ceremonies which took place at the approach to the entrance of the Holy Place in order to determine whether the worshiper possessed the indispensable moral qualifications required of those who came to worship. The two psalms are distinguished by the same unusual feature: a question-and-answer procedure that sets forth the desirable standards.

Psalm 15 opens with the question,

> Lord, who may sojourn in Your tent,
> who may dwell on Your holy mountain?

Psalm 24 poses a similar query,

> Who may ascend the mountain of the Lord?
> Who may stand in His holy place?

In both compositions there follows a series of responses defining the ethical attributes. They are framed both positively and negatively, and they close with a promise of reward. It seems certain that these psalms were chanted antiphonally, that is, with alternating voices, one making the inquiry, and the other voice or group of singers giving the response.

In Psalm 15 the essential, initial question is addressed to the Lord Himself, and the response is to be understood as emanating from Him. The underlying idea of this literary technique of a verbal exchange with God is to emphasize that the rejection of deeds inimical to virtue and the affirmation of actions necessary for the acquisition of virtue—how one ought and ought not live one's life— are not humanly devised utilitarian requirements for social living, but divinely ordained imperatives, of eternal validity.

In Psalm 24, the question is styled impersonally. Significantly, however, the list of attributes closes with a declaration of divine favor and a turning directly to God in the second person (verses 5–6). There can be no doubt that here, too, the psalmist understands that the ethical requirements are the expression of divine will.

Ostensibly, the designation "liturgy of entrance" for these two psalms provides a satisfactory explanation for their function within the framework of the religious life of ancient Israel. Is there any documentary support for such a hypothesis?[2] One possible precedent that comes to mind is the Egyptian *Book of the Dead*, as that funerary composition has come to be known, although its original name was "Chapters of the Going Forth by Day."[3]

The inevitability of death, the stark reality of the finite nature of the human body, the mystery of the unresolved tensions between good and evil—inescapable characteristics of human existence—and the intriguing possibility of some form of survival after death have all been subjects of religious inquiry, philosophical speculation, and ritual practices. The Egyptian *Book of the Dead* provides the most explicit and detailed knowledge of how one ancient people responded to these dilemmas. That work was actually a series of magic spells believed to enable the deceased to overcome obstacles to perpetual survival after death. A papyrus roll inscribed with these texts was frequently deposited in the tomb at the time of burial as a kind of *vade mecum* for the interred. The Egyptians took for granted that their actions in this world were under divine scrutiny. Hence, they imagined a judgment taking place before they could enter paradise. The deceased had to appear in the "Hall of Two Truths" before a tribunal consisting of forty-two divinities presided over by Osiris, lord of the netherworld. Here, they were formally interrogated, and passage to the abode of the blessed depended upon supplying the correct responses to the questions. The potent magical spells were supposed to save them from any pitfalls that might stand in the way. Chapter 125 of this "Book of the Dead" lists a series of offenses that the deceased declared he had not committed in this world. The protestation of guiltlessness includes the following among many other items:

> "I have not committed crimes against people, I have not mistreated cattle, . . . I have not blasphemed a god, I have not robbed the poor . . . I have not killed, . . . I have not committed adultery, . . . I have not added to the balance weights, . . . I have not taken milk from the mouth of children."[4]

It seems likely that this question-and-answer session reflected some actual situation in this life. Discoveries in Egyptian temples lend credence to the suggestion. Among the best preserved are the temples of Edfu, Dendera, and Kawm Umbu (Kom Ombo) in Upper Egypt. Abbreviated versions of the protestation of guiltlessness have been found in the thickness of each jamb of the main door of the portico of the temple of the god Horus at Edfu, immediately in front of the basic element of the temple—the cella, or chamber, which contained the image of the god. It is believed that the officiating priest who entered to carry out his duties was expected to recite the declaration. Some doors of the temple bear warnings to the priests against entering in a state of impurity, in sin, uttering falsehood, coveting, slandering, accepting bribes, showing partiality between the poor and the great, falsifying weights and measures, and so forth. Similar inscriptions appear in the other two temples. These formulae derive from the time of the Ptolemies, but there can be no doubt that they go back to an early period in the long history of Egyptian religion.[5]

A Sumerian hymn devoted to the god Enlil and his holy city of Nippur in southern Mesopotamia, although not exactly an "entrance liturgy," affords another expression of the tendency in ancient neareastern religions to expect standards of integrity from those who would enter the sacred precincts. The hymn declares that the holy city does not tolerate "hypocrisy, distortion, abuse, malice, unseemliness, insolence, enmity, oppression, envy, force, libelous speech, arrogance, violation of an agreement, breach of a contract, and abuse of a [court] verdict."[6]

It must be pointed out that no evidence is really at hand to prove the existence in practice of such an exclusionary institution as is suggested by the term "liturgy of entrance," with its implications of the enforcement of conditions of admittance to the temples on grounds of moral shortcomings. In Egypt and Mesopotamia, the vast mass of the laity was illiterate, and the above-cited written stipulations would have been wholly inaccessible to the populace. Besides, the nonecclesiastic did not generally enter the temples. It is most likely, therefore, that the admonitions and instructions were directed to a small segment of the population, the literati and the priestly classes. They represented an ideal to be fostered by the officiating clergy.

In Israel, it is true, the use of the alphabet rather than the complicated syllabic cuneiform script or hieroglyphic writing, as well as the devotion to study as a religious obligation, made literacy far more widespread, and a lay person would have had easier access to a text. Further, the ordinary Israelite did have entrée into the Temple. Nevertheless, the idea of a formal, exclusionary procedure must be ruled out, if only for the reason that it was the sinners, especially the violators of ethical norms, who would be most in need of the Temple facilities in order to make atonement and seek reconciliation with God. What, then, would be the point of refusing them admission to the Holy Place?

The likelihood is that this psalm originally was a liturgy connected with the arrival in Jerusalem of assemblies of pilgrims come to celebrate the three great pilgrimage festivals of ancient Israel: the Feast of Unleavened Bread, the Feast of the Harvest, and the Feast of Tabernacles. The purpose of the question-and-answer ceremony was not to exclude anyone, but to impress upon the minds of the worshipers before they entered the Temple precincts, the desirable, important, and enduring values underlying the act of worship in Israel.

It must be stressed that the mere posing of the question as to who may worship in the Temple is of great significance. Presence in the sacred place and the worship of God are not to be mechanical observances or routine formalities, not even simple conformity with religious requirement.[7] The unstated assumption in these psalms is that no one who went to the religious center would fail to bring an offering.[8] The questions about worthiness, therefore, go to the very heart of the biblical conception of worship. Although the elaborate sacrificial rituals constituted the dominant feature of the Temple service, the psalmist knows that the offerings are not of primary importance in the Israelite hierarchy of religious values. They are subordinate to the demands of morality, and they lose all meaning unless those imperatives are obeyed.

Perhaps the earliest explicit statement to that effect comes from the prophet Samuel, when he confronts the errant King Saul after the latter's victory over the Amalekites:

> "Does the Lord delight in burnt offerings and sacrifices
> as much as in obedience to the Lord's command?
> Surely, obedience is better than sacrifice,
> compliance than the fat of rams" (1 Sam. 15:22).

A psalm attributed to King David following his sin with Bathsheba and his condemnation by the prophet Nathan[9] states clearly:

> O Lord . . .
> You do not want me to bring sacrifices . . . ;
> You do not desire burnt offerings;
> True sacrifice to God is a contrite spirit;
> God, You will not despise
> a contrite and crushed heart (Ps. 51:17–19).

Biblical Wisdom literature also has something to say on this subject. The Book of Proverbs very plainly states its hierarchy of values:

> The sacrifice of the wicked is an abomination to the Lord,
> but the prayer of the upright pleases Him.
>
> To do what is right and just
> is more desired by the Lord than sacrifice.
>
> The sacrifice of the wicked man is an abomination,
> the more so as he offers it in depravity
> (Prov. 15:8; 21:3, 27).

The problem of morality versus worship powerfully engaged the great Israelite prophets from the eighth century B.C.E. on. Whether they came from Judea or Northern Israel, these spokesmen of the divine word proclaimed that there were certain permanently valid moral principles that condition God's receptivity to worship. Thus Isaiah, on some great holy day, appeared before the assembled throng of pious worshipers and fearlessly declared in the name of God:

> "What need have I of your abundant sacrifices?"
> Says the Lord.
> "I am sated with burnt offerings of rams,
> > and suet of fatlings.
>
> I have no delight
> > in the blood of bulls,
> > and lambs and he-goats.
>
> When you come to appear before Me—
> > who asked this of you?
>
> Trample My courts no more.
> Bringing oblations is futile,
> > incense is offensive to Me.
>
> New moon and sabbath,
> > proclaiming of solemnities,
> > assemblies with iniquity,
> > I cannot bear.
>
> Your new moons and fixed seasons
> > I detest.
>
> They are become a burden to Me;
> > I cannot endure them.
>
> When you lift up your hands,
> > I will divert My eyes from you;
>
> Though you pray at length,
> > I will not listen.
>
> Your hands are stained with blood.
> Wash yourselves clean;
> > put your evil doings
> > out of My sight.
>
> Cease to do evil;

> learn to do good.
> Seek justice;
>   aid the wronged.
> Uphold the rights of the orphan;
>   Plead the cause of the widow" (Isa. 1:11–17).

Isaiah's contemporary, Amos, similarly rose before the crowd of worshipers in the temple of Bethel in Northern Israel, and likewise denounced them in these terms:

> I hate, I scorn your festivals;
> I take no pleasure in your solemn assemblies.
> If you offer Me burnt offerings—or your meal
>   offerings—
>   I will not accept them;
>   I will not look upon your gifts of fatlings.
> Spare Me the noise of your hymns,
>   and let Me not hear the music of your lutes.
> But let justice roll down like water,
>   righteousness like an ever-flowing stream
>   (Amos 5:21–24).

The prophet Hosea, a northerner, emphasized,

> I desire goodness, not sacrifice;
>   the knowledge of God, rather than burnt offerings
>   (Hosea 6:6).

Micah, a younger contemporary of Isaiah, asks his countrymen,

> With what shall I approach the Lord,
>   do homage to God on high?
> Shall I approach Him with burnt offerings,
>   with calves a year old?
> Would the Lord be pleased with thousands of rams,

with myriads of streams of oil?
Shall I give my first-born for my transgression,
    the fruit of my body for my sins?
He has told you, O man, what is good;
        but what does the Lord require of you?
        —only to do justice
        and to love kindness,
        and to walk humbly with your God" (Micah 6:6–8).

What was considered at the time the most outrageous statement of all on this theme was made by the prophet Jeremiah at the very gates of the House of the Lord in Jerusalem. It was addressed to "all you of Judah who enter these gates to worship the Lord":

> Thus said the Lord of Hosts, the God of Israel: Mend your
> ways and your actions, and I will let you dwell in this
> place . . . If you truly mend your ways and your deeds; if
> you act justly one with another; if you do not oppress the
> stranger, the orphan, and the widow; if you do not shed
> the blood of the innocent in this place . . . then only will
> I let you dwell in this place . . . Will you steal and murder
> and commit adultery and swear falsely . . . and then come
> and stand before Me in this House . . . ? Do you consider
> this House, which bears My name, to be a den of
> robbers?[10]

The two psalms that we are discussing, 15 and 24, do not raise the issue of morality and the Temple cult in the manner of the prophets. Because they address those who come to worship in the Temple, they tacitly assume that the ritual requirements will be satisfied, and the validity and acceptability of sacrifices are taken for granted. What concerns the psalmist is that the worshiper be morally fit and fully aware of the proper scale of values.[11] If there is an issue of hypocrisy, it is left to one's understanding and remains unvoiced. The fiery prophetic oratory, on the other hand, while it by no means denounces or negates the institution of sacrifice as such, does explicitly and forthrightly condemn hypocrisy and forcibly insists that morality is the very essence of religion.[12]

PSALM 15

Psalm 15 opens with the query,

> Lord, who may sojourn in Your tent,
> who may dwell on Your holy mountain?

To call the grand Temple in Jerusalem, built of stone, a "tent"—in Hebrew *'ohel*—might seem odd, but this designation occurs several times in the Bible, always in poetic texts.[13] It harks back to pre-Solomonic times when the religious center of Israel was indeed a tent, beginning with the construction of the mobile Tabernacle in the course of the wilderness wanderings.[14]

The parallel term in verse 1 is God's "holy mountain," referring to Mount Zion, on which the Temple stood. This stereotyped phrase occurs many times in Scripture.[15] In Psalm 24, the site is called "the mountain of the Lord."[16] These appellations, as well as the variant "mountain of God,"[17] all recall a phenomenon widely attested in the ancient world. Throughout the area, mountains were thought to be the natural arena of divine activity. Mount Olympus was regarded by the Greeks as the special home of the chief gods, and Mount Saphon, which is Mons Casius in Syria, played the same role among the Canaanites. The multitiered tower structures known as ziggurats were really artificial symbols of mountains in the flat alluvial plain of Mesopotamia, and they served in mythology as the dwelling place of the god. The mountain, with its peak in the sky, was conceived to be the point of contact between the celestial and terrestrial spheres and the channel of communication between the world of the divine and the world of humanity.

While Israel often borrowed the existing religious terminology of the cultures of the ancient Near East, especially in poetic texts, the identity of language conceals a fundamental difference in conception. The mythological notion of intrinsic, "natural," primeval sanctity of space is rejected, and is replaced in the religion of Israel by the sanctity of time. Both Moses[18] and Joshua[19] unexpectedly encounter "holy ground," but in each incident the sanctity of the site is temporary, derives solely from the immediacy of the divine Presence, and does not endure beyond the theophany. The same is true of Mount Sinai, the scene of the supreme revelation of God to the nation of Israel. Although the experience constitutes the essential foundation on which all future developments are built, the holiness of Sinai does not persist beyond the duration of the event. The mountain did not become a place of pilgrimage; it played no role in the future spiritual life of the people, and even knowledge of its location was lost. The site of the Temple in Jerusalem, which here in Psalm 15 is called God's "holy mountain," acquired sanctity only when King David deposited there the Ark of the Covenant.[20]

The initial question of Psalm 15 employs two verbs, "to sojourn" and "to stay." "Sojourn" is now somewhat archaic and sounds quaint, but the translation accurately reflects the Hebrew original, which means "to stay temporarily." It is the verbal form of the regular term for "a stranger," in Hebrew *ger*, the one who comes from outside to take up temporary residence. It would seem to be a strange word to use of one who comes to a place of worship; but it is not really so if one delves into its rich fund of associated ideas.[21]

In the first place, there is the awareness of the existential situation of human beings in relation to God. The Torah declares that "you are but strangers resident with me."[22] The psalmist echoes these words in a prayer:

> Hear my prayer, O Lord;
>> give ear to my cry;
>> do not disregard my tears;
>> for like all my forebears
>> I am an alien, resident with You. [23]

In another psalm, the author proclaims, "I am only a sojourner in the land."[24] And, according to the Chronicler, in his prayer at the coronation of King Solomon, King David reiterates the sentiment of the above-cited psalm: ". . . for we are sojourners with You, mere transients like our fathers; our days on earth are like a shadow with nothing in prospect."[25]

In light of these passages, use of the particular verb "to sojourn" intimates the appropriate mood of human vulnerability and the resultant attitude of humility expected of one who enters the sacred domain. The use of this verb has another implication: if the Temple, figuratively, is the "House of God," then one who seeks admission is, by analogy, an outsider, a stranger, a would-be guest who may enter only by permission of the Master of the house, and must satisfy the criteria He adopts. In addition, the one who comes to the Temple is, in some measure, estranged from God, and looks to dispel this feeling of alienation by the act of worship that will impart a heightened sense of fellowship and intimacy with Him. Last, but by no means least, the verb in question evokes the issue of the legal status of the stranger in society. In the ancient world, such a one, being without kinfolk, had no claim to protection against violence and exploitation.[26] That is why the Hebrew Bible insistently and repeatedly warns against ill-treatment of the stranger,[27] and why the Israelite is enjoined to love and support the stranger[28] in emulation of God who "upholds the cause of the fatherless and the widow, and befriends the stranger, providing him with food and clothing."[29] Among the semi-nomads of the Near East, and among the Bedouin of the desert to this day, a stranger is a natural enemy unless he enters a tent, in which case it becomes a matter of honor for the host to protect him. However, this assumed obligation of ensuring the inviolability of the guest is only temporary, and does not last for more than three days. [30]

The use of the verb "to sojourn" in Psalm 15 awakens a train of thought that encompasses all the notions set forth above. The worshiper who comes into the Temple is a "stranger" who becomes a "guest" of God and enjoys divine protection as he experiences the intimacy of personal communion with Him. [31]

The second verb in verse 1, in parallel with "sojourn," is "dwell." [32] Once again, the Hebrew uses a word that can be traced back to the pastoral nomadic way of life: originally, it meant "to tent," "to take up temporary abode." [33] Its noun form often is used as a synonym of "tent," [34] and gave its name to the Tabernacle, the mobile tent sanctuary in the wilderness. [35] The postbiblical Hebrew term for the divine Presence in the world, the *shekhinah*, is derived from the same stem.

Verses 2–5 comprise the response to the opening queries. They list the eleven desired, distinctive personal qualities or attributes that should characterize the sincere worshiper in the Temple. [36] A passage in the Talmud states that at Sinai the Israelites received six hundred and thirteen commandments; David came and reduced them to eleven—as set forth in this psalm. [37] To put it another way, the psalm is seen as being representative of the underlying, basic values that inform and animate the entire complex of divinely ordained precepts, prescriptive and proscriptive. The same talmudic passage also relates that the distinguished and saintly sage, Rabban Gamaliel, president of the Sanhedrin, would weep when he read this psalm. His reaction implies that it made him aware of his personal shortcomings, as measured by the criteria listed. It illustrates how the psalms, irrespective of their original function, fostered introspection and self-judgment, and inculcated virtue.

The moral requirements are first expressed positively, by means of three Hebrew participles: "lives . . . does . . . acknowledges." This grammatical form partakes of the character of both noun and verb. It expresses the subject in the continuing exercise of the activity specified in the verb. These are not one-time actions, but the dominant characteristics of the human being, the guiding principles that govern one's entire existence on earth. The one worthy of standing in the presence of God is one who

> . . . lives without blame,
> who does what is right,
> and in his heart acknowledges the truth.

The literal translation of the first Hebrew word is "walk," here used metaphorically in the sense of "lives."[38] The passage from birth to death is viewed as a journey along a path that must be followed without deviation, that is, with integrity, devoid of moral blemish.[39] In general terms, this calls for adherence to a high moral code in one's deeds and for truthfulness of speech. In the Hebrew Bible, the "heart" is not so much an anatomical as a psychological term. It is the seat of the intellect, the will, the inner life.[40] Elsewhere in the Psalm, mention is made of the wicked whose speech is smooth but issues from "a double heart"; it is duplicitous.[41] There are those whose "talk is smoother than butter but whose mind is set on war."[42] The prophet Isaiah castigates the people who approach God with their mouth and honor Him with their lips, but whose heart is far from Him.[43] In response to the one who says, "Read my lips," God responds, "Read his mind and actions." Integrity demands consonance of thought and expression, harmony between action and the conviction of the heart.

Following the three attributes formulated positively come three expressed negatively. Unlike the former, these are not essential attributes of character, but rather specific, sometime offenses. Hence, the grammatical form of the verbs is that signifying completed action in the past (verse 3):

> who has had no slander upon[44] his tongue;
> who has never done harm to his fellow,
> or borne reproach for [his acts toward] his neighbor.

The psalmist recognizes that while truthfulness of speech is requisite, the spoken word, even if true, may have devastating effect if employed for gossip or slander. The faculty of speech is easily abused. In the Bible, the tongue, like the mouth and the lip, is looked upon as an organ of speech,[45] and a powerful one. This formidable instrument, says Proverbs 18:21, controls life and death. The Torah rules unfounded hearsay testimony[46] inadmissible in judicial proceedings, and outlaws talebearing.[47] While no penalty is specified for rumormongering in general, the husband who makes a baseless charge against his bride is severely punished.[48]

The harm that slander causes is damage to another's reputation. This is followed logically by mention of the infliction of physical or material harm.[49]

The third item of the verse is problematical, for the text allows of two possible meanings: "He has not borne disgrace because of his neighbor,"[50] or "He has not cast disgrace against his neighbor." Perhaps we have here an example of deliberate ambiguity intended to convey both possibilities.

The next verse deals with the character and reputation of one's associates, for these lay bare one's own standards and values:

> for whom a contemptible man is abhorrent,[51]
> but who honors those who fear the Lord;
> who stands by his oath even to his own hurt.[52]
> and does not retract.[53]

To consort with disreputable characters jeopardizes one's own integrity. "Woe to a wicked man, woe to his neighbor," warns a rabbinic maxim.[54] By implication, the inclusion of the present item in the inventory of desirable attributes implies the ability to read and evaluate the character of others. In the final analysis, this quality is the touchstone for measuring the character of the assessor. Is one attracted and seduced by outward appearances and the projection of personality, or can one discern that smooth talking and exuding charm may be mere affectations that veil noxious and dangerous underlying characteristics?

It is insufficient, says the psalmist, to spurn potentially pernicious influences on one's life. Essential for the promotion of spiritual, moral, and mental soundness are wholesome role models who serve as a source of inspiration, people whom one can respect and emulate. In the present instance, the preferred exemplars of worthiness are those "who fear the Lord." We discussed the meaning of "fear the Lord" in our exposition of Psalm 19; here, it is the people who possess that quality who are invoked, those whose life style and behavior epitomize the standards God demands of His worshipers.

The third admirable quality listed in verse 4 is fidelity to one's pledged word, fulfillment of an obligation freely undertaken, even if it later turns out to be to one's disadvantage. The kind of oath the psalmist has in mind is not specified, but the context indicates that it is one accompanying a promissory vow.[55] In biblical times, a vow was accompanied by an oath invoking the name of God, often in conjunction with a self-imprecation.[56] These were both intended to strengthen the validity and credibility of the oath, and to reinforce the oathtaker's determination to fulfill it. Interestingly, despite the general belief in biblical times in the potent efficacy of curses, there were still people who remained undeterred and violated oaths they had taken, or knowingly took false oaths.[57]

The Torah legislation mentions the contracting of vows, mostly in cultic or ritual contexts.[58] Deuteronomy 23:22–24 deals with this issue:

> When you make a vow to the Lord your God, do not delay fulfilling it, for the Lord your God will demand it of you, and you will have incurred guilt; whereas you incur no guilt if you refrain from vowing. You must fulfill what your lips have uttered and perform what you have

voluntarily vowed to the Lord your God, having made the promise with your own mouth.

Ecclesiastes goes a step further, advising,

> When you make a vow to God, do not delay to fulfill it.
> For He has no pleasure in fools; what you vow, fulfill. It is
> better not to vow at all than to vow and not fulfill.[59]

In the period of the Second Temple, forbearing to take an oath was often regarded as an attribute of piety. Josephus reports of the sect of Essenes that their word had greater force than an oath, and that they avoided swearing, regarding it as worse than perjury. They argued that one who is not believed without an appeal to God stands self-condemned.[60]

The last two virtues involve taking interest and bribery:

> who has never lent money at interest,[61]
> or accepted a bribe against the innocent.

These two sins are paired because they are two facets of a single grave offense—the misuse of assets.[62] In one case, it is done to profit from the disadvantaged of society; in the other, to profit by corruptly influencing the course of justice. Both undermine the very foundations of a civilization.

The lending of money or produce on interest is strictly forbidden in the Torah. This prohibition is rooted in the conception of a loan as a humanitarian act, not a commercial transaction. The passages that deal with this subject clearly indicate the social context. Exodus 22:24–26 reads:

> If you lend money to My people, to the poor among you,
> you shall not act toward them as a creditor; exact no inter-
> est from them. If you take your neighbor's garment in
> pledge, you must return it to him before the sun sets; it is

> his only clothing, the sole covering for his skin. In what
> else shall he sleep? Therefore, if he cries out to Me, I will
> pay heed, for I am compassionate.

Leviticus 25:35–37 repeats the prohibition in a different form and similarly presupposes that the need for the loan is destitution:

> If your kinsman, being in straits, becomes dependent
> on you . . . let him live by your side. Do not exact from
> him advance or accrued interest, but fear your God . . .
> Do not lend him money at advance interest, or give him
> your food at accrued interest.

The third pentateuchal source, Deuteronomy 23:20–21, which explicitly outlaws the taking of interest on a loan, does not specify poverty, but that this is the presupposed background of the law is determined both by the restrictions on the rights of the creditor detailed in 24:10–13, and by the succeeding laws which are designed to protect the rights of the poor.

The Book of Proverbs 28:8 warns that people who seek to increase their wealth by exacting interest on loans ultimately will forfeit it to those who are generous to the poor. The idea is that these benefactors redistribute that wealth by giving charity to the indigent from whom it was derived in the first place.[63] The prophet Ezekiel includes abstaining from lending at interest among the defining attributes of the righteous person, and calls the opposite practice a self-ruinous "abomination" of the wicked, placing this evil among the sins that doomed Jerusalem and caused the exile of its inhabitants.[64]

The reason why the Bible is so antagonistic to the taking of interest is because ancient Israel operated largely on a village-agricultural economy, most of its population living at little above subsistence level. The rainy season in the land of Israel was short, and if precipitation, always precarious, fell markedly below average, drought ensued and famine threatened. In these circumstances, the poor would be forced to borrow money, grain, or seed. For a lender to exact interest would be to exploit human misery and to disregard flagrantly one's responsibility to a fellow Israelite. Furthermore, because paying interest, let alone repaying the capital, was unfeasible in most instances, the charging interest would pave the way to the enslavement of the debtor and his family.

In order to guard against abuse of the unfortunate poor, the Torah enacted several laws designed to protect their dignity, privacy, and freedom. A creditor is permitted to take a pledge to secure repayment of a loan, but may not enter the borrower's premises to collect it.[65] The garment of a widow may not be taken as a pledge,[66] and a garment accepted from other than a widow must be returned by sunset.[67] Whatever would deprive the poor of their means of subsistence is outlawed as a pledge.[68] Finally, in order to break the cycle of poverty, the institution of the sabbatical year mandated the remission of debts, so that each individual could make a fresh start in life, unencumbered by indebtedness.[69]

At various times in the history of biblical Israel these laws were ignored in practice, and creditors hounded debtors, even enslaved them. David's private militia of about four hundred outlaw desperados included many "who were in debt."[70] In the days of Elisha, an impoverished widow complained to the prophet that a creditor was on his way to seize her two children for slaves.[71] Amos lists among the social vices of his time the lender's use of garments taken in pledge.[72] As noted above, Ezekiel testifies to the violation of the prohibition on taking interest. When Nehemiah returned to Jerusalem from the Babylonian exile to be governor of the reconstituted community about the middle of the fifth century B.C.E., he was confronted with a great outcry from the common folk that the wealthy were pressing their sons and daughters into slavery for nonpayment of loans. He forcefully put a stop to these abuses.[73]

Rounding out the list of the desirable qualities of the worshiper who is worthy to enter the presence of the Lord is that "he has not accepted a bribe against the innocent." The corruption of the judicial process through bribery has been a problem in every society since the beginning of civilized life on earth. In the Torah, the prohibition on bribery is given as a divine command, not just as prudent wisdom of utilitarian value. In Exodus 23:8, repeated in Deuteronomy 16:19, the injunction is formulated as follows: "You shall not take bribes, for bribes blind the clear-sighted and subvert the cause of those who are in the right." In the first source, the prohibition immediately follows other regulations outlawing practices that lead to miscarriage of justice. It would appear to be directed to judges. In Deuteronomy, it is plainly addressed to them. Because bribery is performed in private, the proscription is reinforced by a curse upon the violater. Furthermore, in conformity with the biblical conception of *imitatio Dei*, that is, the human obligation to emulate God's ways to the best of one's ability,[74] God's total impartiality and incorruptibility are emphasized:

> For the Lord your God . . . shows no favor and takes no
> bribe, but upholds the cause of the fatherless and the
> widow, and befriends the stranger, providing him with food
> and clothing.[75]

When King Jehoshaphat of Judah (873–849 B.C.E.) reformed the Judiciary, he charged them:

> "Consider what you are doing, for you judge not on behalf
> of man, but on behalf of the Lord, and He is with you
> when you pass judgment. Now let the dread of the Lord be
> upon you; act with care, for there is no injustice or favorit-
> ism or bribe-taking with the Lord our God."[76]

Evidence of the corruption of public officials by bribery even in the times of the Judges is given by Samuel in his farewell speech to the people; he finds it necessary to stress that he had never accepted bribes.[77] His own sons, who sat as judges in Beer-sheba, had done so, and had "subverted justice."[78] It was during the monarchy period, however, especially in the eighth century B.C.E., that the problem became acute, and was the subject of severe castigation by the prophets of the time. Amos, in northern Israel, proclaimed in the name of God:

> For I have noted how many are your transgressions,
> and how numerous your sins—
> you who are hostile to the righteous,
> who take bribes,[79]
> who subvert in the gate
> the [cause of] the needy![80]

In Judah, Isaiah condemned the rulers and judges for loving bribes and chasing after gratuities, while the causes of the orphan and the widow never received a hearing;[81] in return for bribes, he said, the judges vindicated the guilty and withheld justice from those in the right.[82] Micah, Isaiah's younger contemporary, likewise accused the rulers in Jerusalem of giving judgment under the influence of a bribe.[83] Ezekiel, the prophet of the Babylonian exile, charged that bribes had been taken in order to shed blood,[84] and the Book of Proverbs describes the wicked man who "draws a bribe out of his bosom to pervert the course of justice."[85]

On first reading, the "virtue" of not taking bribes against the innocent, included in our psalm among the desirable attributes of the worshiper, would seem to be restricted to those individuals actually engaged in litigation, whether as judges, parties to the legal action, or witnesses. However, this would put it in sharp contrast to the ten preceding qualities, which have universal application. It is possible, therefore, that taking a bribe is paradigmatic of the corruption of the judicial process in general, the most flagrant example being emblematic of the whole.[86] It must be remembered that the administration of justice was carried out in the open plaza in front of the city-gate. The area served as the municipal center, the focus of public life. Commerce and trade were conducted there, and justice administered—hence the phrase, "justice in the gate." The negotiations between Abraham and the citizens of Hebron over the purchase of a burial site took place at the gate;[87] the dealings of Hamor and Shechem with Jacob's sons, following the rape of Dinah, were centered at the gate;[88] Absalom's revolt against his father David began at the city-gates where people came for adjudication of their claims;[89] and Boaz went to the gate to redeem the estate of Elimelekh.[90] Amos calls on the people to "establish justice in the gate,"[91] and Isaiah speaks of those "who cause men to lose their lawsuits, laying a snare for the arbiter at the gate,"[92] while in post-exilic times, Zechariah tells the people in Jerusalem, "These are the things you are to do: Speak truth to one another, render true and perfect justice in your gates."[93]

Excavations at Tel Dan have concretely illustrated the role of the gate area as the forum, the center of civic life. The city-gate was uncovered, and a fifteen-foot-long (4.6m) stone bench was discovered around the wall of one of its towers.[94] Doubtless, here was the permanent seat of the "elders" who were often responsible for the administration of justice, as several biblical passages mention.[95]

The point of all this is to stress that in ancient Israel, the entire citizenry was intimately involved in the administration of justice; therefore the corruption of the courts would have had an immediate impact on the entire society.

Psalm 15 concludes with the confident assurance that those who conduct their lives in conformity with the moral and ethical standards set forth above "will never be shaken." This verb is often used in the Bible in contexts that describe seismic activity: when "the earth's foundations tremble" and the earth itself is said to "totter," to "sway like a drunkard,"[96] and "mountains move and the hills are shaken,"[97] "the earth reels, and mountains topple into the sea, the waters raging and foaming,"[98] and "all the foundations of the earth totter."[99] In each phrase, the Hebrew verb *mwt* is employed as in verse 5 of our psalm. Hence, if the decent human being "will never be shaken,"[100] we understand an image of stability, solidity, firmness, and strength. This is what is meant when the psalmist declares that

God's universal sovereignty ensures that "the world stands firm; it cannot be shaken," and that God "has established the earth on its foundations so that it shall never totter."[101] Transferred from the structural to the intellectual, emotional, and psychological spheres, the same verb with a negative adverb connotes stability, the strength of character to withstand the pain of disappointment, the moral fortitude to cope with ill fortune, the patient courage to deal with frustration and failure.[102] Such, says the psalmist, is the reward of morality—the only reward he can promise.

PSALM 24

The Greek translation of the Bible made for the Jewish community of ancient Alexandria, Egypt, and popularly known as the Septuagint, carries a heading to this psalm, which reads: "A psalm for David for the first day of the week."[103] This cryptic note becomes intelligible in the light of rabbinic traditions[104] that list the different psalms sung each day of the week in the second Temple in Jerusalem by a choir of Levites. This liturgy took place while the wine libation was being offered.[105] Psalm 24 appears in these lists as the selection for Sundays.

It may be assumed that the choice was determined by the initial two verses, which tell of God's creation of the world, a theme thoroughly appropriate to Sunday, the first day of creation.[106] Perhaps, in addition, the sixfold use of the divine name YHVH, the most sacred Hebrew name of God, was also taken as an intimation of the six days of creation.[107]

The psalm comprises three distinct stanzas:

I. Verses 1–2 declare that by virtue of His creation of the world, God retains exclusive ownership of it.

II. Verses 3–6 set forth the ethical standards expected of those who would gain access to His sanctuary.

III. Verses 7–10 call upon the gates to admit the "King of glory."

The interconnections of these three parts are not readily apparent; to see how they cohere, we must inquire further.

God's sole proprietorship of the world is expressed this way in verse 1:

> The earth is the Lord's and all that it holds,
> the world[108] and its inhabitants.

Given the uncompromising monotheism of the religion of the Bible, and its concept of God, this assertion is axiomatic.[109] The same affirmation is made in connection with the laws of land tenure in Leviticus 25:23: "But the land must not be sold beyond reclaim, for the land is Mine; and you are but strangers resident with Me." According to this understanding of the divine-human relationship, human beings have possession of the earth but not ownership, which belongs forever to God. The relationship is that of landlord to tenant. The power, the authority, and the rights of humankind are restricted and limited, and are in subordination to God, who holds title absolutely and in perpetuity.

The second verse of the first stanza reads:

> For He founded it upon the ocean,
> set it on the nether-streams.[110]

We noted in our discussion of Psalm 8 that biblical poetic texts have preserved fragments of a lost Israelite myth about creation.[111] It was pointed out that those items which tell of mutinous forces of primeval chaos at the onset of the cosmogonic process possess a deeper meaning. They really deal with the tension between order and chaos, respectively symbolized by God the Creator and the unruly primeval waters. It will be remembered that Genesis 1:2 presupposes the existence of "the water" prior to the appearance of earth. (The water is mentioned again in verses 6, 7, and 9.) In Psalm 136:6 it is explicitly stated that God "spread the earth over the water" at the time of creation. Psalm 104:5–9 is somewhat more expansive in excerpting this popular variant Israelite account of creation:

> He established the earth on its foundations,
>> so that it shall never totter.
> You made the deep cover it as a garment;
>> the waters stood above the mountains.
> They fled at Your blast,
>> rushed away at the sound of Your thunder,
>> —mountains rising, valleys sinking—
>> to the place You established for them.
> You set bounds they must not pass
>> so that they never again cover the earth.

The first stanza of Psalm 24 affirms God's absolute sovereignty over the earth, an obvious concomitant of His creative acts. Sovereignty confers the power and the authority to impose standards of behavior upon those who reside in His realm. The Israelite conception of deity as an absolute moral Being necessarily implies that God demands of His "tenants" adherence to moral principles. This line of thinking explains the nexus of thought that links the first two stanzas of the psalm.

The second stanza, verses 3–6, is quite complex, and suggests an antiphonal mode of recitation. Someone, apparently the leader of the company of would-be worshipers standing at the foot of Mount Zion, asks:

> Who may ascend[112] the mountain of the Lord?
> Who may stand in His holy place?[113]

The welcoming priest responds:

> He who has clean hands and a pure heart,
>> who has not taken a false oath by My life
>> or sworn deceitfully.

And he adds the following assurances:
> He shall carry away a blessing from the Lord,
>> a just reward[114] from God, his deliverer.

The leader of the would-be worshipers now assures the priest that the members of the group do possess the stated qualifications:

> Such is the circle[115] of those who turn to Him,
>> Jacob, who seek Your Presence.

The stipulated prerequisites for acceptable worship in the Temple comprise four criteria, two stated positively and two framed negatively. The first two are similar to those of Psalm 15: hands unsoiled by dishonest practice and a mind unsullied by insincerity.[116] In other words, there must be integrity of deed and integrity of motive. The negatively formulated rules reject the one who makes profane or frivolous use of the divine Name in oath-taking and the person who commits perjury in order to practice deceit.

Psalm 24, like Psalm 15, does not view religion and morality as two distinct phenomena. Rather, religion is seen as encompassing morality, informing it, defining it, and being meaningless without it. Again as in Psalm 15, no mention is made of any ritual requirements, because it is taken for granted that anyone going to the Temple would be doing so for purposes of worship, and could be expected to fulfill those necessities. What concerns the two psalms is a false notion of worship. The conduct of human affairs and interpersonal relations and the inviolability of the moral law are all matters of vital import in the economy of religion. They are the indispensable ingredients of the spiritual communion the Temple is meant to inspire. The desired personal encounter with the divine, says the priest, must be preconditioned by the dictates of morality. If it is not, the endeavor is unwarranted and unwelcomed.

The members of the congregation are described as "those who turn to the Lord," "who seek God's presence." The two different Hebrew phrases are often used in the Bible in parallel,[117] but they are not identical in meaning.[118] The verb in the first phrase is multivalent, and in the present context can mean "to consult" or "to enquire of God," and especially to turn to Him in prayer and worship.[119] The parallel phrase, "to seek God's presence," most likely derives from the rhetoric of the royal court. In the early period of the monarchy, as in the days of the Judges before that, the ruler exercised judicial powers. Petitioners would seek an audience with the king in order to present their case. The technical expression for this is "to see the face of " the king. The way a citizen would approach the monarch is well illustrated by "the clever woman" from Tekoa whom Joab, commander of David's army, sent to the king, as told in 2 Samuel 14:1–11. That ordinary folk might expect to obtain redress of grievance through the monarch's personal intervention is evidenced by the tactic of Absalom, David's son, in his attempt to seize the throne. According to 2 Samuel 15:2–6, he would curry favor with "every Israelite who came to the king for judgment." King Solomon's famous adjudication of the dispute between the two harlots who claimed maternity of the same baby provides another example. The narrative in 1 Kings 3:28 testifies that, "When all Israel heard the decision that the king had rendered, they stood in awe of the king; for they saw that he possessed divine wisdom to execute justice." Among the imposing structures erected by Solomon was a "throne portico, where he would pronounce judgment—the Hall of Judgment."[120]

True, the expression "to see the face of the king" does not actually appear in these texts, but that it was standard phraseology can be deduced from the instances that tell of denial of an audience. Thus, Joseph warned his brothers that Benjamin must accompany them on their next journey to Egypt from Canaan in order to procure food; otherwise, he said, "You shall not continue to see my face,"[121] meaning, "I will not grant you an audience." The intransigent Pharaoh dismisses Moses from his presence, saying, "You shall not see my face again."[122] King David refused to allow Absalom "to see his face" for a number of years;[123] that is, he denied him access to his person.

These and several other biblical texts, show that the idiom "to see the face of" a king or powerful dignitary signifies the granting of admittance to the royal or official presence.[124] The biblical image of God as King led to a literary development wherein the standard rhetoric of the royal court was in large measure theologized and transferred to God.[125] In this context, the phrase "to seek God's presence" conveys the desire for intimate fellowship with Him; in Psalm 24, this means communion with God[126] within the precincts of the Temple.[127] As in Psalm 15, the purpose of the ceremony of inquiry-and-response is educational. It is meant to arouse the conscience of the worshipers, to promote self-examination on their part, to inculcate a true understanding of God's demands on humankind. This provides the appropriate setting and is conducive to the proper frame of mind for worship.

The third section of Psalm 24 raises some perplexing questions. It reads:

> O gates, lift up your heads!
> Up high, you everlasting doors,
>> so the King of glory may come in!
> Who is the King of glory?—
>> the Lord, mighty and valiant;
>> the Lord, valiant in battle.
> O gates, lift up your heads!
> Lift them up, you everlasting doors,
>> so the King of glory may come in!
> Who is the King of glory?—
>> the Lord of Hosts,
>> He is the King of glory!

The antiphonal nature of this section should be noted: clearly, there are alternating voices, though one of them seems to belong to "the gates"! Moreover, and strangely, it is not the company of the would-be Temple worshipers for whom admittance is sought, but "the King of glory," identified as "the Lord of hosts." The divine epithet "King of glory" is repeated five times here but is found nowhere else in the Hebrew Bible. It recalls the title "the God of glory"—similarly unique—used in Psalm 29:3.

The dictionaries define "glory" as "lofty praise, honor, admiration, high renown, worshipful praise, great beauty, splendor, aureole, radiance." In truth, none of these terms does justice to the Hebrew behind the word "glory"—*kavod*, when used of God—for it is most frequently associated with the idea of His self-manifestation, often as indicated by some visible symbol of His presence. For instance, in the course of Israel's wanderings in the wilderness after the exodus from Egypt, a cloud[128] served this function, as did fire[129]—actually, the two were one and the same, a fire-encased cloud.[130] This picturesque language is intended to convey that at a particular moment, the people experienced a heightened consciousness of the immediacy, or immanence, of the divine Presence.

In the wilderness Tabernacle and later in the Temple at Jerusalem, the permanent material symbol of the divine Presence was the Ark of the Covenant, which contained the two tablets of stone incised with the Decalogue. This item of furniture, placed in the inner sanctuary called the "Holy of Holies," was much more than a mere receptacle for those tablets. It possessed a cover adorned with two golden cherubim, one at each end. It is explicitly stated that God communicated with Moses "from above the cover between the two cherubim that are on top of the ark . . . ,"[131] and that "When Moses went into the Tent of Meeting to speak with Him, he would hear the Voice addressing him from above the cover that was on top of the Ark of the Pact between the two cherubim."[132] The divine Presence was conceived as settling, as it were, in the space between the two cherubim above the Ark. This space was thus imagined to be the invisible throne of the invisible, noncorporeal God. That is why we encounter in the Bible the oft-repeated epithet of God as "Enthroned on the Cherubim," and why reference is made to "the Ark of the Covenant of the Lord of Hosts Enthroned on the Cherubim" and to "the Ark of God to which His Name was attached, the Name Lord of Hosts Enthroned on the Cherubim."[133] Employing synecdoche, the figure of speech that uses the part for the whole, Jeremiah calls the Temple "the throne of glory."[134]

With this in mind, we can understand why, in the days of Samuel, following Israel's defeat at the hands of the Philistines, the dying widow of the slain priest Phineas named her newborn son Ichabod, meaning "The glory has departed from Israel . . . for the Ark of God has been captured."[135] The Ark symbolized the immediacy of the divine Presence. Hence, the epithet "King of glory" in Psalm 24 may be associated with the Ark, a line of reasoning that allows commentators to interpret the psalm as a liturgy accompanying the ceremonial transporting of the Ark to the Temple.

This interpretation is found in rabbinic sources that construed the composition as having been created for a procession connected with King Solomon's dedication of his newly built Temple. The ceremony is described at length in 1 Kings, chapter 8. Solomon convoked a great assembly consisting of the elders of Israel, the tribal heads, and the ancestral chieftains. The high point of the occasion was the installation of the Ark, as recounted there in verses 1–11. Rabbinic legend[136] marvelously embellished this report to transform it into a parable about royal arrogance.

The great king, "wisest of men,"[137] suddenly found himself acutely embarrassed in the presence of the assembled throng. It was discovered that the dimensions of the Ark were such that it could not be gotten through the entrance to the Holy of Holies where it was to be permanently housed. Verses 7–9 of Psalm 24 are interpreted as the verbal give-and-take between King Solomon and the portals of the inner sanctuary. The king ordered them to accommodate that Ark, but to no avail—a rebuke to monarchical pride and a reproof meant to underscore that he was but fallible flesh and blood. The king then uttered no fewer than twenty-four prayers, all in vain. The gates proceeded to interrogate him to insure that he knew who was the true "King of glory." Finally, having humbled Solomon's vanity, and been satisfied with his response, they admitted the Ark.

A different occasion for the presumed processional march headed by the priests carrying the Ark is suggested by the medieval biblical commentator, David Kimḥi (= RaDaK 1160?–1235? C.E.) of Narbonne in southeastern France. He refers to the narrative in 2 Samuel 6:12–15, which recounts how King David transferred the Ark to the City of David, that is, the fortress Zion.[138] In order to consolidate his power, following his acclamation in Hebron over all the tribes of Israel after the death of Saul, David captured Jerusalem from the native Jebusites and turned it into the new national capital of his kingdom. This was a stroke of genius in that the city had no previous tribal history and was not involved in intertribal rivalries. It was also strategically highly defensible. By transferring the Ark to his new, politically neutral capital city, David simultaneously turned it into the religious center of all Israel. The Bible describes the joyous, enthusiastic scene as the Ark was carried into Jerusalem. According to David Kimḥi, Psalm 24 was composed for the occasion.[139]

Still another theory to explain the life experience that generated the psalm sees it as a victory procession following a war. According to this, it was customary in Israel to transport the Ark to the battlefield. The military function of the Ark is attested or clearly implied in a number of biblical texts. During the wanderings in the wilderness prior to the conquest of Canaan, the priest carried the sacred object at the head of the marching columns of tribes. Numbers 10:35 has preserved for such occasions what certainly looks like a liturgy that preceded a battle:

> When the Ark was to set out, Moses would say:
> Advance, O Lord!
> May Your enemies be scattered,
> and may Your foes flee before You![140]

Similarly, a liturgy is recorded for the return of the Ark:

> Moses would say,
> Return, O Lord,
> You who are Israel's myriads of thousands.

A variant version of this formula is to be found in Psalm 132:8,

> Advance, O Lord, to Your resting-place,
> You and Your mighty Ark.

Another text—Numbers 14:39–45—tells how the Israelites, heedless of Moses' opposition, launched a reckless and foolhardy assault upon a coalition of Amalekites and Canaanites, and suffered a grievous defeat. The narrative makes a point of emphasizing that "the Ark of the Covenant" had remained in the camp; on that occasion, it did not accompany the attacking troops.

The well-known story of Joshua's capture of Jericho plainly illustrates the use of the Ark in warfare,[141] and the account of the Battle of Aphek (ca. 1050 B.C.E.), where the Israelites engaged the Philistine army, tells how, at a desperate moment, the Israelites declared, "Let us fetch the Ark of the Covenant of the Lord from Shiloh; thus He will be present among us and will deliver us from the hands of our enemies."[142]

When the Ark appeared, the Israelites burst into a great shout. The Philistines were terror-stricken. This text implies that the Ark was not routinely transported to the field of battle; it also indicates, as do other biblical texts, that it was a potent symbol of the divine Presence[143] that was taken out at critical times to boost the morale of the troops.

In light of the foregoing examples, it is understandable that

Psalm 24 could be interpreted as reflecting a victory procession after the defeat of an ememy in battle, when the Ark was returned to its regular abode in Jerusalem. The epithets of God used here in verses 8 and 10—"mighty and valiant," "valiant in battle," and "the Lord of Hosts"—would seem to lend support to this interpretation. In fact, a report of a victory procession is preserved in 2 Chronicles, chapter 20. This relates that in the days of King Jehoshaphat, Judah was attacked by a coalition of its hostile neighbors, who were soundly defeated. "All the men of Judah and Jerusalem with Jehoshaphat at their head returned joyfully to Jerusalem . . . to the House of the Lord, to the accompaniment of harps, lyres, and trumpets."[144] However, no mention is made there of the transportation of the Ark, and it is not known that the Ark was ever removed from the Holy of Holies, unless through hostile action, once the Temple was built.

The foregoing, varying explanations for the origin of the psalm flow from the presumption that it originated in response to a special historic event. None, however, responds to the question of how the composition came to be preserved.[145] In the introduction of this book, it was emphasized that a literary work had little chance of preservation in the ancient world unless there was repeated occasion for its public recital over quite a period of time. Unless we postulate an annual commemoration of the original occasion for the composition of the psalm—and we have no corroborating evidence for such an unlikely assumption—we have to look elsewhere for a solution, one that would also show the coherence of all three stanzas. It is the last stanza that holds the key to the entire composition. Four items in particular stand out: (i) Martial terminology is applied to God. He is "strong and mighty," "mighty in battle," "Lord of Hosts"; (ii) God's kingship is emphasized; (iii) He enters the Temple via gates; (iv) Strangely, the gates do not swing sidewards but open upwardly, much like trapdoors to an attic.

The martial characterization of God found in verses 8 and 10 is not unique to this psalm. An ancient, no longer extant, "Book of the Wars of the Lord," apparently a collection of popular war songs describing victories over Israel's enemies, is mentioned in Numbers 21:14. The now lost "Book of Jashar" cited in Joshua 10:11–14 seems to have been a composition of the same kind to judge from the context, although 2 Samuel 1:18 would indicate that defeats too were recorded. The tribes of Israel who departed from Egypt are called "the hosts of the Lord."[146] At the shore of the Sea of Reeds, Moses tells the fearful Israelites, "The Lord will battle for you,"[147] and in the "Song at the Sea" that Moses and the people sang in celebration of their deliverance from the Egyptians, the Lord is termed "the warrior."[148] Later, after the unprovoked aggression of the Amalekites in the wilderness against a defenseless Israel, God says that He "will be at war with Amalek throughout the ages."[149] The "Song of Deborah," lauding Israel's great victory over a Canaanite coalition, declares,

> The stars fought from heaven,
> From their courses they fought against Sisera.[150]

This poetic imagery evokes the divine epithet "the Lord of Hosts," for the heavenly bodies constitute "the host of heaven."[151] This same designation is given to the angelic beings,[152] and as we noted above, the tribes of Israel are called "the hosts of the Lord."[153] Finally, the enemies of Israel are, on that account, enemies of the Lord, and Israel's wars of survival are portrayed as "the wars of the Lord."[154]

The martial terminology applied to God reflects one aspect of the national conception of the divine in ancient Israel. It is a singular way of expressing God's omnipotence. Surrounded by aggressive enemies, rarely at peace, and constantly forced to defend its territorial integrity and independence, inhabiting a land situated at the crossroads of the ancient world, the target of imperial rivalries, Israel desperately needed the psychic reinforcement and sense of security provided by the concept of a divine warrior. Doubtless, the ancient Israelite epic about God's decisive suppression of the mutinous chaotic waters at the onset of the cosmogonic process, discussed in our interpretation of Psalm 8 and alluded to in verse 2 of Psalm 24 above, harmonized with the historical situation and inspired and influenced its literary expression. However, it needs to be stressed that the warrior God of Israel is never depicted in battle with other gods or with mythical divine forces as in the pagan mythologies, but only as guardian and protector of Israel in an existing grim reality of present hostilities.[155]

The foregoing establishes the connection between the initial stanza and the last one. God's creation of the world and His absolute mastery over nature and history accord Him the status of "Sovereign of the universe," to express it in human terms. He is the "King of glory," symbolically represented by the Ark.

The notion of His entering the Temple via the gates is paralleled in the vision of the prophet Ezekiel about the rebuilt Jerusalem. At one point, he is taken to the Temple gate that faced east, "and there, coming from the east with a roar like the roar of mighty waters, was the Presence of the God of Israel" who "entered the Temple" by that very gate.[156] At another point, the prophet was led "back to the outer gate of the Sanctuary that faced eastward; it was shut." Then the Lord said to him, "No one shall enter by it because the Lord, the God of Israel, has entered by it."[157]

The Ark, in fact, had disappeared some time before the destruction of the first Temple. Jeremiah alludes to this in chapter 3, verse 16, and Ezekiel does not include the Ark in his blueprint for the restored edifice in chapters 40–48. Hence, his above-cited text cannot refer literally to the entry of the Ark.[158] Rather, the prophet has a mystical vision of the divine chariot bearing God's throne borne by the cherubim, which scene he describes in detail in the first chapter of the book that bears his name (cf. 10:19–20).

This brings us to the last perplexing item of the final stanza, the gates opening upward instead of sideways. Such a structural arrangement suggests not a terrestrial, but a celestial temple. The notion of a gate in heaven is conveyed by Jacob's dream at Bethel, when the patriarch exclaims, "This is the gateway of heaven."[159] Psalm 78:23 has God opening "the doors of heaven."[160] The Scriptures feature several references to a "place"/temple in heaven. Of course, the two temples, the earthly and the heavenly, cannot really be separated, for in the thought-world of ancient times, that which is below is the counterpart of that which is above. The celestial temple is the ideal, transhistorical model of which the terrestrial temple is a replica,[161] and just as there is a ritual practiced in the Temple of Jerusalem, so is there a ritual in the temple above, as the vision of Isaiah, chapter 6, illustrates.

In light of all this, we must postulate that Psalm 24 was a liturgy for an annual festival.[162] This explains how it came to be preserved. On that occasion, throngs would appear at the Temple, and a ritual would take place at the foot of Mount Zion designed to inculcate the lesson that morality is a religious category of the highest order. God's kingship is highlighted, and He is conceived as entering His Temple above and below—the two blend imperceptibly. He enters via "the everlasting doors" to ascend His throne of glory in order to judge the world. In postbiblical Judaism, Rosh Hashanah, held in the Fall on the first of the seventh month, is the New Year festival and it encompasses precisely these very themes. However, the Bible is silent on the matter. It prescribes that on that date, the Israelite is to "observe complete rest; it is a sacred occasion commemorated with loud blasts [on the horn],"[163] but the rationale of the festival is not given.

Some psalms feature a combination of two or even all three of the themes of blowing the horn, divine kingship, and judgment of the world, and, most likely, were the liturgies for that annual festival. Thus, Psalm 47 describes God as "great King over all the earth," who "ascends . . . to the blast of the horn" (vv. 3,7,6); Psalm 96 says, "Declare among the nations, The Lord is King! . . . He judges the peoples with equity . . . He will rule the world justly, and its peoples in faithfulness" (vv. 10, 13); and Psalm 98 has, "With trumpets and the blast of the horn, raise a shout before the Lord, the

King . . . for He is coming to rule the earth; He will rule the world justly, and its peoples with equity" (vv. 6, 9).

It would appear, then, that although the biblical texts do not mention a New Year festival, for whatever reason, there was such an institution, and that Psalm 24 played a role in the liturgy of the day, probably as a prelude to the main service, and was sung as the procession of worshipers reached the foot of Mount Zion.

Chapter 5

PSALM THIRTY

Thanksgiving for Recovery from Illness

A psalm of David. A song for the dedication of the House.

²I extol You, O Lord,
    for You have lifted me up,
    and not let my enemies rejoice over me.
³O Lord, my God,
    I cried out to You,
    and You healed me.
⁴O Lord, You brought me up from Sheol,
    preserved me from going down into the Pit.

⁵O you faithful of the Lord, sing to Him,
    and praise His holy name.
⁶For He is angry but a moment,
    and when He is pleased there is life.
One may lie down weeping at nightfall;
    but at dawn there are shouts of joy.

⁷When I was untroubled,
    I thought, "I shall never be shaken,"
    ⁸for You, O Lord, when You were pleased,
    made [me] firm as a mighty mountain.
When You hid Your face,
    I was terrified.
⁹I called to You, O Lord;
    to my Lord I made appeal,
    ¹⁰"What is to be gained from my death,
    from my descent into the Pit?
Can dust praise You?
Can it declare Your faithfulness?
¹¹Hear, O Lord, and have mercy on me;
    O Lord, be my help!"

> [12]You turned my lament into dancing,
>> you undid my sackcloth and girded me with joy,
>> [13]that [my] whole being might sing hymns to You
>>> endlessly;
>> O Lord my God, I will praise You forever.

A straightforward reading of this psalm conveys the picture of a pious worshiper who gives thanks to God for recovery from a deadly illness.[1] Hence there is a bewildering discrepancy between the content and its title as recorded in verse 1: "A song for the dedication of the House."

The structure of the psalm is typical of biblical thanksgiving psalms in general. An opening declaration of intent to extol God is followed by the immediate reason for it,[2] and the praise is succeeded by a fuller and more specific elucidation of the occasion that prompted it (verses 2–4). The second stanza features a call to the worshipers present to join in praise of God. It narrates the psalmist's harrowing experience and his recuperation (verses 5–6).

The final stanza is a reminiscence of antecedent thoughts, prayers, and developments (verses 7–11). The psalm ends on the note on which it began (verses 12–13), the intent always to extol God.

This composition is a distinctively Israelite version of a genre of thanksgiving hymns widespread in the ancient neareastern world. A striking parallel is provided by a votive stela found at a site called Deir el-Medina, near ancient Thebes, which was a workmen's village for those who labored on the royal tombs in the Valley of Kings during the nineteenth Egyptian Dynasty (ca. 1306–1200 B.C.E.). A draftsman named Neb-Re composed a hymn to his god in gratitude for the recovery of his son, Nakht-Amon, from serious illness. Its structure is similar to that of Psalm 30, and it also has some notable stylistic parallels.[3]

Psalm 30 opens:

> I extol You, O Lord,
>> for You have lifted me up,
>> and not let my enemies rejoice over me.
> O Lord, my God,
>> I cried out to You,
>> and You healed me.
> O Lord, You brought me up from Sheol,
>> preserved me from going down into the Pit.

It is apparent at once that the psalmist is expressing gratitude for deliverance. Yet it may come as a surprise to learn that biblical Hebrew possesses no verb or noun that, in and of itself, carries as its primary meaning the expressing of thanks.[4] A person in ancient Israel expressed gratitude by means of praise of the benefactor.[5] Like the English word "extol," which derives from the Latin *ex-tollere*, "to raise up," and has come to mean "to praise highly," the original Hebrew behind that rendering really means "to raise on high," and underwent the same semantic development.

The grammatical form of the opening verb is declarative: "I proclaim that You are exalted."[6] Recognition of this proclamatory nature of the statement is important for understanding both the religion of Israel in general, and the background of verse 5 of Psalm 30 in particular. Although the verse is addressed directly to God, it presupposes the presence of a congregation. The psalmist is not talking to himself; he is sharing his personal experience with a group. In turn, each congregant partakes of the experience of the celebrating worshiper. The religious experience achieves its fullest expression, not in an individual, private setting, but in a public social context. The group becomes a corporate entity, and the act of worship is a communal act that nourishes and reinforces social solidarity without in any way diminishing the spiritual, inward, personal nature of the outpouring of the human heart in prayerful approach to God.

The immediate reason for the laudation of God is that "He lifted up" the celebrant. This may appear to be a strange expression to use; indeed, it is a biblical rarity. The verb, in its simplest form, means "to draw up water from a well,"[7] and here is used figuratively to conjure up the vivid image of a person extricated from a pit in which he seemed doomed to face certain death.[8] That the metaphorical imagery of our verse was far more widespread in ancient times than the sparse biblical usage would indicate is clear from the proper name Delaiah, which means "The Lord drew up," that is, rescued, a name probably given to a desperately sick newborn baby who survived in defiance of dire prediction.[9] The psalmist's choice of this word to describe his own situation is very subtle, for it produces a kind of literary symmetry: man "raises up"—extols—God in response to God's "lifting up" of man. Note also how an abstract term is used in relation to God, whereas a concrete image is employed for the psalmist's own situation.

The complementary sentence in verse 2 seems to introduce a discordant note. By rescuing the sufferer, God has deprived his enemies of a cause for rejoicing. We can no longer know who these enemies were or the reason for their enmity. Many biblical texts similarly refer to malicious gloating over an adversary's misfortune.[10] We may simply be dealing with an idiomatic expression that belongs to the rhetoric of jubilation in this instance, and to lamentation in other cases.[11] In any event, the phrase, whether literal or not, must have had its origin in a social reality. The pressures of crowded living conditions—most cities were walled and had little room for expansion as population grew—generate complex emotional tensions and disruptive relationships. Irascibility, frayed tempers, contentiousness, the harboring of private grudges and enduring animosities, become typical of human relationships, and individuals and families find reason to regard others as enemies. This is as true of the modern world as it was of the ancient.

The suffering psalmist who thought he was at death's door had "cried out" to God. The phrase used is much stronger than ordinary praying. It connotes an impassioned entreaty in what appears to have been an utterly hopeless situation.[12] God responded; the sufferer was restored to health. The extraordinary recovery is portrayed in quasi-mythical language which, if taken literally, is internally contradictory, for Sheol and the Pit are synonymous.

Sheol is the biblical Hebrew term for the realm of the dead. The origin of the word is unknown and the cognate languages offer no help. With rare exception,[13] the word takes a verb or adjective in the feminine form,[14] and it never appears with a definite article. This suggests that Sheol is a feminine proper name. The Greek Hades provides an analogy. Originally the name of the lord of the underworld, it came to be used for the world of the dead itself. "Sheol" must be a carryover from pre-Israelite times, though why it should be exclusive to Hebrew is a mystery.[15]

The Hebrew Bible is perplexingly vague about the matter of an afterlife. It has left us no clear conception of the netherworld and hardly a record of the mortuary customs of ancient Israel. This is in sharp contrast to the Egyptians, who conceived of human survival after death as a happy continuation of the conditions of this world. They fashioned funerary rites in accordance with this belief, including the preservation of the body—for eternity, as they thought—by means of mummification.[16] Furthermore, the Hebrew Bible, in contrast to postbiblical sources, presents neither notions of heaven and hell nor any distinction between the postmortem abode and the destiny of the righteous and the wicked. There is simply the subterranean Sheol deep beneath the earth.[17] It is

> . . . a land of deepest gloom;
> a land whose light is darkness,
> all gloom and disarray,
> whose light is like darkness[18] (Job 10:21–22).

It is "the house assigned for all the living"[19] irrespective of one's station in life,[20] a site furnished with gates[21] and divided into compartments.[22] "The Pit" is an alternative term for Sheol, although originally it may have signified the passageway in the earth by which the dead were thought to descend to Sheol. At any rate, the cliché for the dead is "those who go down into the Pit."[23]

Anyone familiar with Mesopotamian conceptions of the after-life[24] will recognize at once the affinities with the biblical descriptions, most of which appear in poetic texts. In Akkadian literature, the realm of the dead is "the place of darkness,"[25] "the land of no return."[26] It is surrounded by walls, and its innermost section is reached by passage through seven gates.[27]

Certainly, the biblical poetic references carry no doctrinal authority, and later Judaism developed an entirely different portrayal of the afterlife with its own specialized nomenclature. Moreover, the surface similarity between the biblical and Mesopotamian descriptions hides the fact that biblical law distanced the religion of Israel from that of its neighbors by prohibiting necromancy, the practice of communicating with the dead (to predict the future or for other purposes),[28] and by outlawing sacrifices to them.[29]

To return to the two clauses of verse 4: how can the psalmist declare at one and the same time that God brought him up from Sheol and preserved him from going down into the Pit? The first clause implies an actual descent into the realm of the dead, while the second asserts escape from death.[30] The answer is that Sheol in this context is a metaphor for imminent mortal danger.[31] Hence, verse 4 has nothing to do with the late doctrine of the bodily resurrection of the dead. The identical idiomatic usage occurs in Mesopotamian literature in which the Akkadian divine epithet *muballit miti*, literally "giving life to the dead," connotes "healing the mortally sick."[32]

We have previously observed that the expression of gratitude through the medium of praise takes place in the presence of an assembled congregation, and that what appears to be a private event is inseparable from the life of the community. All the worshipers share each other's joys and sorrows, and so our psalmist summons them to celebrate with him:

> O you faithful of the Lord, sing to Him,
> > and praise His holy name. [33]
> For He is angry but a moment,
> > and when He is pleased there is life. [34]
> One may lie down weeping[35] at nightfall;
> > but at dawn there are shouts of joy. [36]

The "faithful" are those who are loyal to the demands of the covenant between God and Israel. [37] The "singing" involves the accompaniment of musical instruments[38] such as the lyre, [39] the ten-stringed harp, [40] or the timbrel[41] either alone or in combination, [42] and there may have been wind instruments as well. [43]

The psalmist grounds his call for congregational praise in a generalized inference about the nature of God's governance of the world, a conclusion he seems to draw from his recent experience. Human suffering, which to him is a consequence of divine anger, is of limited duration; harmony between God and man is life-sustaining. An alternative understanding contrasts "a moment" with "lifelong" just as "angry" contrasts with "pleased": God's ire is short-lived, His approbation lasts a lifetime. Either way, the implication is that misfortune should not generate despair. A tearful, desolate outlook at eventide may give way to joyous singing as the new day dawns.

The psalmist now reverts to reflections on his personal experience. He confesses:

> When I was untroubled, [44]
> > I thought, [45] "I shall never be shaken,"
> > for You, O Lord, when You were pleased,
> > made [me] firm as a mighty mountain. [46]

The reason for the divine anger that occasioned his desperate sickness was the sin of hubris. Arrogant self-satisfaction with his comfortable lot, his prosperity and wellbeing, had blinded him to the sober realities of life, and had deluded him into believing that he was invulnerable and that his good fortune would last forever. His serene self-confidence was shattered when misfortune suddenly beset him:

> When You hid Your face,
> I was terrified.

The "hiding of God's face" is a figure of speech much used in the psalms.[47] It connotes God's self-willed withdrawal of His favor and providential care. This is how the psalmist interpreted his sudden, severe illness. He recognized that he had alienated God and that his suffering was purposeful, not a matter of happenstance. This acknowledgment of his own sin and vulnerability enabled him to deal with the situation by reestablishing the bond with God by means of prayer. He shares with the congregation his responses to his newly sensitized awareness of his utter dependency on God.

> I called to You, O Lord;
>> to my Lord I made appeal,
>> "What is to be gained from my death,
>> from my descent into the Pit?[48]
> Can dust[49] praise You?
> Can it declare Your faithfulness?[50]
>> Hear, O Lord, and have mercy on me;
>> Lord, be my help!"

Note how "the Lord"(YHVH) has become "my Lord," just as in verse 3 it was "my God," when engaged in earnest, fervent prayer. The possessive pronoun gives voice to seclusive intimacy with God; the term "Lord"—Hebrew *'adonai*—is an acknowledgment of God's mastership and the psalmist's total self-surrender to Him. The ordeal has humbled him; he is a chastened man who no longer would believe that "my own power and the might of my own hand have won this wealth for me"—as the admonitory words of Deuteronomy 8:17 have it.

At the critical, agonizing moment when his disease had reached its peak, with life and death seemingly locked unpredictably in convulsive struggle, the sick man asked desperately, what would be gained by his demise?[51] Were it not for the succeeding clauses, the question would be quite unintelligent, for the same could be posed of the death of almost any human being. The second part of the verse gives it meaning. One recalls the similar positive sentiment expressed in psalm 118, verse 17:

> I shall not die but live
> and proclaim the works of the Lord.

The desire for life is not an exercise in egoism, but is prompted by the consciousness that death irrevocably severs contact and communication with God. Such a concept, abandoned or perhaps transformed in later Judaism, is repeated several times in the Hebrew Bible. King Hezekiah of Judah, who at the very point of death was granted fifteen extra years of life, voices the belief this way in his thanksgiving hymn in Isaiah 38:18–19:

> For it is not Sheol that praises You,
> Not [the Land of] Death that extols You;
> Nor do they who descend into the Pit
> Hope for Your grace.
> The living, only the living
> Can give thanks to You
> As I do this day;
> Fathers relate to children
> Your acts of grace.

The Book of Psalms, in particular, features this same tenet. Gravely ill, the psalmist pleads,

> O Lord, turn! Rescue me!
> Deliver me as befits Your faithfulness,
> For there is no praise of You among the dead;
> in Sheol, who can acclaim You? (Ps. 6:5–6)

Elsewhere in Psalms, there is the following from one who finds
himself in desperate straits:

> For I am sated with misfortune;
>> I am at the brink of Sheol.
>
> I am numbered with those who go down to the Pit.
>> I am a helpless man
>> abandoned among the dead,
>> like bodies lying in the grave
>> of whom You are mindful no more,
>> and who are cut off from Your care. . . .

> Do You work wonders for the dead?
>> Do the shades rise to praise You?
>
> Is Your faithful care recounted in the grave,
>> Your constancy in the place of perdition?
>
> Are Your wonders made known in the netherworld,
>> Your beneficent deeds in the land of oblivion?
>> (Ps. 88:4–6, 11–13)

Formulated not as a rhetorical question, but with absolute certainty,
is the following from Psalm 115, verse 17:

> The dead cannot praise the Lord,
>> nor any who go down into silence.

With the pleas of verse 11, the psalmist completes the retelling
of the prayer he had uttered at the height of his sickness. He reverts
to the theme with which Psalm 30 opened:

> You turned my lament into dancing,[52]
>> you undid my sackcloth and girded me with joy,
>> that [my] whole being might sing hymns to You
>>> endlessly;
>> O Lord my God, I will praise You forever.

Obscured by the English translation is that the term "lament"[53] belongs to the vocabulary of mourning rites, as the "sackcloth" pertains to the mourning apparel. The "lament" is the dirge, usually intoned over the dead by relatives and friends. Here, the sick psalmist has been reciting it over himself! The "sackcloth" was a coarse material, most likely made of goat or camel hair, and was worn as a symbol of sorrow, suffering, humiliation, and penance.

The transformation of mourning into dancing is more than mere rhetoric. Dance involves the rhythmic movements of the body: in fact, the stem of the Hebrew term used here means "to writhe, whirl." Hence, the clause in verse 12 expresses the extraordinary change from a state of torpidity to a condition of energetic bodily vigor. Furthermore, the dance is not only the expression of exuberant joy, but is itself also a mode of worship, a means of extolling God, as Psalms 149:3 and 150:4 affirm:

> Let them praise His name in dance.

> Praise Him with timbrel and dance.

The psalms' headings generally shed no light on the content of the psalm, the particular circumstance that inspired their original composition, or the appropriate liturgical occasion that called for their periodic repetition. The strange caption to Psalm 30 appears to be an exception.

For the sake of clarity, the English translation of verse 1 inverts the word order of the Hebrew, and reads smoothly, "A psalm of David. A song for the dedication of the House." Actually, the literal rendering is barely intelligible: "A psalm; a song [of?]; the dedication of the House; of David." Not only is the content of the title perplexing in relation to the subject matter of the psalm; its structure is unparalleled. The only other composition whose heading preserves information about the occasion of its composition or its recitation is Psalm 92. This reads, "A psalm, a song for the Sabbath day."[54] There, the preposition "for" is determinative; here in Psalm 30, the preposition is lacking in the Hebrew. Another complication is that our psalm places "of/for David" in the final position, whereas this is never the case with the other compositions that bear the title "A psalm, a song" together with a proper name.[55] Furthermore, the designation "a song" does not otherwise appear in the titles of the first book of the Psalter.[56]

These anomalies suggest that the original title was "A psalm of David." At some period, the composition was wholly reinterpreted so that the worshiper became the entire community viewed as a collective personality. The implied sickness was understood as a metaphor for a national calamity, and the remarkable recovery was construed in terms of a great experience of national deliverance followed by the joyous rededication of the Temple at which the people voiced its eternal gratitude to God. This adaptation of the psalm led to the expansion of the superscription in commemoration of the great event, and "A song[57] of the dedication of the Temple" was inserted parenthetically between "A psalm" and "of David."

What historic event occasioned this reinterpretation? Two possibilities come to mind. The first is the dedication of the Second Temple following completion of its rebuilding on the third day of the month of Adar in the sixth year of the reign of the Persian King Darius, that is, in the spring of 515 B.C.E. As told in Ezra 6:15–18, the entire people "celebrated the dedication of the House of God with joy."[58]

The other possibility for locating the specific occasion for the communal use of Psalm 30 and its reinterpretation is the purification and rededication of the Temple in the autumn of 164 B.C.E. following the victory of Judah Maccabee over the Syro-Greeks. The events, which have been celebrated by Jews ever since in the annual eight-day festival of Hanukkah ("dedication"), are described in I Maccabees 4:36–59.[59] The post-Talmudic minor tractate called Soferim prescribes Psalm 30 as a liturgical reading for the festival.[60]

Rabbinic literature has preserved another tradition about the liturgical use of the psalm. According to the Mishnah Bikkurim 3:4,[61] when the procession of pilgrims to Jerusalem in celebration of the first fruits festival[62] arrived at the approach to the Temple court, the Levitical choir would greet them with the singing of Psalm 30. It is clear that in Second Temple times the composition was no longer understood in its literal sense, but was used more generally for occasions of communal thanksgiving.[63]

Chapter 6

PSALM FORTY-EIGHT

A Zion Hymn

A song. A psalm of the Korahites.

²The LORD is great and much acclaimed
    in the city of our God,
    His holy mountain—
    ³fair-crested, joy of all the earth,
    Mount Zion, summit of Zaphon,
    city of the great king.
⁴Through its citadels, God has made Himself known as a
    haven.
⁵See, the kings joined forces;
    they advanced together.
⁶At the mere sight of it they were stunned,
    they were terrified, they panicked;
    ⁷they were seized there with a trembling,
    like a woman in the throes of labor,
    ⁸as the Tarshish fleet was wrecked
    in an easterly gale.
⁹The likes of what we heard we have now witnessed
    in the city of the LORD of hosts,
    in the city of our God—
    may God preserve it forever!

¹⁰In Your temple, God,
    we meditate upon Your faithful care.
¹¹The praise of You, God, like Your name,
    reaches to the ends of the earth;
    Your right hand is filled with beneficence.
¹²Let Mount Zion rejoice!
Let the towns of Judah exult,
    because of Your judgments.

> [13]Walk around Zion,
>   circle it;
>   count its towers,
>   [14]take note of its ramparts;
>   go through its citadels,
>   that you may recount it to a future age.
> [15]For God—He is our God forever;
>   He will lead us evermore.

Zion is lauded many times in the Book of Psalms.[1] It is God's holy mountain,[2] His chosen site[3], the object of His desire[4] and love,[5] His abode,[6] the seat of His sovereign rule[7] whence come His blessings and deliverance,[8] the symbol of permanence[9] and of consummate beauty.[10] Psalm 48 is the most prominent and exemplary of the compositions that focus on the city.[11]

The adoration of Zion can trace its origin, as we shall soon see, to King David's capture of the city.[12] It gradually grew in intensity as a consequence of the studied policies of Judean kings and of some decisive historical events. What the name "Zion" means, no one knows for sure. It might derive from a word meaning "a dry place, parched ground,"[13] or, more plausibly, it could perhaps indicate "rugged, stony ground," "rocky mountain," from a root meaning "strong, sharp, hard."[14] What is certain is that the name originally attached exclusively to the Jebusite fortress on the ridge southeast of Jerusalem[15] which, when it passed into Israelite hands, was renamed "the city of David."[16] The earlier name was not displaced, however, and as Judean penetration of the area expanded, "Zion" lent its name to an ever-wider region. It came to encompass the Temple site as well[17] and eventually became synonymous with the whole of Jerusalem.[18]

Situated astride the central mountain range, the crossroads of both main highways that traversed the land, the north-south and east-west routes, the city was the natural center of the entire country.

It also enjoyed an excellent strategic position. Its topography made it an ideal for defense against assault from outside. Lying some 2500 ft (760m) above sea level, it is surrounded on three sides by steep valleys, and the approach to the city is protected by numerous hills.[19]

The invading Israelites under Joshua's command "were unable to dispossess the Jebusites, the inhabitants of Jerusalem,"[20] and while at some point the Judahites did attack and hold the city, causing much devastation,[21] it was a short-lived success. Years later, a traveling Israelite would want to avoid entering Jerusalem because it was "a town of aliens who are not of Israel."[22] The unconquered city remained a thorn in the side of Israel for hundreds of years. The Jebusite enclave isolated the tribe of Judah from the rest of Israel, an embarrassing and perilous situation reflected in the poem known as Moses' farewell blessing on Israel,

> And this he said of Judah:
>> Hear, O Lord, the voice of Judah
>> And restore him to his people.[23]

How extraordinarily difficult it was for Israel to conquer Jerusalem is indicated by David's waiting more than seven years to undertake the formidable task after he was crowned king at Hebron following the death of King Saul.[24] When he finally set out to assail the city, his effort was met with scorn and derision on the part of the local Jebusite defenders. Supremely confident in their strategic assets, they taunted him saying, "You will never get in here! Even the blind and the lame will turn you back."[25] The brief account of David's capture of "the stronghold of Zion," as told in 2 Samuel 5:7–9,[26] shows that the exploit was regarded as a feat of unusual heroism and skill.

Paradoxically, the very victory that invalidated Jebusite confidence in the impregnability of Zion, by virtue of the daunting magnitude of the achievement, actually led Israel to fall heir to that same belief. Popular trust in the invincibility of Jerusalem was reinforced by the building program on which David embarked, expanding the city northward, and by the massive new fortifications he erected. It was bolstered and nurtured immeasurably by David's brilliant move in transferring the sacred Ark of the Covenant to the site. Zion was now the political and religious center of all Israel. It was looked upon as the abode of God, and as such was thought to be under His permanent and effective protection—unconquerable.[27] When King Solomon built his grandiose Temple, the status and prestige of the city were vastly enhanced, and popular notions about its being God's domicile on earth became further entrenched.[28]

Although Psalm 48 is a paean to Zion, it is the glorification of God's greatness and beneficence and the acknowledgment of His eternal divinity that begin and end it, and form its center.[29] These are the realities that accord Zion its distinctive qualities, its spiritual magnetism.

> The Lord is great and much acclaimed[30]
>> in the city of our God,
>> His holy mountain—[31]
>> fair-crested,[32] joy of all the earth,
>> Mount Zion, summit of Zaphon,
>> city of the great king.
> Through its citadels, God has made Himself known [33]
>> as a haven.

Zion is termed God's "holy mountain." Recall that, in Israelite religious conceptions, there exists no intrinsic, "natural" holiness apart from the innate holiness of God. Any material object or terrestrial site regarded as being "holy" acquires this characteristic solely on account of its being so endowed by Him. Since He chose Zion as the place where the immediacy of His Presence is to be most intensely experienced, it is His holy city, His sacred mountain. (The role of the mountains as the locale of temples in the ancient world has been discussed in chapter 4 in connection with Psalm 15.)

To the psalmist, Mount Zion is "fair-crested." The image is that of a mountain rising to a great height.[34] In fact, it is of rather modest, unimpressive elevation. Of course, no biblical writer or audience would have failed to realize that the language employed was poetic and mythic, not intended to be understood literally. Sacred mountains were conceived to be channels of communication between the world of the divine and the world of human beings. This conception is well illustrated by the names of temples in Mesopotamia, those ziggurats, or temple towers, that were architectural representations of mountains. Thus, the temple of Inanna in Nippur was known as Dur-anki, "The Bond of Heaven and Earth"; that of Marduk in Babylonia was called E-temen-anki, "The House, Foundation-Platform of Heaven and Earth." At Assur, there was "The House, Mountain of the Universe," and at Larsa, "The House, Link of Heaven and Earth." In light of this ancient neareastern tradition, also reflected in Jacob's dream at Bethel,[35] our psalmist can refer to Mount Zion rhetorically and ideally as a place of high elevation, irrespective of its actual height.[36]

Similarly mythopoetic is the designation of Zion as the "summit of Zaphon." This latter term is the regular Hebrew word for "north," a compass point, in itself devoid of any religious or mythological significance. Indeed, many English translations render the phrase "the far-reaches of the north." But how can Zion possibly be so mislocated in a biblical text? Obviously, Zaphon here is a toponym, or place-name, not a directional indicator. In his famous taunt-song over the downfall of the "king of Babylon," the prophet Isaiah ridicules the overweening arrogance of that monarch in these words:

> Once you thought in your heart,
> "I will climb to the sky,
> higher than the stars of God
> I will set my throne.
> I will sit in the mount of assembly,
> on the summit of Zaphon."[37]

This passage clearly describes Mount Zaphon in a way that makes it the equivalent of Mount Olympus, the special abode of the higher gods of Greek mythology, where Zeus had his throne and the assemblies of the gods took place. In Ugaritic literature, Zaphon is the name of a holy mountain on which Baal, the foremost Canaanite god, had his palace, and to which the gods were summoned to assemble. In classical sources, the site is known as Mons Casius, a corruption of the Hittite and Akkadian name Khaz(z)i. It is the present Jebel-el Aqra at the mouth of the Orontes River in Syria.[38] An echo of Zaphon as the home of the Canaanite deity is to be found in the place-name Baal-Zephon, mentioned in Exodus 14:1, 9 and Numbers 33:7 in connection with the first stage of the itinerary of the Israelites as they departed from Egypt. The toponym is evidence of the existence of a temple to Baal in the eastern Delta of the Nile. That this Canaanite deity was worshiped by some residents of Egypt is confirmed by an extant letter sent from Tahpanhes to Memphis some time in the sixth century B.C.E. It carries this line, "I wish you blessing from Baal-zephon and from all the gods of Tahpanhes."[39]

To return to the phrase "Mount Zion, summit of Zaphon" in Psalm 48:3: in Israel, the term Zaphon, like Olympus in English, lost its geographic denotation, was divested of its pagan origins and mythical associations, and became purely metaphorical for the divine abode,[40] the "city of the great King." This last phrase, "great King," in its unusual Hebrew form, is another expression that belongs to the common linguistic heritage of the ancient Near East, where it is a term for a sovereign or suzerain.[41] It appears as a standard royal title among the Hittites, from whom it was borrowed by the Assyrians, and it then passed into Aramaic and other languages. In Ugaritic, *mlk rb* is used both of a god and of a human king. However, here in Psalm 48:3, its sole usage in biblical Hebrew, *melekh rab* is a divine title connoting God's sovereignty over the entire earth. In contrast to other neareastern cultures, no king in Israel is ever called "the great king." It is a title reserved exclusively for God.[42]

The last verse of the stanza—"Through its citadels God has made Himself known as a haven"—is transitional. The city has withstood some massive enemy assault, and the victory is ascribed to divine protection:

> See, the kings joined forces;[43]
>> they advanced[44] together.
> At the mere sight of it they were stunned,
>> they were terrified, they panicked;[45]
>> they were seized there with a trembling,
>> like a woman in the throes of labor,
>> as the Tarshish fleet was wrecked
>> in an easterly gale.

Who are these kings, and to what historic event if any does the psalmist refer? The question is qualified because medieval Jewish commentators, as well as several moderns, have treated the psalm eschatologically,[46] that is, as referring to Messianic times, while others take the reference to the kings as a purely literary device, rather than historic reality.[47] Several scholars, however, see Sennacherib's invasion of Judea and siege of Jerusalem as the real background to verses 4–8.[48] To the present writer, these passages, together with the emphasis in verses 4, 13–14, on the city's defenses, appear to make a plausible case for this last interpretation.

The story begins in the year 745 B.C.E., when Tiglath-pileser III usurped the throne of Assyria. Once he had consolidated his power, this vigorous king campaigned repeatedly in the west against the several petty states in the region. In 732 B.C.E. he occupied Damascus, despoiled the city, and deported its inhabitants.[49] By the time of his death in 727 B.C.E., he had carved out for Assyria an extensive empire. His successor, Shalmaneser V, continued his father's imperialist policies, annexed most of the territory of the northern kingdom of Israel, and laid siege to its capital.[50] It is unclear whether it was he or Sargon II, who seized the throne on his death in 722 B.C.E., who completed the reduction of the city. At any rate, Samaria fell in 722/721 B.C.E., bringing to an end the kingdom of Israel. Much of the population was deported, and foreigners were settled in the land.[51]

The fall of Samaria was both a warning signal and a tempting opportunity to King Hezekiah of Judah (715 B.C.E.–687 B.C.E.). The danger of further Assyrian advance southward was ever-present, and as long as Sargon lived, Judah was a vassal-state. On the other hand, the destruction of the northern kingdom removed any rival to Jerusalem's predominance, and Hezekiah adopted several measures that were designed to reunite the two components of the people of Israel under Jerusalem's hegemony. He launched a religious reform that included rehabilitation of the Temple, the purging of idolatrous practices throughout the land, north and south, and the centralization of sacrificial worship in Jerusalem. He also held a great national Passover celebration in the capital, in which both Israel and Judah were included.[52]

This promotion of Zion, that is, Jerusalem, was supported and furthered by the prophet Isaiah, who assigned it an exalted role in the world. He foretold that in days to come, the Mount of the Lord would stand firm above the mountains and tower above the hills, and that all the nations would acknowledge the spiritual centrality of the city and seek instruction there. As a result, an era of universal peace and disarmament would be inaugurated.[53]

After the year 720 B.C.E., Sargon halted his campaigns against the west. This hiatus encouraged Egypt to organize an anti-Assyrian coalition, but the rebels soon were crushed. International trade flourished during this period, and Jerusalem, occupying an advantageous position between the two great powers, benefited greatly.[54] Hezekiah, anticipating a renewal of Assyrian aggression, buttressed the defenses of the city. He acted with vigor, rebuilding the whole breached wall, raising towers on it, and building another wall outside it.[55] He secured the water supply of Jerusalem by diverting the flow of a spring outside the walls into the city by means of a newly built underground tunnel.[56]

The death of Sargon in 705 B.C.E. and the accession of his son Sennacherib to the throne marked a turning point in Assyrian-Judean relationships. Four years later, Sennacherib invaded Judea, wrought widespread devastation throughout the land, and laid siege to Jerusalem.[57] It was the prophet Isaiah who assured Hezekiah that the city would not fall to the Assyrian:[58]

"He shall not enter this city:
he shall not shoot an arrow at it,
or advance upon it with a shield,
or pile up a siegemound against it.
He shall go back
By the way he came,
he shall not enter this city
　　　—declares the Lord;
I will protect and save this city for My sake,
and for the sake of My servant David."[59]

Isaiah's prophecy was fulfilled. The biblical narrator tells us: "[That night] an angel of the Lord went out and struck down one hundred and eighty-five thousand in the Assyrian camp, and the following morning they were all dead corpses. So King Sennacherib of Assyria broke camp and retreated, and stayed in Nineveh."[60] Interestingly, in his annals Sennacherib reports on his campaign against Judea, boasts of all his conquests, of the massacres he perpetrated, of the booty he took, how he besieged Jerusalem, and made "Hezekiah the Judean" "a prisoner . . . like a bird in a cage"; but he makes no claim to have captured the city.[61]

Whatever the reality behind the biblical report, whether the invading Assyrians were struck by bubonic plague[62] or by some other epidemic, the fact is that of the great cities along Sennacherib's path, Jerusalem alone did not fall. It can be readily understood how this spectacular deliverance made an indelible impression on the popular mind. It appeared to validate the prevailing belief in the city as God's special protectorate, and entrenched the myth of Jerusalem's invulnerability. A century later, the prophet Jeremiah attempted unsuccessfully to eradicate this false theology from the minds of the people. He regarded it as injurious to the spiritual and moral welfare of the kingdom; and he almost paid with his life for his fearless preaching.[63] The psalm under discussion certainly holds to the basic conception of Zion as God's holy city, but whether its author also believed in its invulnerability as God's protectorate is unclear; the last clause of verse 9 may be either affirmative or prayerful.

The psalm mentions the kings—in the plural—who forgathered and advanced on Jerusalem. These most likely would have been the vassals of the Assyrians, who were frequently recruited to participate in the suzerain's campaigns, and who willingly plundered the victims of his aggression. In his Annals, Sennacherib reports that he handed over Judean towns to the kings of Ashdod, Ekron, and Gaza.[64] Our psalmist seems to say that the kings, who themselves weakly succumbed to Sennacherib's threats, converged on Jerusalem in expectation of an easy conquest. They witnessed in astonishment God's awesome power and, terror-struck, they retreated in headlong flight.

Our author employs two similes to depict their situation. The first, "like a woman in the throes of labor," is a fairly common biblical way of portraying uncontrolled, spasmodic bodily convulsions caused by terror.[65] The second simile used to describe the sudden disaster that overtook the invaders is one of unruly nature, drawn from the world of seafaring.[66] In the Bible, the phrase "east wind" very frequently has lost its directional force and is simply a metaphor of a devastating windstorm. In the Canaanite-Syrian region the dangerous, tempestuous winds blow in from the west, and in Egypt the hot, destructive, withering winds come from the south; yet the same Hebrew term *kadim* is used for both.[67]

Two other biblical passages refer to the destruction of "Tarshish ships" in storms. King Jehoshaphat constructed such vessels to sail to Ophir for gold, but they were wrecked at Ezion-geber in the Gulf of Aqaba;[68] and the prophet Ezekiel, in an oracle against the Phoenician city of Tyre, tells that a Tarshish fleet carrying precious cargo was wrecked by a tempest on the high seas.[69]

What is a "Tarshish" ship? The Table of Nations in Genesis, chapter 10:4–5, mentions Tarshish together with Elishah, Kittim, and Dodanim, all descendants of Javan. It is noted there that "from these the maritime nations branched out."[70] Javan is none other than the home of the Ionians, a branch of the Greeks, who colonized the west coast of Asia Minor; Elishah is Alashiya, an ancient name for Cyprus (or part of that island); the Kittim are the inhabitants of Kition, modern Lanarca on the southeastern coast of Cyprus; and the Dodanim most likely are the people of Dardania,[71] the modern Dardanelles (or, if we accept the alternative reading Rodanim,[72] the inhabitants of the isle of Rhodes). Hence, Tarshish must be sought in the Mediterranean region. This accords with the story of Jonah, the fugitive prophet who "went down to Joppa (i.e. Jaffa), and found a ship going to Tarshish."[73] Moreover, several biblical texts mention Tarshish in connection with Phoenician maritime enterprises.[74] In fact, from extra-biblical sources we can document three Mediterranean coastal towns that bore names similar in sound to Tarshish. These are: Tarsus, called Tarsis in the records of the Assyrian conqueror Esarhaddon[75] (680–669 B.C.E.), which was the capital of Cilicia in Asia Minor; Tartessus, a Phoenician settlement on the coast of Spain, west of Gibraltar; and a site consonantally spelled *trshsh* in a Phoenician inscription found in Nora,[76] an ancient port of the Mediterranean island of Sardinia. These sources would seem to settle decisively the problem of the location of a place-name Tarshish within the Mediterranean region, even though a precise identification remains problematical. However, the issue is complicated by the above-mentioned story about King Jehoshaphat's Tarshish ships, which were wrecked in the Gulf of Aqaba. This would place the site somewhere on the coast of the Red Sea. At any rate, ships so named would have been those capable of sailing to faraway places.

To unravel the mystery of the descriptive "Tarshish," scholars have offered several possibilities. One is that the word really derives from the Greek *thalasses*, "sea";[77] hence a ship that plied the high seas. Another suggestion associates the term with the Greek *tarsos*, "an oar,"[78] referring to ships propelled by oars in addition to sails. Such a combination yielded advantages of greater stability, speed, and distance traveled. Places named "Tarshish" would have been coastal maritime sites in which the seafarers were especially skilled in handling such large vessels. Still a third explanation that has been put forward points out that in biblical Hebrew *tarshish* is also the name of a precious stone,[79] and may well be connected with the word *tirosh*, "new wine";[80] this brings to mind Homer's poetic phrase, "the wine-dark sea."[81] This implies that these vessels were designed and used for transporting heavy freight. It is noted that Akkadian *rašašu* means "to be burning hot," a verb particularly appropriate to the smelting and refining of metals. Thus, Tarshish would be a metal-smelting site and this would explain why several sites in different locations bore the same name.[83]

The next stanza, verses 9–12, seems to be the observations of pilgrims enjoying their first view of Jerusalem.[84] The occasion most likely is the anniversary celebration of the raising of the siege of the city. The pilgrims affirm:

> The likes of what we heard we have now witnessed
>> in the city of the Lord of hosts,
>> in the city of our God—
>> may God preserve it forever!
>
> In Your temple, God,
>> we meditate upon Your faithful care.
> The praise of You, God, like Your name,
>> reaches to the ends of the earth;
>> Your right hand is filled with beneficence.
> Let Mount Zion rejoice!
> Let the towns of Judah exult,
>> because of Your judgments.

The lifting of the siege of Jerusalem and the retreat of the Assyrian army enable the pilgrims once again to make their way to Jerusalem. On arrival at their destination, the same sight that struck fear into the hearts of the invaders fills the pilgrims with wonderment and awe. Inside the Temple, engaged in devotional worship, the community reflects upon the marvelous events that recently unfolded. The meditating is not a self-centered or ecstatic experience, but an intellectual focusing of the consciousness by one and all upon the divine reality behind what had occurred. The effect is the transcendent awareness of God's faithful care for the city and its population. Praise of God in gratitude extends beyond the confines of Zion. All peoples throughout the hated, far-flung Assyrian empire rejoice and extol Him. The deliverance of Zion brings them hope and cheer, while the invincible power of divine righteousness is demonstrated and vindicated.

The pilgrims are now exhorted—in all probability by a priest or Levite—to make a circuit around the walls of the city.

> Walk around Zion,
>> circle it;
>> count its towers,
>> take note of its ramparts;
>> go through[85] its citadels,
>> that you may recount it to a future age.

At first glance, this charge appears to have no other purpose than to encourage the tourist-pilgrims to view and admire the city's defenses, except that ritual "circumambulation," as such circuits are called, is a well known ceremony of great antiquity in many cultures. In ancient Egypt, for example, a newly installed pharaoh had to undertake a circuit of the wall in a festal procession as an essential part of the coronation rites on the day of his enthronement.[86] In Israel, the circuit of the walls appears, of course, in the account of Joshua's conquest of Jericho, as set forth in chapter 6 of the biblical book named after him.[87] In Second Temple times, the worshipers, carrying their palm branches, would walk around the altar once each day, and seven times on the seventh day on the festival of Tabernacles [Sukkoth].[88] Following the destruction of the Temple, this practice was transferred to the synagogue service.[89] It would appear from Psalm 26:6,

> I wash my hands in innocence
> and walk around Your altar,

that a ritual procession around the altar was already in vogue in
Israel in biblical times.[90] In many Jewish communities, even in
modern times, it is customary for a bride to make three or seven
circuits around her groom during the wedding ceremony.[91] In ancient Rome, circuiting the city was enacted in time of danger.[92] In
Islam, a sevenfold circumambulation of the sacred Ka'abah sanctuary is a central feature of the hajj, the obligatory pilgrimage to
Mecca that constitutes the fifth "pillar" of that religion.[93] In each
instance, one of two objectives is involved. The circuiting may set
up a "magic circle" around the targeted site or person in order to
provide protection from the intrusion of evil spirits; or it can be to
assert or affirm sovereignty over the area encompassed.

The all-enclosing city walls assumed profound psychological
significance in ancient times. Their defensive military function,
acting as a concrete barrier to the unwanted penetration of hostile
elements, provided a sense of security and an assurance of stability.
Further, the visible, tangible, physical limits encouraged domestic
organization, sustained social, political, and sacerdotal institutions,
and fostered a municipal spirit. They demarcated the sacred, enclosed area from the profane open countryside. The walls often were
enormous, reaching to a height of thirty feet, and could be as much
as twenty feet thick. They were strengthened by ramparts and towers
and monumental gateways. All in all, the walls enjoyed a quasi-
sacred status, were a source of immense pride to the citizens, and
were an index of the magnificence, grandeur, and power of the city.
Such an attitude is well illustrated in the famous Babylonian Epic
of Gilgamesh, which speaks of "the ramparted wall" of Uruk, and
bids one to ascend and take a walk on the walls and inspect the
foundation terrace and examine the brickwork,[94] an exhortation very
similar to that of our psalm. This last recalls the rhetorical question
of the prophet Isaiah, "Where is the one who would count the
towers?"[95] That is to say, the defense towers are too numerous to be
counted—another way of stressing the great might and defensive
power of the city.

The recognition and acceptance of this satisfactory condition is not an end in itself, as valuable as that may be as a means of fortifying morale. Our psalmist has a broader educational agenda in mind. The pilgrims must transmit the memory of their experience to future generations. In this way, the nation's historical heritage is preserved,[96] and the fundamentals of Israel's faith are inculcated in the young. But it is not the glorification of military might and massive defenses that are to be at the center of consciousness. The psalm concludes with an acknowledgment that all human affairs are under the direction and governance of God:

> For God—He is our God forever;
> He will lead us evermore.[97]

This is the message that the psalmist wishes to communicate to the pilgrims to Jerusalem, and to all future generations.

Chapter 7

PSALM EIGHTY-TWO

A Judgment on the Judges

A psalm of Asaph.

God stands in the divine assembly;
    among the divine beings
    He pronounces judgment.
[2]How long will you judge perversely,
    showing favor to the wicked?
[3]Judge the wretched and the orphan,
    vindicate the lowly and the poor,
    [4]rescue the wretched and the needy;
    save them from the hand of the wicked.

[5]They neither know nor understand,
    they go about in darkness;
    all the foundations of the earth totter.
[6]I had taken you for divine beings,
    sons of the Most High, all of you;
    [7]but you shall die as men do,
    fall like any prince.

[8]Arise, O God, judge the earth,
    for all the nations are Your possession.

This psalm was sung by the Levitical choir in the Temple on Tuesdays.[1] The reason for this selection is unknown. The composition itself is extraordinary. It exhibits the principal characteristics of biblical poetry, but were it not for the last verse—an appeal for divine intervention—we would not identify it with the psalms literature. Rather, it is a vision of a celestial scene, much like that of Isaiah, chapter 6, in which the prophet beheld the Lord seated on a high and lofty throne surrounded by angelic beings. It recalls several other prophetic visions, some of which we shall mention later on. In conception and content, Psalm 82 is a courtroom scene; some of its phraseology is drawn from the world of mythology.[2] The opening verse sets the tone.

> God stands in the divine assembly;
> among the divine beings He pronounces judgment.

The first anomaly that engages our attention is that the Hebrew employs the same term for "God" as for "divine beings." The word is *'elohim*; used in the Bible as a comprehensive term for supernatural beings.[3] Our psalm begins with this word, and not with "Lord" (YHVH), because it belongs to the collection within the larger book known to scholars as the "Elohistic Psalter." This comprises Psalms 42–83, which are distinguished by the infrequent use of YHVH in contrast to the frequent appearance of *'elohim*; the reverse is true in the rest of the book.[4] Whatever the original significance of the stylistic preferences in designating the deity, it is clear that the opening word connotes YHVH, "the Lord," the personal, ineffable name of the God of Israel.

In his vision, the psalmist sees God "standing" amidst a celestial assembly. The actual Hebrew phrase used for this convocation literally means "assembly of God." It is never found again in the Hebrew Bible, but does occur in Ugaritic texts.[5] This would seem to indicate an ancient Canaanite, pre-Israelite origin of the phrase.[6] The idea of the celestial court, or of gods in assembly, was widespread in the ancient world, neareastern and classical, and particularly in Phoenicia.[7] In biblical monotheism, which admits of no deities independent of the one, sovereign Creator, this idea has been transformed into the notion of a celestial council. Thus, in I Kings 22:19–23 there is the narrative about the prophet Micaiah son of Imlah who was summoned before King Jehoshaphat of Judah and the King of Israel. He sees "the Lord seated upon His throne, with all the host of heaven standing in attendance to the right and to the left of Him." The Book of Job features two such heavenly sessions when "the divine beings presented themselves before the Lord."[8] In that same book, Eliphaz the Temanite, one of the hero's friends, asks Job, "Have you listened in on the council of God?"[9] Jeremiah similarly refers to standing "in the council of the Lord,"[10] and in Psalm 89:8 there is mention of "the council of holy beings." In light of these references, it is clear that in his vision, our psalmist pictures to himself an assembly of heavenly beings presided over by God.

Who these supernal beings might be, we shall later discuss. First, we must consider still another strange aspect of the opening verse: God is represented as standing, whereas judges are always described as sitting. When Jethro, the Midianite priest, observes Moses, his son-in-law, acting in the capacity of magistrate, he found him seated;[11] Deborah used to sit under a palm tree administering justice;[12] Isaiah 28:6 refers to "the one who sits in judgment"; Joel declares that in the future time God "will sit in judgment on all the nations";[13] the psalmist has God "seated on a throne as righteous judge," for "He has set up His throne for judgment," and he declares that the thrones of judgment of the house of David are placed in Jerusalem;[14] finally, the Book of Proverbs speaks of "the king seated on the throne of judgment."[15]

If the sitting posture is the norm for a judge, why does our psalm portray God in a standing position? The answer is that it opens, as it were, after the legal proceedings are over, and it remains only to pronounce the sentence. God "stands" or "rises" to do this because His word inherently carries with it the absolute certainty of fulfillment, and terms of "standing up" or "rising" in Hebrew express imminent action.[16] That is why in the psalms God is so frequently called upon "to arise," that is, to execute judgment,[17] as here in verse 8. For instance, in Psalm 12:6, God declares,

> "Because of the groans of the plundered poor and
>   needy,
> I will now act (literally, "arise")," . . .
> I will give help."

Similarly, in Psalm 76:9–10 we find,

> In heaven You pronounced sentence:
> > the earth was numbed with fright,
> > as God arose to execute judgment,
> > to deliver all the lowly of the earth.

What is the aggravating situation that dictates the need for divine judgment and action? This is made abundantly clear in the next three verses.

> How long will you judge perversely,
> > showing favor to the wicked?
> Judge the wretched and the orphan,
> > vindicate the lowly and the poor,
> > rescue the wretched and the needy;
> > save them from the hand of the wicked.

The corruption of the judicial system and the decay of social morality prompt God to intervene and convoke the celestial court. This indictment is a recurring theme in the mouths of the classical prophets from the eighth century B.C.E. on. The causes and history of this lamentable deterioration can be traced in large measure as a consequence of several interacting factors.

The conquest of Canaan had transformed the life of the semi-nomadic tribes. They became settled farmers, concentrated mainly in the highlands and contending with difficult climatic conditions, precarious seasonal rainfall and periodic drought. Much of the soil was uncongenial for cultivation, and the topographical complexities of the land created problems of distribution, aggravated by the primitive means of transportation. Yet the clan and the tribal affiliations supplied efficient support systems, and society was largely egalitarian. In the course of time, the social balance came to be disturbed. The increase in population, the gradual domination and then settlement of the plains and valleys, the growth of urbanization, the increasing centralization of government stimulated by the need to face formidable enemies from without, and finally, the establishment of a monarchy, radically transformed the social picture. A new power structure was created in which service to the crown became a means of increasing wealth and influence. In addition, the expansion of commerce gave rise to a merchant class, while great building projects necessitated the introduction of the corvée system, compulsory unpaid labor required by the state. Society became fractured.

Following the death of Solomon, the united monarchy came to an end, and the nation was divided between the kingdom of Israel in the north and that of Judah in the south. The two entities were engaged in frequent hostilities. During the ninth century B.C.E., the Arameans of Syria exerted great pressure on Israel. A series of Aramean-Israelite wars ensued, which lasted on and off for nearly a hundred years. The cities were devastated, the population became impoverished, and the social cleavage was greatly intensified. Toward the end of the century, Assyrian imperialist ventures in the west, especially on the Arameans, eased the situation of Israel, allowing a measure of recovery.

The first half of the eighth century B.C.E. was a period of decline for Assyria. Israel and Judah were at peace, and enjoyed independence. Unprecedented prosperity flowed through the land mainly from international trade. Both kingdoms greatly benefited. However, the lives of the impoverished masses did not improve. The wealth that was generated did not trickle down, but rather remained within the confines of a small affluent class which gained still greater wealth.

It was this situation which gave rise to the classical, literary prophetic movement in the middle of the century. The books of Amos, Hosea, Isaiah, and Micah all testify to the shameful pauperization of the masses and to the contrasting irresponsibly lavish life style of the rich. They paint a picture of licentious dissipation, sordid luxury, wanton extravagance, dishonest business practices, corruption of the judiciary, exploitation of human misery, total insensitivity to the plight of society's disadvantaged.[18] Verses 2–4 in our psalm reflect this scandalous state of affairs, with special emphasis on the inability of the vast, vulnerable underclass to obtain justice or even to have recourse to the legal processes.

In the mind's eye of the psalmist, God has decided to intervene in response to the massive injustice that is rife in the world; He has convoked the celestial council. At this point, the interpretation of the psalm becomes equivocal. Two possibilities may be advanced. One sees the culprits as human judges who are castigated from on high for malfeasance; they are called upon to exercise their judicial duties with integrity, and to redress the grievances of the oppressed. The other interpretive possibility is more complicated. The reprobates who are addressed in this vision are the members of the divine assembly themselves, those mentioned in verse 1.

To understand this alternative explanation, it must be realized that in the ancient world it was widely believed that each people, even each city-state, had a divine protector. This polytheistic conviction was obviously unacceptable to Israelite monotheism, but it was not rejected in its entirety. Instead, it was transformed into the notion that each people had on high an angelic patron, a subordinate tutelary spirit allotted it by God. The Book of Deuteronomy 4:19 first gives clear expression to this notion:

> When you look up to the sky and behold the sun and the moon and the stars, the whole heavenly host, you must not be lured into bowing down to them or serving them. These the Lord allotted to other peoples everywhere under heaven.[19]

It is uncertain when such a belief first appeared in Israel. The mysterious "man" who wrestled with Jacob, and who is described as "a divine being" (*'elohim*), as told in Genesis 32:25, 29, 31, may be identified as the celestial patron of Esau, that is, of the Edomite people. However, not until post-exilic times does the evidence for such notions become explicit. The Book of Daniel (10:13, 20–21) refers to the celestial "prince of the Persian kingdom," "the prince of Greece," and "Michael, a prince of the first rank," who is the prince of Israel. Thus, behind the text of our psalm may be the conceptual presupposition that the guardian angels of the nations, who are expected to be responsible for overseeing justice, have failed in their charge and abused their assigned function.[20] The moral law has been violated. Conditions have deteriorated to the point when God must intervene.

Whichever interpretation is favored, it is clear from verse 5 that the speaker, be he God or the psalmist, has despaired of the ability of the judicial authorities, celestial or terrestrial, to reform themselves and remedy the intolerable state of affairs.

> They neither know nor understand,
>> they go about in darkness;
>> all the foundations of the earth totter.

Those responsible are incorrigible and benighted individuals, enveloped in intellectual, moral, and social darkness. The corruption they have caused undermines the very foundations of civilization. The world order has been disturbed by them, and they must be removed. So the psalm continues,

> I had taken you[21] for divine beings,
>> sons of the Most High,[22] all of you;
>> but you shall die as men do,[23]
>> fall[24] like any[25] prince.

If the first interpretation given above be favored, those humans responsible for the grievous injustices are being addressed sarcastically as "divine beings" and as "sons of the Most High." These dishonorable judges give themselves haughty airs, display despotic arrogance, and generally act as though they are superior individuals, not subject to ordinary human frailties and limitations; they think they are above the law and are accountable to no one. The psalmist (or God) therefore reminds them that they are but common mortals, fated to fall from power just like any of the princes or governors[26] whose abuse of power has brought them ruin.

The alternative mode of interpretation that views the corrupt individuals as celestial beings, the tutelary angels of the nations, connects verses 6–7 with the myth about fallen angels.[27] This appears in Genesis 6:4, which tells of divine beings who cohabited with human women. Isaiah 14:12 refers to the "shining one, son of Dawn" who was "felled to earth." The same prophet states that "the Lord will punish the host of heaven in heaven and the kings of the earth on earth" (24:21). Job 4:18 mentions that God "cannot trust His own servants, and casts reproach on His angels," and further that "He puts no trust in His holy ones; the heavens are not guiltless in His sight" (15:15). All these passages must refer to the same myth, now lost, about rebellious supernatural beings who forfeited their angelic status. The "divine beings" addressed in our psalm would appear to be those who fell short of divine standards and as a result were destined to die like mortals, to "fall" like the angelic princes of old who were expelled from heaven.

With the conviction and sentencing of the miscreants, the vision is over. Now, the stark, unresolved reality of the wanton injustice that abounds on earth fills the consciousness of the psalmist. Seeing that continuation of the present course must inevitably lead to the collapse of society, and despairing of the ability of human agency to effectuate fundamental change, he takes his case directly to God. Hence, the urgent closing appeal,

> Arise, O God, judge the earth,
> for all the nations are Your possession.

By virtue of His unchallengeable sovereignty over all the nations, God alone possesses the power to execute judgment on earth. Divine sovereignty and divine judgment: these are twin themes of the Jewish New Year festival of postbiblical times. If such existed also in biblical times, then it is possible that our psalm was preserved because it belonged to the liturgy of that sacred day.[28]

Chapter 8

PSALM NINETY-THREE

The Lord Is King!

The LORD is king,
> He is robed in grandeur;
> the LORD is robed,
> He is girded with strength.
The world stands firm;
> it cannot be shaken.
[2]Your throne stands firm from of old;
> from eternity You have existed.
[3]The ocean sounds, O LORD,
> the ocean sounds its thunder,
> the ocean sounds its pounding.
[4]Above the thunder of the mighty waters,
> more majestic than the breakers of the sea
> is the LORD majestic on high.
[5]Your decrees are indeed enduring;
> holiness befits Your house,
> O LORD, for all times.

According to rabbinic sources, Psalm 93 was sung each Friday in the Temple by the Levitical choir.[1] This tradition is reflected in the superscription to the psalm that appears in the Greek version of the Jews of Alexandria, Egypt. It reads, "For the day before the Sabbath when the earth was [first] inhabited . . ." A talmudic source[2] connects the selection of this psalm for Fridays with the Genesis cosmogony, according to which active creation was completed on the sixth day with the formation of human beings; thereafter, God exercised His sovereignty over the world. This interpretation of the psalm makes it complementary to Psalm 24, the liturgy for Sunday when the cosmogonic process began. Indeed, there are several points of connection between the two.[3] Both psalms mention the kingship of God,[4] the primeval waters,[5] God's might,[6] and the sanctity of His House.[7]

The psalm opens with an emphatic declaration affirming God's kingship. It shares this distinctive feature with Psalms 97 and 99, and the same acclamation occurs in Psalm 96:10. Of course, the metaphor of God as king occurs many times in the Hebrew Bible, and is standard imagery in the Book of Psalms, where it expresses the conception of God's absolute sovereignty over nature and history.

In the present state of our knowledge there is no way of deciding conclusively how early in the history of Israel the projection of the human political institution onto God took place. All we know is that this conception and designation was pervasive in the ancient Near East long before Israel arrived on the scene of history. Yet the biblical sources offer precious little evidence for a similar early usage in Israel. Moses' Song at the Sea in Exodus chapter 15 singularly closes with the triumphant declaration, "The Lord will reign for ever and ever!"[8] Nevertheless, it is highly significant that the account of God's supreme revelation at Sinai contains not a hint of the metaphor. This is remarkable when viewed in light of the findings of modern scholarship that the concept and formulation of the covenant between God and Israel are modeled on the conventional pattern and style of neareastern treaties between suzerain kings and their vassals.[9] Moreover, if we examine theophoric proper names, that is, names derived from or compounded of a divine name or a divine epithet—and such names are a very important index of religious beliefs and religious history[10]—we find only three Israelite names that are composed of the Hebrew word for "king," *melekh* (*melech*). These are: Malchiel,[11] meaning "El is my king," given to a grandson of Asher, son of Jacob; Abimelech,[12] meaning "the [divine] king is my father"; he was the son of the Judge Gideon-Jerubaal; and Elimelech,[13] meaning "My God is king"; he was the husband of Naomi, mother-in-law of Ruth. All three belong to persons who lived prior to the founding of the monarchy in Israel. However, all three names also appear either in the fourteenth century B.C.E. Tell El-Amaarna tablets from Egypt or in the tablets found at Ugarit-Ras Shamra on the Syrian coast, which derive from the fourteenth to the twelfth century B.C.E.[14] In other words, there is nothing specifically Israelite about them, and they cannot be used to prove a pre-monarchy Israelite conception of God as King. In fact, the extreme paucity of such *melekh* names and a total absence of *melekh* names compounded with the termination *-yah* or with the prefix *yo-*, both abbreviations of the specifically Israelite ineffable name of God, are revealing. The cumulative effect of the evidence set forth above favors the view that the concept of God as king is not borrowed from neareastern culture but is an internal Israelite development attendant upon the introduction of the monarchy, a relatively late phenomenon, and one that initially met with official resistance.

At this point, before we examine the implications of the opening phrase of the psalm, "The Lord is king," it is worth sketching, even if briefly, the course of events which led to this innovation. It is important to note that the monarchy as a sociopolitical institution was firmly entrenched throughout the lands of the ancient Near East.[15] In Mesopotamia, as the Sumerian King List has it, "kingship was lowered from heaven." That is to say, it was taken to be of divine origin and to be the essential and sustaining basis of civilized society, although the king himself was not considered to be a god.[16] The Egyptian experience was quite different. Here, the pharaoh was presented to the public as a divine person, regarded literally as the offspring of the sun god. In the small land of Canaan there were numerous city-states, each with a king of its own. The Book of Joshua, chapter 12, tells how the invading Israelites had to contend with thirty-one such monarchs. In short, the impact of the well-nigh ubiquitous institution, theologically speaking, was that gods, and not just high-gods, received the title "king."

The Israelites, successors to the Canaanites, did not adopt the constitutional model of their predecessors.[17] The new settlers preferred a loose confederation of tribes, each led by "elders" or by a "judge." The latter usually rose to power in response to a crisis. This type of leadership was rarely effective. It produced disunity and instability, and proved to be inadequate to the challenge of recurring attacks by surrounding peoples. The constant state of insecurity was greatly aggravated by the rise of the Philistine menace, which became chronic in the course of the eleventh century B.C.E. It was this situation of recurring crises of ever-increasing severity that finally excited popular clamor for the appointment of a king who would be the center of power and a national unifying force. The concluding verse of the Book of Judges summarizes the prevailing state of affairs eloquently, if succinctly: "In those days there was no king in Israel; everyone did as he pleased."[18]

Two isolated attempts to appoint a king are recorded in the Book of Judges. Following his victory over invading Midianites, Gideon was asked "to rule" over the people.[19] (The usual verb for royal rule is not used here.) He rejected the proposal, but his son, Abimelech, tried to make himself king of the important city of Shechem. The attempt ended in disaster,[20] for he was assassinated by a woman.

Around the middle of the eleventh century B.C.E., the Israelites suffered some humiliating defeats at the hands of the Philistines. Even the central sanctuary at Shiloh was destroyed.[21] The call for a monarchy became irresistible. The people demanded of the aged prophet Samuel that he "appoint a king for us to govern us like all other nations," a call that he strongly opposed until divinely instructed to acquiesce, "for it is not you that they have rejected; it is Me they have rejected as their king."[22] In these words we find for the first time in a narrative text the projection onto God of royal status. It is to be noted, however, that the term "king" is here understood in the limited sense of God's relationship to the people of Israel, and not yet in the extended concept of cosmic sovereignty, as is found in our Psalm 93. It is most reasonable to assume that the impetus to such a broad evolutionary development of the concept came with the extensive territorial conquests of King David and the empire that he carved out and bequeathed to his son, King Solomon.

What would have been the occasion for the composition of Psalm 93 and of similar hymns which celebrate God's kingship?[23] What situation (in the life of the people) would have called for their repeated recitation, thereby ensuring the survival of these compositions? Modern scholars generally give the title "Enthronement Psalms" to the hymns which feature the acclamation,[24] "The Lord is king!" This is because that phrase appears to have been adapted from the coronation rituals of human kings. Admittedly, we know tantalizingly little about such ceremonies in Israel, but two narratives do seem to afford us some supportive evidence for the conjecture. When Absalom raised the standard of revolt against his father, David, in his attempt to usurp the throne, he instructed his agent to tell the people, "When you hear the blast of the horn, announce that Absalom has become king in Hebron."[25] This would indicate that the blowing of the shofar and the proclamation of the name of the would-be successor as the subject of the Hebrew verb *malakh* were essential elements of the rituals of coronation. This inference is confirmed by the story of Jehu's accession to the throne of northern Israel. "They sounded the horn and proclaimed 'Jehu is king.' "[26]

If we turn to the Psalter, we observe that Psalm 47 repeatedly features God's kingship. He is the "great King over all the earth . . . God ascends midst acclamation; the Lord, to the blast of the horn . . ." The peoples of the world are exhorted to "sing to our King; for God is King over all the earth . . . God reigns over the nations; God is seated on His holy throne."[27] Similarly, Psalm 98:6 reads,

> With trumpets and the blast of the horn
> raise a shout before the Lord, the King.

The same two elements of the human coronation rituals, the proclamation of kingship and the blast of the horn, are present. It has been theorized[28] that the aforementioned compositions, together with others that affirm "The Lord is King" (even though not all of them mention the sounding of the horn) originally belonged to the liturgy of an annual festival that centered upon the idea of God's cosmic sovereignty: "He comes to govern the earth . . . justly, with faithfulness and with equity."[29]

The calendars of ancient Israel list the first day of the seventh month, in the autumn, as a sacred occasion commemorated with the blasting of the horn, and with various sacrificial rituals.[30] The Torah gives no other information about the nature of the festival. It is clear, however, that this season was the start of the agricultural year, for Tabernacles, which occurs in the middle of the same month, is referred to as "the feast of Ingathering at the end/turn of the year."[31] Further, the tenth century B.C.E. Hebrew agricultural calendar discovered at Gezer in the northern Shephelah also begins with the months of ingathering.[32] The Book of Nehemiah records that the returnees to Zion from the Babylonian exile observed a solemn assembly on the first day of the seventh month, at which the people were told not to mourn or weep or be sad "because the day is holy to the Lord."[33] Here, again, the narrative leaves unclear the real nature of the occasion or why just that day was chosen for the communal convocation.

As is well known, postbiblical Judaism has always celebrated Rosh Hashanah, the New Year,[34] on the first day of the seventh month, the month known by the name Tishri, derived from the Babylonian *Teshritu*, meaning "beginning [of the year]." The liturgy of the day gives emphasis to the basic themes of God's cosmic kingship, the blowing of the horn, God's judgment of the world, and His deciding the destiny of humanity at that time. These themes coincide with those prominent in the biblical "enthronement psalms." Some also happen to have been central to the ancient Babylonian New Year festival, held in the spring, in which the motif of the seasonal rejuvenation of nature, humankind, and society was foremost.[35] On the fourth day of that festival, the Akkadian epic *Enuma Elish*[36] was read in its entirety, thus connecting the New Year with the theme of creation. In this composition, creation is interpreted in terms of a war between the monstrous goddess of darkness and chaos, Tiamat, and the chief god of the city of Babylon, Marduk. Following his victory over Tiamat, Marduk fashioned the cosmos out of her body. He was enthroned by the other gods as the universal sovereign, and a temple was built for him in heaven. That annual festival also featured the determination of destinies, deciding the fate of society for the coming year.

Based on these analogues, it has been theorized that the biblical "enthronement psalms" constituted the liturgy of a New Year festival in ancient Israel held in connection with the Feast of Tabernacles two weeks later. This New Year festival is thought to have had as its central motif the enthronement of the Lord, the Creator, following His vanquishing of the forces of chaos.[37] The main event is conjectured to have been a great festal procession in which the presence of the Lord was symbolized by the Ark of the Covenant and in which the primeval struggle was reenacted and reexperienced in ritual drama. These cultic acts supposedly had as their purpose the renewal of nature and society.

Although this theory has gained wide currency, it has also come under strong criticism.[38] Our knowledge of Israelite coronation rituals is too fragmentary and too problematical to serve as a secure model for the interpretation of the setting in life of the acclamatory, "The Lord is King." Moreover, not all the psalms in question include each of the basic coronation themes listed above. For instance, the theme of creation does not appear in Psalms 47, 97, 98, 99, and 149, even though God's Kingship is emphasized. To take them collectively and treat them as a unit in order to support the theory is not very convincing. Also, none of the psalms cited contain any mention of the Ark. Further, there is not a shred of evidence that ritual drama was an ingredient of the Temple worship. In addition, because kingship was a late institution in Israel, unlike everywhere else in the ancient Near East, and because its establishment had pragmatic, not ideological underpinnings, it is highly unlikely that it engendered the kind of transfer onto God of the ritualized mythology found in Mesopotamia. It is impossible to imagine that the official monotheistic religion of Israel could have conceived that God's sovereignty required annual renewal. In fact, such an idea is refuted by verse 2 of our psalm. Finally, complete silence of the biblical sources about such an elaborate festival as postulated by the theory is inexplicable.

Still, these objections do not entirely rule out the possibility that some kind of New Year holy day did exist in pre-exilic times, of which the later festival of Rosh Hashanah is the direct, lineal descendant. It might well have been deliberately downplayed in the biblical texts precisely to avoid identification with the pagan, polytheistic, mythological drama of its contemporary neareastern counterparts, which were repugnant to the religion of Israel. The Israelite festival acknowledged, as it still does, God's absolute cosmic sovereignty, His omnipotence, His incontestable governance of the world, and His control and direction of human destiny. The declaration "The Lord is King" (literally, "reigns") is a jubilant celebration of an eternal, indisputable fact.

Psalm 93 elaborates on this royal image,

> He is robed in grandeur;
> the Lord is robed,
> He is girded with strength.
> The world stands firm;
> it cannot be shaken.

This conception of "monarchotheism"[39] entails imaginatively the trappings of kingship,[40] but the biblical texts, with two vague exceptions, forebear to invest God with royal apparel. In Isaiah 6:1 the prophet experiences a vision of the Lord "seated on a high and lofty throne; and the skirts of His robe filled the Temple." Daniel (7:9) sees the "Ancient of Days" seated on His throne and "His garment was like white snow." Our psalm uses the verb "to be clothed" in a figurative, transferred sense, its object being abstract qualities.[41] This literary convention also appears in Akkadian in such descriptions as "clothed in awesomeness," "clothed with terrifying splendor and light," "clothed in loveliness."[42] Homer, too, employs this convention, using such phrases as "one clothed in shamelessness," "clothed in great might."[43] In our psalm, the figurative language "robed in grandeur" carefully avoids compromising God's incorporeality, but does subtly evoke an image of royalty majestically attired in the rich regalia of kingship. The second image suggests both impending action and the accoutrements of war. Ordinary apparel was free-flowing, and any energetic or difficult activity required prior "girding of the loins" to facilitate locomotion.[44] Hence the figurative use of that phrase in the sense of "being ready for action."[45] The soldier or hero wore a girdle or belt for the dual purpose of firming up the body by cinching the waist and of accommodating weapons.[46] In light of the foregoing, the poetic expression that God "girds Himself with strength" suggests the notion of "the divine warrior, " a concept which has been discussed above in connection with Psalm 24:8. Suffice it to note that the phrase refers to a display of divine power, another way of voicing God's omnipotence and invulnerability. Human beings can be assured that the physical world that He created is ordered and stable.[47] This confidence is all the more justified because God's "throne"—a figurative term for sovereignty and justice[48]—is not of yesterday but exists from all eternity, and by implication is not subject to the vagaries of time and change.

> Your throne stands firm from of old;[49]
> from eternity You have existed.

Allusion to time immemorial stimulates thoughts of Creation. In a kind of stream-of-consciousness technique, the psalmist continues his adoration of God with an oblique glance at popular notions about the origins of the universe.

> The ocean sounds, O Lord,
> the ocean sounds its thunder,
> the ocean sounds its pounding.[50]
> Above the thunder of the mighty waters,[51]
> more majestic than[52] the breakers of the sea
> is the Lord, majestic on high.

The ocean (literally, "rivers") and the "mighty waters" refer to the primordial cosmic ocean, the chaotic unruly watery mass that supposedly surrounds the earth, and that popular fancy endowed with mythic status. Numerous fragments of this myth, apparently from an ancient epic, are cited in biblical poetry, as explained in our discussions of Psalms 8 and 24.[53] The mighty roaring of the turbulent, surging waves is construed as the resistance of chaos to creativity and order. Such opposition is unavailing before the overwhelming majesty of God.

The final verse of the psalm gives the appearance of being discontinuous, unrelated to the rest of the hymn:

> Your decrees are indeed[54] enduring;[55]
> holiness befits Your house,
> O Lord, for all times.

In reality, the thought flows naturally from the first two verses. Sovereignty intrinsically entails the prerogative and obligation to assure the stability and welfare of the subject community. It fulfills this function by means of decrees that it authoritatively enjoins on the citizenry. Unlike the case of human kings, whose laws are of limited duration and are subject to change, God's edicts are immutable and perdurable.

Once God is conceived as a cosmic sovereign, the metaphor is extended to include the varied trappings of royalty. God's throne is mentioned in verse 2. This presupposes a locale, a celestial dwelling in which the throne is housed. It projects the imagery of a celestial temple corresponding to the terrestrial one, a fanciful representation mentioned several times in the Bible, as we noted and discussed in chapter 4.[56] Because holiness, that is, a state of moral and spiritual perfection, is an essential attribute of the divine being, the heavenly abode is befittingly holy by virtue of that association; and since God's holiness is eternal, His abode shares everlastingly this sacred quality.

In sum, our psalm opens and closes with declarations about the nature of God. The first affirms His absolute and supreme power. The second asserts His holiness. In between, the psalmist sets forth the implications for humanity that flow from these inherent qualities.

Permanence and stability for the world are assured because God's sovereignty and existence are beyond all limitations of time. Nature's seemingly threatening, noisy, tempestuous fury, which in the pagan religions is personified as an evil divinity, the embodiment of disorder in the universe, is demythologized. It is the commanding majesty of God that is enduring.

PSALM NINETY-FOUR

How Long Shall Evil Prevail?

God of retribution, LORD,
 God of retribution, appear!
²Rise up, judge of the earth,
 give the arrogant their deserts!
³How long shall the wicked, O LORD,
 how long shall the wicked exult,
  ⁴shall they utter insolent speech,
 shall all evildoers vaunt themselves?
⁵They crush Your people, O LORD,
 they afflict Your very own;
  ⁶they kill the widow and the stranger;
 they murder the fatherless,
  ⁷thinking, "The LORD does not see it,
 the God of Jacob does not pay heed."

⁸Take heed, you most brutish people;
 fools, when will you get wisdom?
⁹Shall He who implants the ear not hear,
 He who forms the eye not see?
¹⁰Shall He who disciplines nations not punish,
 He who instructs men in knowledge?
¹¹The LORD knows the designs of men to be
 futile.

¹²Happy is the man whom You discipline, O LORD,
 the man You instruct in Your teaching,
  ¹³to give him tranquillity in times of misfortune,
 until a pit be dug for the wicked.
¹⁴For the LORD will not forsake His people;
 He will not abandon His very own.
¹⁵Judgment shall again accord with justice
 and all the upright shall rally to it.

¹⁶Who will take my part against evil men?
Who will stand up for me against wrongdoers?
¹⁷Were not the LORD my help,
 I should soon dwell in silence.
¹⁸When I think my foot has given way,
 Your faithfulness, O LORD, supports me.
¹⁹When I am filled with cares,
 Your assurance soothes my soul.

²⁰Shall the seat of injustice be Your partner,
 that frames mischief by statute?
²¹They band together to do away with the righteous;
 they condemn the innocent to death.
²²But the LORD is my haven;
 my God is my sheltering rock.
²³He will make their evil recoil upon them,
 annihilate them through their own wickedness;
 the LORD our God will annihilate them.

The Greek translation of the Bible carries a heading to this psalm that is not in the Hebrew. It reads as follows:

"A psalm of David for the fourth day of the week."

This note accords with the rabbinic tradition[1] that the psalm was sung in the Temple each Wednesday by the Levitical choir. Why it was so chosen is presently beyond our ken, but in its basic theme it is analogous to Psalm 82, the liturgy for Tuesdays, and supplements it. Both compositions touch on the massive evil that afflicts society. However, whereas Psalm 82 concludes with an entreaty, this one opens with one. Psalm 82 is a vision about celestial affairs; Psalm 94 treats in greater detail the oppressive reality that obtains on earth.

And it goes further: it tries to understand why the unprincipled scoundrels in power act as they do, and it offers a polemic designed to expose the folly of the kind of theological thinking that produces such wanton behavior.

One of the characteristic literary features of Psalm 94 is the threefold use of anadiplosis,[2] that is, the rhetorical repetition of selected words or phrases. These are: the opening divine epithet, "God of retribution"; the agonizing, searching question "how long?"; and the final, confident, unwavering declaration of faith that God "will annihilate" the evildoers. In each case, the reiteration gives prominence to a key element of the psalm—the nature of God, the intolerable suffering of human beings, and the certainty of the ultimate downfall of evil.

The first two lines are an impassioned plea to God to manifest His quality of retributive justice:

> God of retribution,[3] Lord,
> God of retribution, appear!
> Rise up, Judge of the earth,[4]
> give the arrogant their deserts!

At the outset, the psalmist affirms his concept of an active God. This is needed because, as he states later on, the wicked believe in an essentially inactive deity. The specific epithet used here, "God of retribution," is paralleled in verse 2 by "Judge of the earth." In this way, the understanding of "retribution" is clarified: it is not an arbitrary or vindictive act, but a judicial intervention against the guilty. Moreover, the epithet itself indicates that such is an essential and intrinsic characteristic of the divine personality.

It should be noted that the Hebrew term here translated "retribution" is often misleadingly rendered "vengeance" in many other English versions. But that word conveys to the popular mind a negative, primitive conception of religion. "Vengeance" is usually taken to be synonymous with revenge, and implies actions prompted by base emotions. The Hebrew root, however, means nothing of the kind, for in most instances, it signifies an action worthily motivated, purposeful, intended to serve the ends of justice. Unlike "revenge," which is essentially antisocial, "retribution" is concerned with vindication, not with vindictiveness, with upholding or restoring a just social order, not primarily with retaliation. Leviticus 19:18 prohibits the private exaction of retribution, and Deuteronomy 32:35 affirms that such action is the exclusive prerogative of God.[5]

Our psalmist calls upon the "God of retribution" to "appear," employing a Hebrew verb that means "to shine," "be radiant," with the extended meaning of "be manifest."[6] In Psalm 50:2, God's "appearance" means His active intervention in the affairs of humankind for the purpose of exercising His sovereign judicial authority; in our present psalm, the verb has this same signification. Moreover, it is reinforced here by the addition of the parallel word "rise up," meaning a call for imminent action, a usage which has already been discussed in connection with Psalm 82:1.[7] What the supplicant is here asking for is decisive, overwhelming, timely action in a situation in which the ordinary resources available to decent people are inadequate to the task of restoring the balance of justice. The plea becomes ever more urgent.

> How long shall the wicked, O Lord,
>> how long shall the wicked exult,
>> shall they utter insolent speech,[8]
>> shall all evildoers vaunt themselves?

The wording shows that the psalmist is looking for action in the here and now, not in some vague eschatological future.[9] The questions go to the very heart of the problem of evil in a world that is under divine governance.[10] In brief, the issue hinges upon the nature of God as described in the Hebrew Bible. When, in Exodus 33:13, Moses asks to "know" God's ways, God's responsive self-disclosure is a recital of His own attributes, that is, of His moral qualities, which are the essence of His character. Exodus 34:6–7 lists them as:

> compassionate and gracious, slow to anger, abounding in
> kindness and faithfulness, extending kindness to the thou-
> sandth generation, forgiving iniquity, transgression and sin;
> yet He does not remit all punishment, but visits the iniq-
> uity of parents upon children and children's children upon
> the third and fourth generations.[11]

From the numerous citations of this listing in the Bible in one form
or another—clearly an institutionalized liturgical formula[12]—it is
apparent that the emphases are on the magnanimous and benevolent
divine qualities, rather than on the judgmental and punitive aspects
of God's morality. But these very characteristics raise the serious
problem of divine tolerance of evil, which is essentially what is
behind the vexatious question, "How long, O Lord?" The prophet
Habakkuk (1:2) asked,

> How long, O Lord, shall I cry out
> > and You not listen,
> > Shall I shout to You, "Violence!"
> > and You do not save?
> Why do You make me see iniquity?
> [Why] do You look upon wrong?

The same challenging problem of God's forbearance, His being
"slow to anger," confronted the prophet Jonah. Deeply grieved that
the evil city of Nineveh had repented and thereby escaped punishment, he gave as his reason for trying to flee to Tarshish and avoid
his prophetic mission: ". . . I know that You are a compassionate
and gracious God, slow to anger, abounding in kindness, renouncing
punishment" (4:2). Implicit here is the subtle and perplexing paradox
that it is precisely these benign divine qualities that fortify the conviction of unaccountability, embolden the wicked, and aggravate the
problem of evil. So, to ask of God, "How long?" is to view His
quality of forbearance from the perspective of the victim of humanly

wrought evil, and to demand reduction in the duration of His tolerance.

What are the evils that arouse the psalmist? The following verses grimly detail them.

> They crush Your people, O Lord,
> > they afflict Your very own;[13]
> > they kill the widow and the stranger;
> > they murder the fatherless,
> > thinking, "The Lord does not see it,
> > the God of Jacob does not pay heed."

Who are these "wicked" who perpetrate such heinous crimes? A superficial reading would take them to be foreign, national enemies, because they afflict "Your people." However, closer scrutiny of the text militates against such an understanding. The specification of the oppressed shows that those described as God's "people" are the disadvantaged and most vulnerable segments of society. An invading enemy would hardly regard those elements as posing a great threat to his security. When King Nebuchadnezzar of Babylon advanced on Jerusalem in the year 597 B.C.E., it was the royal family, the courtiers, commanders, officers, and nobles who were deported, together with the warriors, craftsmen, and smiths.[14] Similarly, when he returned and destroyed the city ten years later, it was again the upper classes who were carried off. The poorest of the land were left behind.[15]

God's "people" are the ordinary common folk,[16] and the evil oppressors and exploiters are the corrupt, privileged upper classes in Israel, those whom the prophets denounced repeatedly from the eighth century B.C.E. on.[17]

Of course, a major and pervasive theme of biblical literature is that God is the redeemer from injustice and oppression, and that God's redemptive acts for Israel demand an imitative human response. Numerous biblical texts insist that the experience of the liberation from Egypt must be a motive force for social ethics and the wellspring of moral action. This concept is enshrined in law as a positive prohibition. For instance, Exodus 22:20–23 enjoins as follows:

> You shall not wrong a stranger or oppress him, for you were strangers in the land of Egypt. You shall not ill-treat any widow or orphan. If you do mistreat them, I will heed their outcry as soon as they cry out to me . . .

Similarly, Deuteronomy 24:17–18 commands,

> You shall not subvert the rights of the stranger or the fatherless; you shall not take a widow's garment in pawn. Remember that you were a slave in Egypt and that the Lord your God redeemed you from there; therefore do I enjoin you to observe this commandment.

Elsewhere in the same book (10:17–19), Moses characterizes the God of the people of Israel in these words,

> For the Lord your God is God supreme and Lord supreme, the great, the mighty, and the awesome God who shows no favor and takes no bribe, but upholds the cause of the fatherless and the widow, and befriends the stranger, providing him with food and clothing.—You too must befriend the stranger, for you were strangers in the land of Egypt.

The prophets of Israel severely castigate the people for the infraction of these obligations. Isaiah 1:17 admonishes them,

> Learn to do good.
> Devote yourselves to justice;
> Aid the wronged.
> Uphold the rights of the orphan;
> Defend the cause of the widow.

He goes on to accuse the rulers,

> They do not judge the case of the orphan,
> And the widow's cause never reaches them.

A century later, Jeremiah argues that the only way to prevent the otherwise inevitable destruction of the kingdom of Judah is to ensure social justice. He exhorts the people (7:6):

> If you really mend your ways and your actions; if you exe-
> cute justice between one person and another; if you do not
> oppress the stranger, the orphan, and the widow; if you do
> not shed the blood of the innocent . . . then only will I let
> you dwell in this place . . . .

The prophet reiterates this theme in 22:3,

> Thus said the Lord: Do what is just and right; rescue from
> the defrauder the one who is robbed; do not wrong the
> stranger, the fatherless, and the widow; commit no lawless
> act, and do not shed the blood of the innocent in this
> place.

Once the threatened destruction became a reality and the people were in exile, Ezekiel, the spiritual leader of the Babylonian community, reflected aloud upon the tragic past. He harangued the exiles:

> Every one of the princes of Israel in your midst used his
> strength for the shedding of blood. Fathers and mothers
> have been humiliated within you; strangers have been
> cheated in your midst; orphans and widows have been
> wronged within you (22:7).

After the return from exile and the reconstitution of the Jewish state, Zechariah and Malachi stressed the same theme. The former (7:9–10) has,

> Thus said the Lord of Hosts: Execute true justice; deal loy-
> ally and compassionately with one another. Do not defraud
> the widow, the orphan, the stranger, and the poor . . .

Malachi (3:5), in the name of God, declares,

> I will act as a relentless accuser against those who have no
> fear of Me . . . who cheat laborers of their hire, and who
> subvert [the cause of] the widow, orphan, and stranger . . .

In the Psalms, God is described as "the Father of orphans, the
champion of widows" (68:6); He "watches over the stranger; He gives
courage to the orphan and widow" (146:9).

In light of this fundamental conception of a compassionate God
who displays intense concern for the unfortunates of society, and
considering the covenantal, humanitarian imperatives of the religion
of Israel that flow from such an understanding, it is not surprising
that judicial corruption, as in Psalm 82, and the cruel and oppressive
excesses of tyrannical rulers, as in Psalm 94, would be the subject
of prayer and entreaty to God.

The precise historical circumstances that called forth the psalmist's accusations can no longer be determined with certainty, but
they are consistent with the references in the books of Jeremiah and
Ezekiel to bloodshed in the land on a large scale.[18] These would
seem to point to the reign of King Manasseh (687/6–642 B.C.E) of
whom 2 Kings 21:16 records that he "put so many innocent persons
to death that he filled Jerusalem [with blood] from end to end," and
whom 2 Kings 24:4 blames for the destruction of Jerusalem "because
of the blood of the innocent that he shed. For he filled Jerusalem
with the blood of the innocent, and the Lord would not forgive."[19]

The psalmist tells us that the horrible crimes perpetrated by the
wicked oppressors are grounded in the conviction that there is no
accountability. That these people do not actually repudiate the existence of God is clear from the psalmist's rebuttal in verses 8–11,
which otherwise would hardly be relevant. It is not the reality of

God that is denied, but rather His providence. At issue is the nature of this creator God. The wicked conceive of an otiose deity, an absentee God, one who, having created the world, thereafter withdrew from it, and remained remote and aloof from the affairs of humankind. A like theological doctrine is recorded in Psalm 10, which complains of the arrogance of the wicked who oppress the poor and who openly and brazenly boast of their unbridled lust. They assume that God "does not call to account," that "He does not care," that He "is not mindful, He hides His face, He never looks" (vv. 4, 11). Similarly, in Psalm 14[20] "the benighted man thinks" that God does not care how he acts (v. 1). In each of these two instances the psalmist uses the phrase "there is no God" to express the supposed divine indifference and unconcern. The image of the otiose deity is best drawn by the prophet Zephaniah (1:12), who tells that the wicked say to themselves, "The Lord will do nothing, good or bad."[21]

The conviction of the psalmist is that people act wickedly because they do not believe in divine supervision over human society. This is practical, not philosophical, atheism.[22] If God is not the center of their religious life, if He is not the source of their value system and the upholder of the moral order, then the imperatives of the moral law are ineffective. Sordid self-interest becomes the sole motivating force in human behavior; restraint is dispelled, inhibition discarded, and evil given free reign.

The poet now turns from describing the miscreants to reprimanding them directly for their foolishness. He says that the assumptions that underlie their actions defy logic.

> Take heed, you most brutish people;
>> fools, when will you get wisdom?
> Shall He who implants[23] the ear not hear,
>> He who forms the eye not see?
> Shall He who disciplines nations not punish,
>> He who instructs men in knowledge?
> The Lord knows the designs of men to be futile.

The evildoers are termed "brutish," an apt translation of the Hebrew, which derives from a word meaning "a beast."[24] However, it should be noted that by so characterizing them the emphasis is not on boorish social behavior but on senseless, unreasoning, unconsidered actions. Also, in labeling them "fools" there is no suggestion of an innately disordered mind or of intellectual impairment. As we have previously pointed out, the stress is on the lack of wisdom, and the terms for "folly" and "fool" are overwhelmingly employed in the Bible in antithesis to "wisdom" and "the wise."[25] The fool is accused of willful rejection of discipline and knowledge.[26] He spurns advice[27] and disdains words of wisdom.[28] If he is exhorted to gain instruction,[29] the obvious assumption is that he does not lack innate intelligence. That is why he may be disciplined[30] although he may be incorrigible.[31] At any rate, it is certain that those described as being fools bear responsibility for their actions. Hence, the psalmist tries to reason with them in order to disabuse them of their false conception of God.

The Creator cannot be inferior to His creation. If He possesses the power to confer on human beings the faculties of hearing and seeing, then He Himself must be endowed with the same faculties.[32] The notion of an otiose deity is a manifest absurdity. Moreover, adds the psalmist, this conclusion is confirmed by the lessons of history, which demonstrate that the fate of nations is subject to divinely imposed discipline. Perhaps he had in mind the well-known narratives about the Flood and the destruction of Sodom and Gomorrah, both of which teach that violation of the moral law inevitably leads to disaster.[33] If such be the case with whole nations, it must also be so in regard to the individual. God endowed people with intelligence; therefore, He must Himself be an intelligent Being. He knows that the machinations of the human mind are ultimately futile: they cannot prevail against the divine will.

It follows from the foregoing that the psalmist is convinced that God will exact retribution from the wicked, and he reiterates this belief repeatedly. Their ultimate downfall is inevitable. In the meantime, however, their powerless victims continue to suffer, and their undeserved ordeal raises profound philosophical questions. The psalmist, who is himself among the victims, addresses their ever-pressing concerns. His answers are intended to give meaning to the painful experiences and to offer a measure of consolation.

> Happy is the man whom You discipline, O Lord,
>> the man You instruct in Your teaching,
>> to give him tranquillity[34] in times of misfortune,
>> until a pit[35] be dug for the wicked.
> For the Lord will not forsake His people;[36]
>> He will not abandon His very own.
> Judgment shall again accord with justice[37]
>> and all the upright shall rally to it.

It is at once apparent that the poet, like the author of Job, does not subscribe to the doctrine that there is a necessary correlation between suffering and sin; the former by no means presupposes the latter. He does, however, hold to the view that the travail of the innocent is divinely wrought, and is not mere happenstance. This being so, there must be meaning to the suffering. Here, he falls back on the explanations given in Deuteronomy 8:5: "Bear in mind that the Lord your God disciplines you just as a man disciplines his son."[38] The same interpretation is given in Proverbs 3:11–12:

> Do not reject the discipline of the Lord, my son;
> Do not abhor His rebuke.
> Whom the Lord loves, He rebukes
> As a father a son whom he favors.

It should be noted that the Hebrew root that underlies the word rendered "discipline" refers primarily to religious and moral instruction, rarely to the development of the intellectual faculties. Suffering, says the psalmist, rather than being a penalty for sin, may be an expression of God's fatherly love. It may serve an educational function as a test of character. When accompanied by instruction in God's teaching (*torah*), it molds and elevates one's personality, providing the moral fiber that enables one to bear adversity with endurance and serenity, secure in the conviction that the wicked will receive their just deserts and tyranny will be overthrown.

Most interesting is the faith expressed in verse 15 that judgment will once again be united with justice. The wicked have severed the one from the other. The decisions and deliberations of the courts no longer are informed by the ends of justice, for the judicial institutions have become mere instruments of the wicked who control the levers of power. Yet, this terrifying situation does not cause the psalmist to lose faith in divine governance of the world. Unable to obtain redress in law, he asks,

> Who will take my part against evil men?
> Who will stand up for me against wrongdoers?
> Were not the Lord my help,
> > I should soon dwell in silence.[39]
> When I think my foot has given way,
> > Your faithfulness, O Lord, supports me.
> When I am filled with cares,
> > Your assurance soothes my soul.

It seems that the psalmist himself is the victim of some fabricated charge; the judges are corrupt, and would-be witnesses to his innocence are too intimidated by the reign of terror to testify in his behalf. In this terrible predicament, only unshakable faith in God saves him from complete collapse.

In his desperation, our psalmist turns directly to God, asking in a different form the same basic question with which he began: How is it that God tolerates the evil? By so doing, He allows an impression of acquiescence to be conveyed.

> Shall the seat of injustice be Your partner,
> > that frames mischief by statute?
> They band together to do away with the righteous;

> they condemn the innocent to death.
> But the Lord is my haven;
>> my God is my sheltering rock.
> He will make their evil recoil upon them,
>> annihilate them through their own wickedness;
>> the Lord our God will annihilate them.

The prophet Isaiah (10:1–2) similarly excoriated those who occupy the seat of power for perpetrating evil under the sanction of law.

> Ha!
> Those who write out evil writs
> And compose iniquitous documents,
> To subvert the cause of the poor,
> To rob of their rights the needy of My people;
> That widows may be their spoil,
> And fatherless children their booty!

Such has ever been the practice of tyrants and dictators, in ancient and modern times. A fictional impression of legality is created by cloaking injustice in robes of law. As noted in verse 15 above, a veneer of legitimacy is laid on, but law is separated from morality so that judicial decisions do not conform to the demands of justice. In fact, the judges conspire to condemn to death their innocent victims.

Despite all this, and in the face of a seemingly hopeless situation, when monstrous evil appears to be all powerful and hideous brutalities are the order of the day, our psalmist continues to place his faith in God and affirms again and again his abiding optimism that the moral order that has been disturbed will be set right, and the wicked will be destroyed.

Afterword

The subtitle of this book is "An Introduction to the Book of Psalms." To some, this description may seem to make too presumptuous a claim, seeing that I have selected but a limited number of compositions, and have deliberately avoided discussion of several important issues of Psalms research that generally engage the attention of scholars. Omitted are such weighty topics as the musicological terminology, textual variants, the implications of numerous parallels between the style and phraseology of the psalms and the prophetic writings, the question of pre- or post-exilic origins, and the identity of the speaker who refers to himself as "I" (whether that "I" represents an individual or the worshiping community conceived of as a collective entity, a corporate personality). All these are serious issues of a highly technical nature, and properly find their way into the conventional introductions to the Bible and the many biblical dictionaries and encyclopedias. However, rarely is there any consensus in regard to these matters. Only occasionally do such concerns yield insights into the meaning and message of a psalm. And it is the meaning and the message that primarily interest me here.

If I have used the term "introduction," it is because I have tried to lay before the reader something of the thought-world of the authors and the worshipers. I have endeavored to present their animating ideas and concepts, the values they held dear, the truths they adhered to, the ideals that stirred them, the convictions they firmly and passionately cherished. My purpose has been, not to sate the reader's appetite for knowledge about these matters, but to sharpen it.

The first distinguishing feature of the biblical psalms is the direct, personal approach to God. There are no intermediaries, human or celestial, no being or beings who facilitate the ascension of prayer to the divine realm. Nor is there any notion of angelic intercession or influence. Then, there is the unqualified conviction that prayer is heard, that the Deity is approachable and responsive to the pleas of humankind, though not necessarily immediately or always favorably. In this connection, it is important to emphasize that the psalmists were acutely aware of the dangers of hypocrisy and the perils it holds for true religiosity. They warn the would-be worshiper that God probes the mind and the conscience, that He discerns the contrast between profession and deed, promise and performance.

It is taken for granted that history has meaning because the processes of history are under the sovereign control of God. It is regarded as axiomatic that His governance of the world is based upon foundations of justice and righteousness, that there is a divinely ordained moral law of universal application operative in the concatenation of events, and that there are positive ethical imperatives for the violation of which human beings are held accountable. Given such a system of beliefs, the psalmists inevitably possess unshakable faith that evildoing must in the end be punished, and the wicked overthrown. They inveigh against the flagrant abuses rife in the land. Their special concern is the corruption of the judicial processes. They cry out against the exploitation of the disadvantaged and vulnerable of society: the stranger, the poor and the needy, the orphan, and the widow.

Another interesting and perhaps surprising feature of the psalms is that despite the frequent expression of basic human concerns, there is a complete absence of personal pleas for power or wealth. If there ever were any, they have not survived. On the other hand, instances of a victim of false accusations who suffers the hostility and machinations of foes and desperately implores God for vindication are not uncommon. The vagaries and dilemmas of the human condition find expression in abundance. The vexing problems of life, the fearful insecurities of existence, the troubles and travails that afflict every human being—all are reflected in the psalmist's work. Always, the psalmist, and thus the worshiper, too, finds solace and comfort in adversity; he is sustained and strengthened by his faith and musters the courage to continue with life. Moreover, the joys and sorrows of the individual are shared by the entire community, for the psalms were recited in the Temple in the presence of a congregation. The sorrows are thereby ameliorated and the joys enhanced. Man is recognized to be essentially a social being even if, at times, he is an island unto himself.

For thousands of years, the biblical psalms have nourished, sustained, and elevated the spiritual and moral life of peoples of many faiths. In this age of spiritual and moral chaos they still have something to teach us.

Abbreviations

AB	Anchor Bible
AHW	W. von Soden, *Akkadisches Handwörterbuch*
Akk.	Akkadian
ANEP	J. B. Pritchard, ed., *Ancient Near East in Pictures*
ANET	J. B. Pritchard, ed., *Ancient Near Eastern Texts*
An. Or.	Analecta Orientalia
Arab.	Arabic
Aram.	Aramaic
Av. Zar.	Avodah Zarah
BA	*Biblical Archeologist*
BAR	*Biblical Archaeologist Reader*
BARev	*Biblical Archaeology Review*
BASOR	*Bulletin of the American Schools of Oriental Research*
BB	Bava Batra
BDB	F. Brown, S. R. Driver, and C. A. Briggs, *Hebrew and English Lexicon of the Old Testament*
Bek.	Bekhorot
Ber.	Berakhot
BJRL	*Bulletin of the John Rylands University Library of Manchester*
BM	Bava Metsia
BZ	*Biblische Zeitschrift*
BZAW	*Beihefte Zur Zeitschrift für die alttestamentliche Wissenschafft*

CAD	*The Assyrian Dictionary of the Oriental Institute of the University of Chicago*
CAH	Cambridge Ancient History
Cant. R.	Canticles Rabba
CBQ	*Catholic Biblical Quarterly*
CD	Damascus Document from the Cairo Genizah
Dem.	Demai
Deut. R.	Deuteronomy Rabba
EM	*Encyclopaedia Mikra'it*
ER	*Encyclopaedia Biblica*
ER	*Encyclopaedia of Religion*
Eruv.	Eruvin
Exod. R.	Exodus Rabba
Gen. R.	Genesis Rabba
Gk.	Greek
GKC	*Gesenius' Hebrew Grammar*, ed. E. Kautzsch and trans. A. E. Cowley
Heb.	Hebrew
HTR	*Harvard Theological Review*
HUCA	*Hebrew Union College Annual*
IEJ	*Israel Exploration Journal*
JAOS	*Journal of the American Oriental Society*
JBL	*Journal of Biblical Literature*
JCS	*Journal of Cuneiform Studies*
JJS	*Journal of Jewish Studies*
JNES	*Journal of Near Eastern Studies*
JPS	*Jewish Publication Society*
JQR	*Jewish Quarterly Review*
JSOT	*Journal for the Study of the Old Testament*
JSOTSup	*Journal for the Study of the Old Testament: Supplement Series*
JSS	*Journal of Semitic Studies*
JTS	*Journal of Theological Studies*
KAI	H. Donner and W. Röllig, *Kanaanäische und Aramäische Inschriften*
Ker.	Keritot
Ket.	Ketubbot

Kid.	Kiddushin
Lam. R.	Lamentations Rabba
Lev. R.	Leviticus Rabba
LXX	Septuagint
Meg.	Megillah
Mid.	Midrash
Mish.	Mishnah
MT	Masoretic Text
NJPS	New Jewish Publication Society translation
NSI	*North Semitic Inscriptions*
Num. R.	Numbers Rabba
OSA	Old South Arabic
PdRE	Pesikta de-Rav Eliezer
PEQ	*Palestine Exploration Quarterly*
Pes.	Pesahim
Pesh.	Peshitta
Pesik.	Pesikta
Phoen.	Phoenician
Q	Qumran
RA	*Revue d'Assyriologie et d'Archéologie Orientale*
RB	*Revue Biblique*
RH	Rosh Ha-Shanah
Sam.	Samaritan
Sanh.	Sanhedrin
Shab.	Shabbat
Shek.	Shekalim
Shev.	Shevi'it
Sif.	Sifrei
Sifra	Sifra
Sof.	Soferim
Sot.	Sotah
Suk.	Sukkah
Sum.	Sumerian
Symm.	Symmachus
Syr.	Syriac
Ta'an.	Ta'anit
Tam.	Tamid

Tanh.	Tanhuma
Targ.	Onkelos
Targ. Jon.	Targum Jonathan
Targ. Yer.	Targum Yerushalmi
TDOT	G. J. Botterweck and H. Ringgren, eds., *Theological Dictionary of the Old Testament*
Tosaf.	Tosafot
Tosef.	Tosefta
Ugar.	Ugaritic
UT	C. H. Gordon, *Ugaritic Textbook* (1965)
VT	*Vetus Testamentum*
VTSup	*Vetus Testamentum: Supplements*
Vulg.	Vulgate
Yal.	Yalkut
ZAW	*Zeitschrift für die alttestamentliche Wissenschaft*

NOTES

INTRODUCTION

1. *Midrash Tehillim* to Ps. 18:1, ed. S. Buber, 135.

2. Ber. 57b.

3. M. Gilbert, *Shcharansky, Hero of Our Time*, 363, 392f., 401f., 412, 416.

4. Rabbi Israel Lau reported this in the *Jerusalem Post*; it was reprinted by the Wexner Heritage Foundation in its *Jewish News Anthology*, June–October, 1988.

5. Gen. 4:20–22, on which see N. M. Sarna, *JPS Commentary on Genesis*, 37–38.

6. On the Beni Hasan paintings, see *ANEP*, pp. 2–3, No. 3 and p. 249; W. F. Albright, *Archaeology and the Religion of Israel*, 5th ed., 96, 121; *CAH* 1, 2: 503f., 516, 541.

7. So Targ. Jon., *ad loc.*; cf. Gen. R. 23:4.

8. Cf. 2 Sam. 23:1; Ps. 81:3; 135:3; 147:1; see also *UT* 2225; Ben Sira 45:9, ed. M. H. Segal, 310, and the note *ad loc.* p. 314. In rabbinic Hebrew the root is used in the sense of "sing, chant," and the noun *ne'imah* means "a tune."

9. See *Oxford Classical Dictionary*, 2nd ed. (Oxford, 1970), 242.

10. A. D. Kilmer, *RA* 68 (1974): 69–87; see *BARev* 6/5 (1980):14–25.

11. *UT* 19:1274, 2164.

12. Gen. 4:3–4.

13. Gen. 4:26.

14. This was pointed out by Y. Kaufmann, *Toledot Ha-'Emunah Ha-Yisre'elit*, 2:476–78; Kaufmann, *The Religion of Israel*, 302–4.

15. A. Leo Oppenheim, *Ancient Mesopotamia*, 175; cf. S. Mowinckel, *The Psalms in Israel's Worship*, 1:52; W. W. Hallo, "The Cultic Setting of Sumerian Poetry," *Actes de la XVIIᵉ Rencontre Assyriologique Internationale*, 1969:116–34.

16. Ezra 3:2,10; Neh. 12:24, 45–46; 2 Chron. 23:18; cf. 2 Chron. 8:12–14.

17. See Kaufmann, *Religion of Israel*, 302–4.

18. Cf. P. Ber. 4:3 (8a); P. Ta'an. 2:2 (65c); P. Shab. 16:1(15a). In Akkadian *zamāru* is a song or literary composition to be sung with or without instrumental accompaniment; see *CAD* 21:35–38, which points out that singing for ritual or ceremonial purposes was always done to the accompaniment of musical instruments. Ugaritic text 602.3f., *yšr wydmr bknr*, "he sings and plays on the lyre," shows that *dmr* refers to the musical accompaniment; see C. H. Gordon, *Supplement to UT* (An. Or. 38): 55-19:727a. On this text, see S. E. Loewenstamm, "The Lord Is My Strength and Glory," *VT* 29 (1969): 464–70. In biblical Hebrew, *mizmor* never appears in the plural or with the definite article; "musical instruments" are *klei shir* (Amos 6:5, Neh. 12:36; 1 Chron. 16:42; 22:19 (18); 2 Chron. 5:13; 7:6; 23:13; 34:12), but never *klei zemer*; "singers" are *sharim* (2 Sam. 19:36; 1 Kings 10:12; Ezek. 40:44; Eccl. 2:8; 2 Chron. 35:25) and *meshorerim*, but never *zammarim*. The Annals of Sennacherib, ed. D. D. Luckenbill, 70, line 32, designates the male and female singers sent by King Hezekiah of Judah to Nineveh by the terms *zammerê* and *zammerâte*. Further, although Hebrew *mizmor le-david* occurs frequently in Psalms, *shir le-david* never appears. I have found no explanation for these oddities.

19. Cf. the Syriac title *kethaba' de-mazmurē*.

20. BB 14b; Av. Zar. 19a; P. Suk. 3:12 (53d); P. Ket. 12:3 (35a) (shortened).

21. Only Ps. 145 has *tehillah* in the title.

22. Professor Jonas C. Greenfield kindly made this text available to me. For the date of the letter, see L. Schiffman, "The New Halakhic Letter (4QMMT) and the Origin of the Dead Sea Sect," *BA* 53 (1990):66.

23. See J. Goldstein, *II Maccabees*, AB 1983: 156; for the date, see pp. 71–83.

24. *De Vita Contemplativa* 3:25.

25. *Contra Apion* 1:40.

26. On this topic, see M. I. Finley, *The World of Odysseus*, 9. For the statistics given here, see the articles on these authors in *The New Century Classical Handbook*, ed. C. B. Avery, 162, 698.

27. See N. M. Sarna, *Understanding Genesis*, xvii–xix.

28. For a list of such works, see S. Z. Leiman, *The Canonization of Scripture*, 17–20.

29. The original Hebrew text of this supernumerary psalm turned up in Qumran; see J. A. Sanders, *The Psalms Scroll of Qumran Cave 11 (11QPS*ᵃ *)*, 53–64.

30. On 146 psalms, see A. Berliner, *Magazin für die Wissenschaft des Judentums* (Berlin), vol. 7 (1880): 112. For 147 psalms, cf. P. Shab. 16:1 (15c), *Massekhet Soferim*, Sof. 16:11, ed. M. Higger, 292f. and n. 60 for other sources; to which add *Mid. Tehillim*, ed. Buber, 190 to Ps. 22:19 and the editor's n. *ad loc.*, also 439 to Ps. 104:2; Yal. to Ps. 22:4 (Salonika), 1521–26; Baal Ha-Turim to Gen. 47:28; see also C. D. Ginsberg, *Introduction to the Massoretico-Critical Edition of the Hebrew Bible*, 18 n.1, 777 n.1. For 149 psalms, see "Mishael b. Uzziel's Treatise on Differences Between Ben Asher and Ben Naphtali," ed. L. Lipschütz, *Textus* II (1962):43. The same number appears in a poem by Samuel Ha-Nagid (993–1056) in H. Schirmann, *Ha-Shirah Ha-'Ivrit Bi-Sefarad U-bi-Provence*, 1:92, poem no. 25, line 139; cf. also 101, poem no. 27, line 140; see also I. Joel, *Kirjath Sefer* 38 (1962): 125. For 151 and 159 compositions, see Ginsberg, *Massoretico-Critical Edition of Hebrew Bible*, 584, 536.

31. With Ps. 106:47–48, cf. 1 Chron. 16:36.

32. Noted by H. B. Swete, *Introduction to the Old Testament in Greek*, 254.

33. On the problems of the "five books of Psalms," see M. Haran, "The Four Blessings and the Five 'Books' in the Book of Psalms" [Hebrew], *Proceedings of the Israel National Academy of Sciences*, 8, 1 (1989):1–32.

34. P. Lagard, *Analecta Syriaca* (1858), 86; Jerome, *Prologus Galeatus*.

35. Kid. 33a.

36. P. Kahle dates Mishael to ca.1050, J. Mann to the twelfth century; see L. Lipschütz, "Kitab al-Khilaf. The Book of the Ḥillufim," *Textus* IV (1960): 1. Mishael refers to each "scroll" by the initial word or phrase of the first psalm of each "book."

37. See Haran, "Four Blessings."

38. *Mid. Tehillim*, ed. Buber, 1[2], p. 3.

39. 2 Chron. 8:13–14; 23:18.

40. If this is the correct meaning of Hebrew *la-menatse'ah*.

41. It should also be pointed out that the Psalms scroll from Qumran (11QPs^a) contains selections from "Book Four" interspersed with some psalms from "Book Five." However, this scroll may not be a canonical text, but a liturgy or hymn book.

42. Meg. 29b.

43. The liturgical poet Yannai, composing apparently in the fifth century C. E., based his *piyyutim* on the *sedarim* of the triennial cycle. That system was still in vogue in the synagogues of Palestinian Jews in Egypt in the late twelfth century, as attested by the traveler Benjamin of Tudela, *Itinerary*, ed. A. A. Asher, 98; and by Moses Maimonides, *Hilkhot Tefillah* 13:1. If the chronicle of Joseph b. Isaac Sambari (1640–1703) is reliable on this point, it would seem that the practice still existed vestigially in his day; see A. Neubauer, *Medieval Hebrew Chronicles*, 118.

44. J. Heinemann, *Tarbiz* 33 (1964): 362–68; I. Joel, *Kirjath Sefer*, 126–32; B. M. Lewin, *Otsar Hilluf Minhagim*, 96 n. 5, 98.

45. I. Yeivin, "The Divisions into Sections in the Book of Psalms," *Textus* VII (1969):76–102.

46. E. A. King, "The Influence of the Triennial Cycle upon the Psalter," *JTS* V (1904):203–13, on which see I. Abrahams, "Critical Notices," *JQR* 16 (1904):579–83; N. H. Snaith, "The Triennial Cycle and the Psalter," *ZAW* 51 (1933):302–7. Professor John H. Hayes kindly let me read his unpublished manuscript, "The Psalms and the Triennial Cycle," from which I learned much.

47. 1 Chron. 16:4–5. The psalms that bear his name are 50, 73–83.

48. Num., ch. 16.

49. Num. 26:11; 1 Chron. 16:22. The psalms that bear their name are 42, 44–49, 84, 85, 87, 88.

50. Ps. 121 has *shir la-ma'alot*.

51. Pss. 122, 124, 131, 133.

52. Codex Vaticanus (G^B) also adds Ps. 67, making fourteen more than the Hebrew.

53. Pss. 72, 127; Ps. 90; Ps. 88; Ps. 89.

54. So called in Av. Zar. 24b. Pss. 39, 62, 77 carry "Jeduthun" in the superscription, but the first two also add *le-david*; Ps. 77 adds *le'asaph*. The

Greek adds "Jeremiah" to Ps. 137, and "Haggai and Zechariah" to Pss. 138, 146, 147:1, 147:12, and 148.

55. BB 14b, referring to Pss. 139:16, 110:1, 89:1 (Ethan is identified with Abraham), 90:1, 88:1, 39:1 et al., 50:1 et al.

56. Pes. 117a.

57. Sanders, *Psalms Scroll*, 91–93.

58. 1 Sam. 17:16–23; 19:9.

59. Neh. 12:36; 1 Chron. 23:5; 2 Chron. 29:26–2; cf. Amos 6:5. On this last reference, see D. N. Freedman, "But Did David Invent Musical Instruments?" *Bible Review* I(1965):49–51.

60. 2 Sam. 1:17–22; 3:33 (dirges); 2 Sam. ch. 22 (thanksgiving).

61. 2 Sam. 12:13; cf. Ps. 51; 2 Sam. 24:10–17; 1 Chron. 21:8, 13–17; 2 Sam. 6:2–17; 1 Chron. 13:1–14; 15:1–15; 16:1.

62. 2 Sam. 7:1–2; 1 Chron. 17:1–2; 28:1–3.

63. 1 Chron. ch. 28; 29:1–9, 16.

64. Ezra 3:2, 10; Neh. 12:14, 25; 1 Chron. 6:16–17; 16:4–7, 37–42; chs. 25–26; 2 Chron. 7:6; 8:14; 23:18; 29:25–27, 30.

65. The preposition *le-* might also mean "for/dedicated to/concerning"; cf. Jer. 23:9; 46:2; 48:1; 49:1, 7, 23, 28.

66. Pss. 3, 7, 18, 34, 51, 52, 56, 57, 59, 60, 63, 142. The Greek adds Pss. 27, 71, 143, 144. On this subject, see A. Cooper, "The Life and Times of King David According to the Book of Psalms," in *The Poet and the Historian. Essays in Literary and Historical Criticism*, ed. R. E. Friedman, 117–31.

67. 1 Chron. 6:16; 15:16–24; 23:6, 30; 25:1–8.

68. On the subject of the musical guilds and their dating, see N. M. Sarna, "The Psalm Superscriptions and the Guilds," in *Studies in Jewish Religious and Intellectual History Presented to Alexander Altmann*, 281–300.

69. Ezra 2:41-Neh. 7:44.

70. Ezra 3:10.

71. Y. Aharoni, "Arad: Its Inscriptions and Temple," *BA* 31(1968):11; Aharoni, *Arad Inscriptions* [Heb.], 82, no. 49, line 2. Aharoni assigns the inscription to stratum VII, he dates it to the age of Hezekiah (715–687 B.C.E.). This refutes the theory of G. Wanke, "Die Zionstheologie der Korachiten," *BZAW* 97 (1966):23–31, that the Korahites were post-exilic.

72. Their association with the official cult is said to include the entire period from David to Isaiah; see 1 Chron. 6:16f., 24; 15:3, 17f.; 16:5f.; 2 Chron. 5:12; 29:13; 35:15.

73. 1 Chron. 9:19.
74. 1 Chron. 9:31.
75. 1 Chron. 26:1, 19.
76. 1 Chron. 15:17, 19.
77. 1 Chron. 6:18.
78. 1 Chron. 6:18–23, 24–28.

CHAPTER ONE: PSALM 1

1. Av. Zar. 24b.

2. *'ashrei* occurs in the Hebrew Bible nineteen times in all, ten of which are in Proverbs (3:13; 8:32, 34; 14:21; 16:20; 28:14; 29:18), Job (5:7), and Ecclesiastes (10:17). The phrase *'atsat resha'im* is otherwise peculiar to Job (10:3; 21:16; 22:18; cf. 18:9). *'Etsah* itself belongs to the technical terminology of Wisdom, as is obvious from Jer. 18:8; Ezek. 7:26; Prov. 1:25, 30; 8:14. As to *lets*, fourteen of its sixteen biblical usages are to be found in Proverbs (1:22; 3:34; 9:7, 8; 13:1; 14:6; 15:12; 19:25,29; 20:1; 21:11, 24; 22:10; 24:9). The image of v. 2 is certainly that of a sage immersed in study, and that of v. 3 is paralleled in an Egyptian Wisdom text.

3. *Midrash Tehillim*, ed. S. Buber, 1891, 4 to Ps. 1:3; cf. Ber. 9b–10a in the name of R. Johanan.

4. I have borrowed the terms "anthropotropic" and "theotropic" from A. J. Heschel, *The Prophets*, 439–43.

5. See Introduction, pp. 17–18.

6. On this topic, see *Encyclopaedia Judaica*, 15:1386–89, "Triennial Cycle"; N. M. Sarna, *JBL* 87(1968):100–106.

7. *Mid. Tehillim*, ed. Buber, 1:2 (p. 3), 1:5 (p. 7).

8. Deut. 33:29.

9. This was noted by L. Liebreich, *HUCA* 25 (1954):37f., n. 3.

10. On this subject, see below p. 39 and n. 89.

11. See W. Jansen, " '*Ašre* in the Old Testament," *HTR* 57 (1965):215–26; H. Cazelles in *Theological Dictionary of the Old Testament*, eds. C. J. Botterweck and H. Ringgren, trans. J. T. Willis, 1:445–48 (hereafter cited as TDOT).

12. So noted by Kimḥi, *ad loc*. On the "plural of intensity," see *Gesenius*'

Hebrew Grammar, edition Kautzsch-Cowley, Oxford, 1910, §124, (hereafter cited as GKC.)

13. Ps. 33:12.
14. *Ibid.*, Ps. 89:16; 144:15.
15. Eccl. 10:17.
16. Ps. 32:2; 84:6, 13; Prov. 3:13; 8:34; 28:14.
17. Ps. 34:9; 40:5; 94:12; 127:5.
18. Isa. 56:2; Job 5:17.
19. For the use of *'ish* or its plural form in this sense, see Gen. 32:29; Exod. 16:16, 18, 21, 29; Num. 23:19; Josh. 10:14; Judg. 9:9; Isa. 31:8; Jer. 17:10; 32:19; Ezek. 18:8; Hos. 11:9; Prov. 5:21; 19:22; Job 12:10; 32:13; 38:26.
20. Cf. 1 Sam. 4:9; 26:15; 1 Kings 2:2. A similar usage occurs with Akk. *amīlu;* see CAD, AII: 54 2a); 55 3a).
21. Prov. 1:15; 4:14; 5:8; 22:24, 26; cf. M. Avot 1:7, "Keep your distance from a bad neighbor, and do not associate with a wicked person"; cf. Suk. 56b.
22. Cf. Isa. 33:15–16; Pss. 15, 24 for similar negatively formulated virtues.
23. This phrase otherwise is peculiar to Job (10:3; 21:16; 22:18; cf. 18:19). It is true that the preferred Hebrew term for evil counsel is *mo'etsot*, as in Jer. 7:24; Hos. 11:6; Mic. 6:16; Ps. 5:11; 81:13; Prov. 1:31, but the form *'etsah* is also so used; see Ps. 106:43; Isa. 29:15; Ezek. 11:2. Just as *hlkh b-* is used with *mo'etsot*, as in Jer. 7:24; Mic. 6:16; Ps. 81:13, so can it occur with *'etsah*, as in 2 Chron. 22:5 (cf. Ps. 73:24). The reading of our received Hebrew text is found 4Q Florilegium from Qumran; see J. M. Allegro, "Fragments of a Qumran Scroll of Eschatological Midrashim," *JBL* 77 (1958):353. The emendation of *'atsat* to *'adat* suggested by A. B. Ehrlich, *Die Psalmen*, 1, and by J. Kennedy, *An Aid to the Textual Amendment of the Old Testament*, 17, is gratuitous, as is the attempt of M. Dahood, *Psalms*, AB, 1:1f. to take *'etsah* in the sense of "council," based on its supposed usage in the Qumran texts. See J. Worrel, "עצה 'Counsel' or 'Council' at Qumran," *VT* 20 (1970):65–74.
24. E.g., Exod. 23:7; Num. 35:31; Deut. 25:1; Isa. 5:23; Prov. 17:15; 18:5; 24:24; cf. also 20:4; 38:26.
25. Ps. 10:2–4; 31:19; 36:12; 73:6; 75:6.
26. Ps. 94:4, Prov. 18:3; 21:29.
27. Ps. 36:5; 37:12; 73:8; Prov. 12:6.
28. Ps. 11:5; 17:23.
29. Ps. 73:6; 140:5; Prov. 10:6, 11.
30. Ps. 10:2, 8–9, 18; 11:2; 37:14, 32; 94:6.

31. Ps. 10:3; 140:9.

32. Ps. 28:3.

33. Ps. 10:7; 31:19; 36:4; 109:2 (3); Prov. 10:31; 12:5; 19:28.

34. Ps. 109:4–5.

35. Ps. 37:21; 73:12.

36. Prov. 29:26.

37. Prov. 12:10.

38. Ps. 10:6,11; 94:4,7; cf. Ezek. 8:12.

39. Ps. 32:10; 36:7.

40. See N. M. Sarna, *Exploring Exodus*, 25–26.

41. Ps. 14:2-53:2. On the question of whether true atheism existed in the ancient world, see A. B. Drachman, *Atheism in Pagan Antiquity*.

42. Prov. 15:8; 21:27.

43. For *'ashrei* associated with the verb *h-l-kh*, "to walk," or with *derekh*, "way," cf. Ps. 2:12; 84:12–13; 89:16; 119:1; 128:1; Prov. 20:7; cf. Prov. 3:16–17.

44. For the verb *'-sh-r*, "to walk, advance," see Isa. 3:12; 9:15; Prov. 4:14; 9:6; 23:19. For the noun forms meaning "footstep," see Ps. 17:5, 11; 37:31; 40:3; 44:19; 73:2; Job 23:11; 31:7; cf. Ugar. verb *'tr*, "to march," Arab. *'itr*, "footstep, track."

45. In Judg. 20:16 *ḥṭ'* is used in a military context meaning "to miss a target." In Gen. 31:39 the verb in the *pi'el* means "to make good what is missing." In Prov. 19:2 and Job 5:24 the *qal* form means "to fail." In Isa. 65:20, *ḥote'* means "to miss," i.e., fail to reach the age of 100. In Ps. 25:8 *ḥ'atta'im* are those who stray from the right path. In Prov. 8:35–36 *ḥ'ote'iy*, "who misses me," is the antonym of *motse'iy*, "who finds me"; cf. CAD 6:156 *ḥaṭû*, "to make a mistake, neglect, miss (the boat)."

46. Cf. Eccl. 7:20.

47. Ps. 25:8; 26:9; 51:15; 104:35; cf. Prov. 1:10; 13:21; 23:17.

48. See GKC §84b, p. 233.

49. See Prov. 1:10–19.

50. For Hebrew *'-m-d*, "to linger, tarry," cf. Gen. 19:17; 45:9; Deut. 10:10; Josh. 10:19; 1 Sam. 20:38; 2 Kings 15:20; Eccl. 8:3.

51. On the stem, see F. Buhl, "Die Bedeutung des Stammes *lwṣ* oder *lyṣ* im Hebräischen," *BZAW* 27 (1914):81–86; H. N. Richardson, "Some Notes on ליץ and Its Derivatives," *VT* 5(1955):163–79, 434–36; T. D. Donald, "The Semantic Field of Folly in Proverbs, Job, Psalms, and Ecclesiastes," *VT*

13(1963):285–92. M. Heltzer, "The Inscription on the Nimrud Bronze Bowl No. 5 (BM91303)," *PEQ* 114 (1982):4–6 finds proof that *lṣ* was a court jester.

52. Prov. 1:22; 9:8; 13:1; 14:6; 15:12; 19:25, 29; 21:11; 24:9; 29:8.

53. Prov. 21:24; cf. Ps. 119:51.

54. Prov. 9:7; 19:28; cf. Isa. 9:20.

55. Prov. 21:24.

56. Prov. 29:8.

57. Prov. 9:1–8; 15:12.

58. Prov. 24:9.

59. Hab. 2:6; Isa. 28:14; Ps. 119:51.

60. In Ps. 107:32 the phrase *moshav zekenim*, "assembly of the elders," parallels "congregation of the people." In Ezek. 28:2 *moshav 'elohim yashavti* seems to mean "I sit enthroned like a god" or "I sit in the seat of gods." In 1 Kings 10:5 *moshav 'avadav* means the "seating of his servants." In each case, *moshav* implies a formal session.

61. See S. Gandz, "Oral Tradition in the Bible," in *Jewish Studies in Memory of George Kohut*, eds. S. W. Baron and A. Marx, 248–69.

62. Cf. Gen. 19:1; 23:10, 18; Ruth 3:11; 4:1ff. See N. M. Sarna, *Understanding Genesis*, 168–69, 178 n. 22.

63. Cf. Jer. 15:17; Ps. 26:4, 5.

64. So noted in Av. Zar. 18b; *Mid. Tehillim*, ed. Buber, 1:7 (p. 28).

65. Ps. 34:15; 37:17.

66. On this word, see H. Yalon, *Pirkei Lashon*, 157–58.

67. Eccl. 3:1,17; 8:6.

68. Isa. 58:3,13; cf. *CAD* 16:167 *ṣibûtu* for the same semantic development.

69. Prov. 3:5; cf. Job 22:3; 31:16.

70. Job 21:21; 22:3.

71. Jer. 8:8–9. On this text, see M. Weinfeld, *Deuteronomy and the Deuteronomic School*, 151n., 158–71.

72. Cf. Ps. 19:8; 37:3; 78:5,10; 105:45; 119 *passim*.

73. So noted by Kimhi in his interpretation of *yehegeh*.

74. Isa. 38:14; 59:11.

75. Isa. 31:4.

76. Ps. 37:30; cf. Job 37:2.

77. Isa. 59:3; Ps. 35:28; 71:24; Job 27:4.

78. Prov. 8:7; cf. Job 31:30; 33:2.

79. Ps. 115:7.

80. Isa. 33:18; 59:13; Prov. 15:28; 24:2; cf. Ps. 19:15; 49:4. On *lev* as an organ of speech, see H. L. Ginsberg, *Encyclopaedia Judaica*, s.v. "heart."

81. Cf. Isa. 16:7; Jer. 48:31; Ps. 2:1; 38:13; 77:13; 143:5.

82. These are *hagut* in Ps. 19:15, Lam. 3:62; *higgayon* in Ps. 92:4, which refers either to the twang of the lyre or to singing to the accompaniment of the lyre; *hegeh* in Ezek. 2:10, Job 37:2, which means "sound," its type depending on the context; similarly, in Ps. 90:9 *hegeh* means "a sigh." The verb *h-g-h* in the sense of "say, speak" has turned up in the Balaam inscription from Deir 'Alla; see J. Hoftijzer and G. Van der Kooij, *Aramaic Texts from Deir 'Alla*, 173 (Combination I, line 9). The term *sefer hhgw*, "the book of the *hgw* (study)" as a synonym for Torah appears in the Dead Sea Scrolls: CD 10:6; 13:2; 14:6–7, undoubtedly because it was invariably recited aloud. On this term see N. Wieder, *The Judean Scrolls and Karaism*, 215–56, esp. n. 5. In QS 1:6–7 a variant spelling *hhgy* occurs, on which see M. Goshen-Gottstein, "Sepher Hagu—The End of a Puzzle," *VT* 8 (1958):286–88. The verbal form of the stem *hgh* is found in 1QH 11.2, 21f. in the sense of "to lament, bewail"; cf. Ezek. 2:10. In rabbinic Hebrew, the verbal form is used with the meaning "to utter," especially the Tetragrammaton, as in M. Sanh. 10:1, Av. Zar. 18a, and Exod. R. 3:9 (to Exod. 3:15). In P. Meg. 4:1 (74d) the same verb is employed with respect to reciting the Torah.

83. Cf. Exod. 13:8–9, 14–15; Deut. 4:9–10, 20–25; 6:7; 11:19; 30:14; 32:7; Josh. 4:6–7, 21–24; Judg. 6:13; Isa. 59:21; Ps. 44:2; 78:1–6.

84. Eli's reaction to Hannah's silent praying, in 1 Sam. 1:12–14, shows that audible prayer was the rule. On oral recitation and audible reading, see S. Krauss, *Talmudische Archaeologie*, 3:227–29; G. L. Hendrickson, "Ancient Reading," *Classical Journal* 25(1929):182–96; E. S. McCartney, "Notes on Reading and Praying Audibly," *Classical Philology* 43(1948):184–87; M. Hadas, *Ancilla to Classical Reading*, 50–60; B. Gerhardsson, *Memory and Manuscript*; D. Zlotnick, "Memory and the Integrity of the Oral Tradition," *JNES* 16–17 (1984–85):229–41; *id.*, *The Iron Pillar—Mishnah: Redaction, Form and Intent*, 51–71; J. Neusner, *The Memorized Torah: The Mnemonic System of the Mishnah*; L. H. Silberman ed., *Orality, Aurality, and Biblical Narration*, *Semeia* 39 (1986).

85. *ANET*, 145 and fn. 7. The Jewish practice of chanting texts as an aid to memorization is reflected in the Targum's rendering of *h-g-h* in Ps. 1:2 and Prov. 15:28 by *r-n-n*. It is mentioned several times in rabbinic texts; cf.

Tos. Ahilot 16:8 and Tos. Parah 4:7, ed. M. S. Zuckermandel, 614, 633: "Rabbi Akiba said, 'Sing me (i.e. the Torah) constantly, sing me.' " The same appears with variants in Sanh. 99 a–b: "Rabbi Akiba said, 'Sing it constantly, every day, sing it' "; cf. Meg. 32a (Sof. 3:13): "Rabbi Shefatiah said in the name of R. Johanan, 'He who reads [the Bible] without a melody or recites [the mishnah] without a tune . . .' " See S. Krauss, *Archaeologie*, n. 84.

86. M. Lichtheim, *Ancient Egyptian Literature*, 2:168.

87. Von Soden, *AHW*, p. 1195; G. R. Driver and J. C. Miles, *The Babylonian Laws*, 2:286; see also J. H. Tigay, *The Evolution of the Gilgamesh Epic*, 102 and n. 72.

88. So *Encyclopaedia Britannica* (Micropaedia), 8:447.

89. Cf. Sif. Deut. 41 to Deut. 11:13, ed. Horovitz-Finkelstein, 87. On study as an act of worship, see R. T. Herford, *The Ethics of the Talmud: Sayings of the Fathers* (repr. 1962), 14–15; G. F. Moore, *Judaism*, 2:239–47; M. Kadushin, *Worship and Ethics*, 36; see also B. T. Viviano, *Study as Worship*.

90. 1 QS. 6:6–7.

91. For an exhaustive discussion of scholarly exegesis of verses 3–4, see M. Weiss, *The Bible from Within*, 135–63. I. Engnell, "Planted by Streams of Water," in *Studia Orientalia Joanni Pedersen Dicata*, 85–96, regards verse 3 as reflecting the language of royal liturgy, the tree being the king. G. Widengren, *The King and the Tree of Life in Ancient Near Eastern Religion*, 42–58, takes the tree to be a cultic symbol of Tammuz.

92. Amos 2:9.

93. Jer. 11:19.

94. Ps. 52:10.

95. Ps. 92:13–15.

96. Jer. 11:20; Job 8:11–19; 15:30; 18:16; 29:19.

97. *ANET*, 422.

98. Cited by Widengren, 42.

99. G. A. Cooke, *A Text-Book of North-Semitic Inscriptions*, 30, No. 5, lines 11–12; H. Donner and W. Röllig, *Kanaanäische und Aramäische Inschriften* (hereafter cited as KAI), 1:3, No. 14, lines 11–12; *ANET*, 662.

100. *Mid. Tehillim*, ed. Buber, n. 11.

101. Citing Jer. 17:8, M. Avot 3:17 states, "He whose deeds exceed his wisdom, to what may he be compared? to a tree which has few branches but numerous roots, so that even if all the world's winds were to blast it, they

would not dislodge it." Interestingly, the commentary on the Mishnah by Yom Tov Lipmann Heller (1579–1654), known as *Tosefot Yom Tov,* defines *shatul* as *mushrash yafeh ba-'aretz,* "well-rooted in the soil." The *Pesikta' Rabbati,* ed. M. Friedman, ch. 3:8b, commenting on Eccl. 12:11, notes, "just as the roots of a tree *mashtilim* in all directions; so the words of the Torah enter and *mashtilim* the entire body." The parallel citation in Num. R. 14:11 replaces *mashtilim* by *mishtarshim,* "become deeply rooted," thus indicating that the two verbs are synonymous; cf. also Yal. Eccl. 12:11. The same meaning of *shatul* is implied in the comments of Rabbis Jannai and Hisda in Av. Zar. 19a on Ps. 1:3 to the effect that "whoever learns Torah from but a single teacher will never achieve great success," that is, his learning will be superficial and not deep-rooted.

102. In Jer. 17:8, "sending forth its roots by a stream" is in synonymous parallelism with "like a tree planted [*shatul*] by waters." In Ezek. 17:8, 10, the point of the parable is that the vine was planted under optimum conditions for flourishing; yet, despite being *shetulah,* it will be uprooted (v. 9). See also M. Greenberg, *Ezekiel 1–20,* AB, 312.

103. Note the plural *palgei,* which intensifies the image of the tree's invulnerability to a lack of rain; cf. Isa. 32:2; Ps. 46:5, also Ezek. 17:8; 31:57. With *peleg* (sing.), cf. Akk. *palgu,* "canal," Arab. *falj,* "a small brook." Ps. 1:3 would seem to constitute one of the earliest precursors of the well-known rabbinic analogy between Torah and water as life-sustaining elements; see Mekhilta to Exod. 15:22; B.K. 17a, 82a; Av. Zar. 5b; Keth. 81a; cf. also Deut. 32:2; Isa. 55:1.

104. Cf. Rev. 22:2.

105. For the verb '-*s-h* in the sense of yielding fruit, cf. Gen. 1:11, 12; 2 Kings 19:30; Isa. 37:31; Jer. 12:2; 17:8; Ezek. 17:8, 23; Hos. 9:16; Ps. 107:37.

106. For the use of the stem *ts-l-ḥ* as an agricultural term, see Jer. 22:30; Ezek. 17:9–10. This usage has survived in rabbinic Hebrew in the sense of "thriving": R. H. 16a; Cant. R. 6:17 (on 6:11); Tanh. Gen., ed. S. Buber, 30: 22. The same is found in the Palestinian Hebrew liturgical poetry of Yannai; see *Piyyutei Yannai,* ed. M. Zulay, No. 33, p. 77, line 68; No. 90, p. 206, line 26; No. 113, p. 275, line 39, the verbs *ts-l-ḥ* and *ts-m-ḥ* appearing in tandem. On *ts-l-ḥ* see further H. Yalon, *Pirkei Lashon,* 239–41; H. Tawil, "Hebrew צלח/הצלח, Akkadian *ešēru/šūšuru:* A Lexicographical Note," *JBL* 95 (1976):405–13. Tawil does not mention Ps. 1:3.

107. For a description of the process, see D. Baly, *The Geography of the*

Bible, 45; J. Feliks, *Agriculture in Palestine in the Period of the Mishna and Talmud*, 288f.

108. Isa. 18:13; 29:5; 41:15; Hos. 13:3; Zeph. 2:2; Ps. 35:5; Job 21:18; cf. Isa. 40:24; 41:2; Jer. 13:24.

109. Targ. renders "the Great Day," which is used of the Day of Atonement. M. San. 10:3 understands it as the hereafter, so Rashi, Ibn Ezra, and Kimḥi. For Christian interpretation, see the comments of C. A. Briggs, *The Book of Psalms*, 1:7.

110. S. Paul, "Unrecognized Legal Idioms of Comparative Akkadian Expressions," *RB* 86 (1979):236–37; cf. Ps. 76:10 *kum la-mishpat* with Josh. 20:6 *'amad la-mishpat*.

111. Pointed out by Y. Kaufmann, *Toledot Ha-'Emunah Ha-Yisre'elit*, 2:521, 705–8. For this use of *mishpat* and the verbal forms of the stem, cf. 1 Kings 8:59; Ps. 25:8–9; 58:12; 75:8; Prov. 16:33; 29:25; Eccl. 8:5–7. The same idea, without *mishpat*, is expressed in Jer. 17:5–11; Prov. 11–31; 12:7. J. Licht, *The Rule Scroll*, 91, points out that *mishpat* in 1Q3:17 is used in this sense.

112. Cf. Jer. 12:1–2; Ps. 73:3–8, 12.

113. Cf. Prov. 2:21–23; 3:33; 5:21; 12:21; 13:9–25; 14:11; 21:13; 24:16, 19–20.

114. On *'edah*, see *EM* 6:83–89 s.v.; J. Milgrom, *JPS Commentary to Numbers*, to Num. 1:2, and Excursus I, pp. 335–6.

115. Cf. Prov. 28:28.

116. Cf. the use of Akk. *idû* in *CAD* 7:20–34, esp. p. 27f., 2.

117. See M. Buber, *Good and Evil*, 55–57; J. Emerton, *JSS* 15 (1970), 145–80; Sarna, *JPS Commentary on Genesis*, to Gen. 4:1; H. Yalon, "Leshonot y-d-', l-m-d," *Tarbiz* 36 (1967):396–400.

118. H. B. Huffmon, "The Treaty Background of Hebrew *yad'a* "BASOR 181 (1966):31-37; Huffmon and S. B. Parker, "A Further Note on the Treaty Background of the Hebrew *yad'a*," *BASOR* 184 (1966):36–38; D. R. Hillers, *Covenant: The History of a Biblical Idea*, 120–24.

119. So Gen. 4:1; 18:19; Exod. 1:8; Deut. 34:10; Jer. 1:5; Hos. 2:22; 13:3, 5; Amos 3:2; Nah. 1:7; Ps. 37:18. For a human being's ideal relationship to God expressed in terms of "knowledge," cf. Isa. 11:9; Jer. 22:16; Hos. 6:6; Prov. 2:5; 3:6; 1 Chron. 28:9.

120. Cf. Ps. 112:10; Prov. 10:28; Job 8:13.

CHAPTER TWO: PSALM 8

1. See Exod. 20:4–5; Deut. 4:19; 5:8–9; 17:2–3; 2 Kings 23:5, 11; Jer. 7:18; 18:2; 44:17–19, 25; Amos 5:26; Zeph. 1:5; 2 Chron. 33:5.

2. On this topic, see Sarna, *Understanding Genesis*, 1–23; Sarna, *JPS Commentary on Genesis*, 3–16.

3. On the inclusio as a form of parallelism, see A. Berlin, *The Dynamics of Biblical Parallelism*, 3, 132. For Abraham ibn Ezra's observations on the inclusio, see E. Z. Melammed, *Bible Commentators*, 2:575f.

4. The full title otherwise appears in the Bible only in Neh. 10:30; *'adoneinu* alone is used in Ps. 135:5; 147:5; Neh. 8:10. It is used of Nabal in 1 Sam. 25:14, 17; and of King David in 1 Kings 1:11, 43, 47.

5. On *'adon*, see M. Z. Brettler, *God Is King: Understanding an Israelite Metaphor* (1989), 40–44.

6. E. Z. Melammed, "Biblical Phrases Unique to God," [Heb.] *Tarbiz* 19 (1948):1–2. See 2 Sam. 2:7; 10:3; 1 Kings 1:11, 43, 47; cf. 1 Sam. 26:5; exceptions are 1 Kings 16:24; 2 Kings 9:7.

7. Cf. Ps. 5:3.

8. For this use of *mah*, cf. Gen. 28:17; Num. 24:5; Ps. 36:8; 66:3; 84:2; 92:6; 104:24; 139:17 et. al.

9. On this use of *mah*, see n. 63 below.

10. Cf. Judg. 5:13, 25; Jer. 14:3; 25:34; 30:21; Nah. 2:6; 3:18; Zech. 11:2; Ps. 136:18; Neh. 3:5; 10:30; 2 Chron. 23:20.

11. Exod. 15:11, cf. v. 6; 1 Sam. 4:8; Isa. 33:21; Ps. 76:5; 93:4. The element of holiness appears in Exod. 15:11. On *'addir*, see Brettler, *God Is King*, 59.

12. On the name, see Sarna, *Understanding Genesis*, 135 and n. 36; *JPS Genesis*, p. 7.

13. A. Heidel, *The Babylonian Genesis*, 18; ANET, 60f.

14. W. Beyerlin, ed., *Near Eastern Religious Texts Relating to the Old Testament*, 7.

15. ANET, 5; M. Lichtheim, *Ancient Egyptian Literature*, 1:54, 55; see also J. A. Wilson in Frankfort, *The Intellectual Adventure of Ancient Man* (1977), 53.

16. Gen. 1:5, 8, 10 (day and night; sky; earth and sea).

17. Gen. 2:19–20.

18. Cf. Gen. 1:28.

19. As Kimḥi expresses it, "His Name is He, and He is His Name." See R. Tournay, "Le psaume VIII et la doctrine biblique du Nom," *RB* 78 (1971):18–30.

20. For God's *hod*, cf. Hab. 3:3; Ps. 96:6; 1 Chron. 16:27; Ps. 104:1; 111:3; 145:5; 148:13; Job 37:22; 1 Chron. 29:11. On *hod*, see Brettler, *God Is King*, 66.

21. In Ps. 148:13 God's *hod* is over the earth as well as the heavens, but the Name is not mentioned.

22. In Isa. 30:30 and Job 39:20 *hod*, exceptionally, is associated with sound, perhaps meaning thunder, a transfer derived from its connection with a lightning discharge. There may also be wordplay with *hed*, "echo, reverberating sound." It is also possible that we are dealing with a homonym: cf. Arab. *hadid*, "crash, roar."

23. Heb. *tehillato*, "radiance," from *h-l-l*, "to shine"; cf. Akk. *ellu* "to shine," *elliš*, "brilliantly."

24. Num. 6:25; Isa. 2:5; Ezek. 1:27f.; Ps. 4:7; 31:17; 36:10; 44:4; 67:2; 80:20; 89:16; 104:2; 118:27; 119:135; Job 27:3.

25. Ezek. 1:27–28.

26. Exod. 34:29–35.

27. A. L. Oppenheim, "Akkadian *pul(u)ḫtu* and *mellamu*," *JAOS* 63 (1943):31–34; E. Cassin, *La splendeur divine. Introduction à l'étude de la mentalité mesopotamienne*, Paris, 1968.

28. *CAD*, 10:9–12.

29. H. Frankfort, *Kingship and the Gods*, 46, 135, 148.

30. *Encyclopaedia Britannica* (Micropaedia), 4:864f., "halo."

31. See E. Magalis, *Encyclopaedia of Religion* 10:446, s.v. "Nimbus"; J. E. Cirlot, *A Dictionary of Symbols*, 135.

32. For *hod* with respect to humans, cf. Num. 27:20, Jer. 22:18; Zech. 6:13, cf. 10:3; Ps. 21:6; 45:4; Dan. 11:21; 1 Chron. 29:25.

33. Num. 27:20, BB 75a et al. interpret *hod* in this passage as "light, radiance": "The face of Moses was like the face of the sun"; see Targs.

34. Zech. 6;13; Ps. 21:6; 45:4; Dan. 11:21; 1 Chron. 29:25.

35. 1 Sam. 8:4–22; Hos. 13:10–11.

36. Cf. Deut. 17:12–20; 1 Sam. 15:10–31; 2 Sam. 7:14; Ps. 89:31–33 etc.

37. The morphology and meaning of Heb. *tenah* are uncertain. Targ., Syr., Sym. Jerome all render as though the reading were *natatta*, from

n-t-n, "to give, put," so that the translation would be, "You have placed." Rashi explains, "It is fitting that You should place Your *hod* . . ." Ibn Ezra takes the form as a feminine infinitive like *redah* in Gen. 46:3. Kimḥi also understands *tenah* to be an infinitive but functioning as a perfect, like *'azov* in Jer. 14:5. Quite a different approach is suggested by Saadiah, who takes the underlying stem to be *t-n-h*, "to recite." This stem is found in Judg. 5:11; 11:40, and possibly in Hos. 8:9 (so *NJPS*). It appears in Ugar. *tny* (*UT* 192705), Aram. *tny*, Syr. *tn'* and tannaitic Heb. S. Morag, *JAOS* 92 (1972):299, points out that occurrences of *tnh* in biblical Hebrew are exclusively attested in texts showing affiliation with northern regions. He does not include *tenah* of our psalm as being definitely subsumed under this same stem (n. 5). H. L. Ginsberg, "Some Emendations in Psalms," *HUCA* 23, 1 (1950–51):98, accepts the emendation *tunnah*, "is praised." This was earlier suggested by H. Gunkel, *The Biblical World* 21 (1903):206–9, and is very convincing. For the syntax, cf. Hos. 14:4; Isa. 49:23; Jer. 32:19; Ps. 71:19–20; 84:4; 95:9; 139:15; 144:12.

38. So Ibn Ezra citing R. Moshe Gikatilla (eleventh century). Kimḥi refers to the ability of babes to feed at the breast.

39. The evidence has been marshalled by U. Cassuto, "The Israelite Epic," in *Biblical and Canaanite Literatures*, 1:62–90. *Kenesseth* 8 (1943): 121–42.

40. Isa. 51:9–10.

41. Hab. 3:8. On the affinities between Hab. chapter 3 and Ugaritic literature in general, cf. U. Cassuto, "Chapter iii of Habakkuk and the Ugaritic Texts," in *Biblical and Canaanite Literatures*, 2:118–28.

42. Ps. 74:13–14; cf. 77:17.

43. Ps. 89:11.

44. Ps. 104:5, 7, 9.

45. Job 7:12.

46. Job 9:13.

47. Job 26:12–13.

48. Job 38:4, 8, 11.

49. Gen. 1:9.

50. Hag. 12a.

51. BB 74b.

52. Exod. R. 15:22.

53. PdRE 5.

54. See Cassuto, *Biblical and Canaanite Literatures*, 1:20–54; 55–61.

55. Isa. 30:7.

56. Ezek. 29:3.

57. Ps. 74:12–14.

58. H. L. Ginsberg, *The Ugaritic Texts*, 76, nn. 8–9; Ginsberg, "Ugaritic Studies and the Bible," *BA* 8 (1945):54–55; N. M. Sarna, "The Psalm for the Sabbath Day," *JBL* 81 (1962):160f.

59. Ps. 29:1; 60:12; 77:15; 78:26; 93:1; 96:7; 105:4; cf. 66:3.

60. Isa. 51:9; Ps. 74:13; 89:11.

61. Lit. "enemy and avenger," a hendiadys.

62. On this literary technique, see *GKC* §167a.

63. For this deprecatory use of the particle *mah*, cf. Exod. 16:7, 8; Num. 16:11; 1 Sam. 9:8; 2 Sam. 6:20; 2 Kings 8:13; Ps. 144:3; Job 6:11; 7:17; 15:14; 21:15. On the phenomenon in general, see G. W. Coates, "Self-abasement and Insult Formulas," *JBL* 89 (1970):14–26. Coates (p. 18) finds no distinction in connotation between questions beginning with *mah* and those prefaced by *miy*, but it seems to me that the deliberate impersonal use of *mah* with a human being does intensify the inflection of abasement.

64. Cf. Akk *enešu*, to become weak, impoverished, etc., *CAD*, 4: 166–67.

65. Cf. 2 Sam. 12:15; Isa. 17:11; 51:12; Jer. 15:18; 30:12; Micah 1:9; Ps. 90:3; 103:15–16; Job 25:6.

66. The terms *'adam* and *ben 'adam* are used in contrast to God in Num. 23:19; Deut. 4:28–32; 1 Sam. 15:29; 2 Sam. 7:14; 24:14; 2 Kings 19:18; Isa. 2:17; 31:3; Ps. 14:2; 82:6–7; 115:16. Cf. Gen. 11:5 *bnei ha-'adam* to emphasize the insignificance of the arrogant tower builders.

67. So Jer. 3:16; 14:10; 15:15; Hos. 8:13; 9:9; Ps. 106:4.

68. For the benevolent use of *z-kh-r*, cf. Gen. 8:1; 19:29; Exod. 32:13; Ps. 9:13; 74:2; 106:4; for the punitive use, cf. 25:7; 79:8. For the benevolent use, of *p-k-d*, cf. Gen. 21:1; 50:24; 1 Sam. 2:21; Ps. 65:10; 80:15; 106:4; for the punitive connotation, cf. Exod. 20:5; 32:34; Ps. 59:6; 89:33. Note that in Ps. 144:3 the verbs *y-d-'* and *h-sh-v* replace the two used in verse 5 and are synonymous with them. Lachish letter II, lines 3–5 feature *z-kh-r* in the same sense as here.

69. LXX, Targ. Syr., followed by Saadiah, Rashi, Ibn Ezra and Kimḥi all render "angels." In Gen. 3:5, 22 *'elohim* takes a plural form of the verb, and certainly refers to the angels; cf. Gen. 28:12 *mal'akh*; 35:7 *'elohim*; 32:25 *'ish*; vv. 29, 31 *'elohim*; Hos. 12:5 *mal'akh*; Judg. 13:3, 9, 13, 15–18, 20, 21 *mal 'akh*; vv. 6, 8 *'ish 'elohim*; v. 22 *'elohim*; cf. Gen. 6:2, 4.

70. The conjoining of the two terms, as here, is unique. They appear in

a construct relationship in Ps. 145:5 (in reverse order) and in v. 12 (cf. v. 10); cf. Isa. 35:2; Ps. 21:6; 29:1–9; 96:6–9; as a royal endowment, cf. Ps. 21:6. In Ps. 45:4, 5 *hod* and *hadar* occur, but not *kavod*. As an attribute of ordinary people, *hadar* appears in Isa. 53:2; Prov. 20:29; Job 19:9. It is likely that *hadar* in Deut. 33:17 in reference to Joseph intimates kingship.

71. For the *'atarah* as an insignia of royalty, cf. 2 Sam. 12:30; Jer. 13:18; Ps. 21:4; as a sign of honor, cf. Zech. 6:11, 14; Song 3:11; Esth. 8:15. It is also frequently used figuratively, e.g., Isa. 28:1, 35; 62:3, etc.

72. Heb. *tahat* can also mean "at" as in Exod. 24:4; Deut. 4:11; 2 Sam. 22:39, cf. v. 43; Ps. 18:39, 43; 45:6; cf. Ugaritic I Aqht: 115–16, etc. However, the cognate examples favor translating *tahat* in Ps. 8:7 as "under."

73. Heidel, *The Babylonian Genesis*, 41; *ANET*, 67.

74. F. Thureau-Dangin, "La fin de la domination gutiene," *RA* 11 (1912):111–20; see *CAH* 1, 2: 461–63.

75. E. Weidner, *Die Inschriften Tukulti-Ninurtas I, AfO* Beiheft 12 (1959), r. 33:35.

76. *ANET*, 199.

77. *KAI*, No. 26, IA, line 16; *ANET*, 500.

78. Cf. *ANEP*, No. 308, 309, 393, 522–24.

79. With the exceptional Heb. form *tsoneh*, cf. Num. 32:24 *tsona'akhem*.

80. Lit. "oxen."

81. Heb. *bahamot sadai* recurs only in Joel 2:22; the nonpoetic form *behemot (ha-) sadeh* occurs in 1 Sam. 17:44; Joel 1:20. For the poetic form *sadai*, cf. Deut. 33:13; Hos. 10:4; 12:12; Isa. 56:9; Jer. 4:17; 18:14; Ps. 50:11; 80:14; 96:12; 104:11; Lam. 4:9.

82. Lit. "birds of the sky"; Heb. *tsippor shamayim* is unique, the usual phrase being *'of ha-shamayim*. Gen. 1:30; 2:19 etc; cf. Akk. *iṣṣur šamê*, Ugar. 52:62 *'ṣr šmm*.

83. Lit. "fish of the sea," so Gen. 9:2; Num. 11:22, etc. In Gen. 1:26, 28 the form is *dgat ha-yam*.

84. This phrase is unique.

CHAPTER THREE: PSALM 19

1. See Sarna, *Understanding Genesis*, 1–80; Sarna, *JPS Commentary on Genesis*.

2. Josh. 15:10; 19:41; 15:7; Judg. 1:35; 8:13.

3. Exod. 20:4–5; Deut. 5:8–9.

4. Deut. 4:19.

5. Deut. 17:3–5.

6. 2 Kings 21:3, 5; 23:4–5, 11–12.

7. 2 Kings chs. 22–23; 2 Chron. ch. 24.

8. Zeph. 1:5.

9. Jer. 7:18; 8:1–2; 19:13; 44:17, 19, 25. Cf. the Old Assyrian version of the Epic of Gilgamesh, Tablet III, ii. 7ff. *ANET*, 81: Ninsun ascends the stairs of the palace to make offerings to Shamash.

10. Ezek. 8:16, on which see T. H. Gaster, "Ezekiel and the Mysteries," *JBL* 60 (1941):289–310.

11. See M. Cogan, *Imperialism and Religion: Assyria, Judah and Israel in the Eighth and Seventh Centuries B.C.E.* See also J. W. McKay, *Religion in Judah under the Assyrians,* esp. 31 ff.; F. I. Hollis, "The Sun-cult in Jerusalem," in S. H. Hooke, ed., *Myth and Ritual,* 87–110; but see the observations of M. Haran, "The Priestly Image of the Tabernacle," *HUCA* 36 (1965):206, n. 31. See also M. Smith, "The Near Eastern Background of Solar Language for Yahweh," *JBL* 109 (1990):29–39.

12. See N. M. Sarna, "Psalm XIX and the Near Eastern Sun-god Literature," in *Fourth World Congress of Jewish Studies Papers,* 171–75.

13. Cf. O. Eissfeldt, *The Old Testament: An Introduction,* trans. P. R. Ackroyd, 446; S. Mowinckel, *Psalms in Israel's Worship,* 1:90f. appears to favor Ps. 19 as a unity, whereas in vol. 2, pp. 190 and 267, he seems to prevaricate on the subject. On the other hand, O. Schroeder, *ZAW* 34(1914):69f., and L. Duerr in *Sellin Festschrift,* 37–48, showed that the two motifs of the psalm intermingle in the Mesopotamian Shamash hymns.

14. The same sevenfold repetition of the tetragrammaton appears in Pss. 29 and 92.

15. See F. M. Cross, s.v. " *'el*" in *TDOT* 1:242–81.

16. See J. R. Bram, s.v. "Sun" *ER* 14:132–43; P. Gelling and H. R. Ellis Davidson, *The Chariot of the Sun*; J. Hawkes, *Man and Sun.*

17. See A. Berlin, *Poetics and Interpretation of Biblical Narrative,* 127, regarding this construction.

18. *GKC* §116a.

19. Lit. "The heaven of heavens"; so Deut. 10:14; 1 Kings 8:27; 2 Chron. 6:18; Ps. 148:4; Neh. 9:6; 2 Chron. 2:5. In R. H. 32a, Men. 39a mention is

made of "seven firmaments (*reki'im*)." Hag. 12b mentions "two firmaments," and also seven such.

20. So Gen. 22:11; Deut. 26:15; Isa. 63:15; 66:1; Ezek. 1:25–26 et al. But 1 Kings 8:27 clearly militates against a literal understanding.

21. Gen. 24:3, 7; Jonah 1:9; Ezra 1:2; Neh. 1:4, 5 et al. For "Heaven" as an epithet for God in rabbinic literature cf. Ber. 53b, Shab. 5a, Shek. 5a, Kid. 33b, Sot. 47b et al. See A. Marmorstein, *The Old Rabbinic Doctrine of God*, 1:56.

22. On *raki'a*, see Sarna, *JPS Commentary on Genesis*, 8, 353 n. 15.

23. Cf. Hag. 12b, based on Gen. 1:14–15, 17.

24. *ANET*, 136c; C. H. Gordon, *Ugaritic Literature*, 19; U. Cassuto, *The Goddess Anath*, 92–93, 128.

25. See S. Sambursky, *The Physical World of the Greeks*, 55f.

26. Heb. *kavvam* has occasioned much scholarly discussion. The context and associated words (*'omer, devarim, kolam, milleihem*) all express audible sound, and thus suggest a meaning for *kavvam* within the same semantic range. The Greek renders the word by *phthongos*, "speech, sound"; Symmachus has "echo, speech, report"; the Vulgate translates *sonus*, "sound." The same understanding appears in Romans 10:18, "their voice." However, Aquila has *kanon*, "line, extent," as in 1 Kings 7:23; Isa. 44:13; Jer. 31:38; Ezek. 47:3; Zech. 1:16; Job 38:5; Lam. 2:8; 2 Chron. 4:2 et al. It is to be noted that Gk. *kanon* is also a musicological term; see H. G. Liddell and R. Scott, *A Greek-English Lexicon*, 875 s.v. *kanon* 10; cf. Italian *corda*, "a string," as of a piano and the musical instruction *una corda*. That sound can be construed as a line was one of the underlying ideas of the Aristoxenian musical theory (fourth cent. B.C.E.); see *The Oxford Classical Dictionary*, 2nd ed. (Oxford, 1977), 708. P. Haupt, *JBL* 38 (1919):180–83 points to "cord, string," hence, "tone, note, sound." The Targum and medieval Jewish commentators, Saadiah, Ibn Janah, Rashi, and Kimhi all take *kav* to mean "line." H. L. Ginsberg, *JAOS* 88 (1968):48 n. 7, understands "muttering, murmuring," based on Isa. 18:2, 7; 28:10, 13. Z. Rin, *Leshonenu* 27 (1963):14, connects with Ugar. *g*, "voice," with infixed *vav* as in *tsah* becomes *tsvah*. The appearance of *kav* in the Hodayot 1:29–30 from Qumran is interesting but not helpful, although A. M. Haberman, *Megilloth Midbar Yehuda*, 202n, accords it "the meaning kol, 'voice,' as in Ps. 19." Similarly unclear is the phrase *mizmor 'al kav* in the Masada manuscript of Ben Sira 44:5. (See Y. Yadin, *Eretz-Israel* 8 (1967):36 n. 45. The Cairo MS B (see M. Z. Segal, *Sefer Ben*

Sira Ha-Shalem, 302 and 305n) reads *ḥok in place of kav*. P. W. Skehan, *BASOR* 200 (1970):69, regards *ḥok* as "inherently superior."

27. The Hebrew employs wordplay or, rather, double entendre. The root *sis* mostly means "to be joyful," but the primary denotation is "to run, to be in a state of great agitation." This sense is still preserved in Zeph. 3:17; Ps. 119:14 (cf. v. 32); Isa. 8:6. This last is a play on Rezin, taken as derived from the root *r-w-ts* "to run." In Job 39:21 *sis* describes the action of the horse. On the root, se T. Noeldeke, *Beiträger zur Semitischen Sprachwissenschaft*, 42; M. Elioenai, "On the Meaning of the Verb *s-w-s/s-y-s*" [Hebrew], *Beth Mikra* 42 (1960):323–26. The Targum to Job from Qumran Cave XI, col. xxxiii, 3, lines 2–3 on Job 39:21 has a conflation of two renderings of *yasis*; see the edition of M. Sokoloff (Ramat Gan, 1976), 92, 155 and N. M. Sarna, *IEJ* 26 (1976):152.

28. Heb. *ḥammato* should be rendered "His sun"; cf. Isa. 24:23; 30:26; Song 6:10; Job 30:28. This was noted by C. A. Briggs, *The Book of Psalms*, 1:167f.

29. *ANET*, 391. On this passage, see A. Jeremias, *Handbuch der Alto-rientalischen Geistkultur*, 20, who interpreted it as a reference to Shamash leaving the house of his beloved Aya each morning and returning thereto at night.

30. S. N. Kramer, "Sumerian Similes: A Panoramic View of Some of Man's Oldest Literary Images," *JAOS* 89 (1969):1–10. The Sumerian term for the sleeping chamber, *ganun*, is echoed in the Targum's rendering of *ḥuppah* by *ginun*—Isa. 4:5; Joel 2:16; Ps. 19:6.

31. Akk. *kallatu*; see K. Tallqvist, *Akkadische Götterepitheta*, 110 ff., 168; *CAD*, 8:81c); D. O. Edzard in H. W. Haussig, ed., *Wörterbuch der Mythologie*, 1:126. An inventory from Ugarit, UT 1175.2, mentions *klt bt špš*, "bride of the Sun-temple." For the bridegroom compared to the sun in Indian mythology, see S. Thompson, *Motif Index of Folk Literature*, 5:Z62.2.

32. Hebrew *'-h-l* is a secondary root of *h-l-l*; cf. Job 25:5. For *h-l-l*, "to shine," cf. Isa. 13:10; Job 29:3; 31:26; 41:10.

33. The Akkadian epithet is *quradu/qarradu*; see Tallqvist, *Götterepitheta*, 162f., 174, 457; Tallqvist, *Der Assyrische Gott*, 99, 107 n. 3. For the pictorial representation, see H. Frankfort, *Ancient Egyptian Religion*, 100f., 105–8. On the sun as warrior, see G. H. Halsberghe, *The Cult of Sol Invictus*.

34. H. G. Güterbock, "The Composition of Hittite Prayers to the Sun," *JAOS* 78 (1958): 241.

35. *ANET*, 365, 367f., 370; M. Lichtheim, *Ancient Egyptian Literature*, 2:87; T. G. Allen, *The Egyptian Book of the Dead*, 86, 285; A. Scharff, *Aegyptische Sonnenlieder*, 32f., 37, 39, 41 et al.; Frankfort, *Ancient Egyptian Religion*, 132.

36. So in the Babylonian Shamash hymn; see W. G. Lambert, *Babylonian Wisdom Literature*, 127 line 20; 129 line 37; cf. 282; Güterbock, "Hittite Prayers," 240.

37. Tallqvist, *Götterepitheta*, 456f.; H. Frankfort, *Kingship and the Gods*, 150–57; *CAD* 3:32, 1) 2–3b; 17i:459, points out that only in referring to Shamash is *shapiṭu* used in the same meaning as *dayānu*. See also G. D. Young, "UTU and Justice: A Neo-Sumerian Proverb," *JCS* 24(1972):132.

38. See F. Guirand in *Larousse Encyclopedia of Mythology* (New York, 1960), 72.

39. Güterbock, "Hittite Prayers," 241.

40. B. Meissner, *Babylonien und Assyrien*, 1:148f.; 2:2, 21, 47.

41. *ANET*, 523.

42. *ANET*, 161.

43. *ANET*, 164f., 178f.; *ANEP*, No. 245, No. 515, and p. 310.

44. *ANET*, 523, 526.

45. *ANET*, 387–89; Lambert, *Babylonian Wisdom Literature*, 121–38.

46. *ANET*, 24, 366f.; J. A. Wilson, *Culture of Ancient Egypt*, 119; Frankfort, *Ancient Egyptian Religion*, 15, 117; Frankfort, *Kingship and the Gods*, 157, 308; E. O. James, *Ancient Gods*, 200f.

47. J. E. Harrison, *Epilegomena to the Study of Greek Religion*, 439; M. K. C. Guthrie, *The Greeks and Their Gods*, 183–87, 203.

48. For the idiom, cf. 1 Kings 17:21; Ps. 35:17; Job 33:30; Ruth 4:15; Lam. 1:11, 16, 19.

49. Lichtheim, *Ancient Egyptian Literature*, 87, 91f., 97f.

50. Tallqvist, *Götterepitheta*, p. 456f.

51. Güterbock, "Hittite Prayers," 239 (variant reading).

52. Cf. Akk. *adû*, *CAD*, 1, i:131–34; 'dy' in Old Aram., cf. *KAI*, No. 222, A, line 7. K. H. Kitchen, *Ancient Orient and Old Testament*, 108, points out that a twelfth century B.C.E. Egyptian text features this word as a Canaanite loanword.

53. Exod. 25:16, cf. v. 22; 26:33–34; 31:18; 39:35; 40:3, 5, 21; cf. also 38:21; Lev. 24:3; Num. 9;15; 17:19.

54. 1 Kings 2:3; Ps. 78:5; 132:15.

55. Tallqvist, *Götterepitheta*, pp. 47, 104–6; cf. 465.

56. *ANET*, 368, line 9; Lichtheim, *Ancient Egyptian Literature*, 88.

57. For the parallelism of *'or*, "light," and the root *s-m-ḥ*, "to shine, be happy," cf. Pss. 97:11; 107:42; 119:74; Prov. 13:9; see J. C. Greenfield, "Lexicographical Notes II," *HUCA* 30 (1959):141–51 for a study of that root; cf. also S. Morag, *Tarbiz* 33(1964): 144.

58. *UT* 1005, lines 2–4; cf. J. Nougayrol, *Le Palais Royal d'Ugarit III* (Paris, 1955):57f., 66, 68, 70, 102, 110f.; *CAD* 17:336, 2)b.

59. Cf. 1 Sam. 14:27, 29; Pss. 13:4; 36:10; 38:11. The same idiom is used in tannaitic Hebrew; cf. M. Yoma 8:6. For "light" as "life," cf. Ps. 56:14; Job 3:20; 18:18; 33:30; Eccl. 11:7. The same image appears in Gilgamesh 10, i:1.

60. On "fear of the Lord," see J. Becker, *Gottesfurcht im Alten Testament*; M. Pope, *Job*, AB, Garden City, N.Y., 1965, to Job 15:4; M. Weinfeld, *Deuteronomy and the Deuteronomic School*, 274–81.

61. S. Langdon, *Building Inscriptions of the Neo-Babylonian Empire*, 98, lines 23–25; *CAD* 4 *elēlu* 1a, p. 81.

62. *UT* 2008.7.

63. *KAI* No. 26, III, i.19; *ANET*, 500.

64. Lambert, *Babylonian Wisdom Literature*, 129, line 64; cf. p. 138, line 199; *ANET*, 388.

65. Lambert, *Babylonian Wisdom Literature*, 233f.

66. E. A. Wallis Budge, *The Book of the Dead*, 112f., 498f.

67. Xenophon, *Memorabilia*, iv, 2, para. 9, p. 274f.

68. Ps. 119:72; Prov. 3:13–14; 8:10, 19; Job 28:15–17.

69. See above to Psalm 1, pp. 36–37.

70. Frankfort, *Kingship and the Gods*, 379, n. 9; 46; cf. 135, 149.

71. Lichtheim, *Ancient Egyptian Literature*, 87; *ANET*, 367.

72. M. Eliade, *The Forge and the Crucible*, 49.

73. Judg. 14:18.

74. Deut. 32:13; Judg. 14:8f.; 1 Sam. 14:25f.; Ps. 81:17.

75. *ANET*, 366.

76. Güterbock, "Hittite Prayers," 243. It is pertinent that in Greek mythology Aristaeus, who taught men the art of agriculture, was the son or servant of Apollo; see R. Graves, *The Greek Myths*, para. 82.1 and n. 6.

77. N. H. Tur-Sinai, *Ha-Lashon Ve-Ha-Sefer II*, 2:93, has plausibly suggested that the use of *nizhar* in v. 12 may have been influenced by the

meaning of "to shine, glow," which the root *z-h-r* can bear in Hebrew (Dan. 12:3), Aramaic, and Arabic.

78. See B. A. Levine, *JPS Commentary on Leviticus*, 19 to Lev. 4:2; J. Milgrom, *JPS Commentary to Numbers*, 122f. to Num. 15:22–31.

79. See Berlin, *Dynamics of Biblical Parallelism*, 59.

80. Hebrew *zedim* more likely means "arrogant men" than sins committed willfully, which would be *zedonot*, as in postbiblical Hebrew.

81. Cf. Gen. 8:21; Jer. 17:9–10; Eccl. 7:20.

82. Cf. Ps. 86:14; Prov. 21:24; Mal. 3:15, 19.

83. Cf. Ps. 119:21, 51, 69, 78.

84. On the verb *hgh*, see Ps. 1 above, pp. 37–39. On *lev* as an organ of speech, see H. L. Ginsberg, *Encyclopaedia Judaica*, 8:7 s.v. "heart."

85. Cf. Exod. 28:38; Lev. 1:3; 7:18; 19:7; 22:19, 20, 21, 23, 25, 27, 29; 23:11.

86. Cf. Exod. 12:5; Lev. 1:3, 10; 3:1, 6; 4:3, 23 et al.

87. On God as "Rock," see M. P. Knowels, *VT* 39 (1989):307–22.

CHAPTER FOUR: PSALMS 15 AND 24

Psalm 15

1. H. G. Gunkel, *Die Psalmen*, 48; Gunkel and J. Begrich, *Einleitung in die Psalmen*, 327ff., 408f.; Gunkel, *The Psalms: A Form-Critical Introduction*, 22; S. Mowinckel, *The Psalms in Israel's Worship*, 1:177–80; O. Eissfeldt, *The Old Testament: An Introduction*, 74, uses the phrase, "Admission Torah"; J. H. Hayes, *Understanding the Psalms*, 44–46.

2. See M. Weinfeld, "Instructions for Visitors in the Bible and in Ancient Egypt," *Egyptological Studies*, 224–50.

3. E. A. Wallis Budge, *The Book of the Dead* [reprint], New York, 1960; T. G. Allen, *The Egyptian Book of the Dead*.

4. Wallis Budge, *Book of the Dead*, 572–84; Allen, *Egyptian Book of the Dead*, 97–99; *ANET*, 34–36; M. Lichtheim, *Ancient Egyptian Literature*, 2:124–32; S. G. F. Brandon, *The Judgment of the Dead*, 6–48; A. J. Spenser, *Death in Ancient Egypt*, 139–64.

5. H. W. Fairman, "Worship and Festivals in an Egyptian Temple," *BJRL*, 37(1954):165–203. See H. Ringgren, *The Faith of the Psalmists*, 120, for an

excerpt in English of Egyptian inscriptions in the temples at Edfu and Dendera from R. Alliot, *Le culte d'Horus à Edfou*, 1:184f., referring to the duties of the priest.

6. *ANET*, 573.

7. In biblical times the Israelite was required to undertake a pilgrimage to the religious center three times a year, as enjoined in Exod. 23:14–17; 34:23; Deut. 16:16.

8. Cf. Deut. 16:16–17.

9. 2 Sam. ch. 11.

10. Jer. 7:3–11.

11. S. Lieberman, *Hellenism in Jewish Palestine*, 164–66, cites the Targum to 2 Sam. 5:8, which states that sinful persons do not enter the Temple.

12. On the prophetic versus the psalmodic attitude to sacrifice and morality, see Y. Kaufmann, *Toledot Ha-'Emunah Ha-Yisre'elit*, 1:31–34; 2:643 and n. 16.

13. Isa. 16:15; 33:20; Jer. 10:20; Ps. 27:5–6; 61:5; Lam. 2:4.

14. Cf. Exod. 26:7 and throughout the Exodus account of the wilderness Tabernacle; cf. 2 Sam. 7:6; Ps. 78:60, 67. The same poetic convention is found in Ugaritic texts, cf. 128:iii:18; 2 Aqht v:32.

15. Cf. Isa. 11:9; 27:13; 56:7; 57:13; 65:11, 25; 66:20; Jer. 31:23(22); Ezek. 20:40; 28:14; Joel 2:1; 4:17; Ob. 16; Zeph. 3:11; Zech. 8:3; Ps. 2:6; 3:5; 43:3; 48:2; 99:9; Dan. 9:16, 20.

16. Cf. Gen. 22:14; Num. 10:33; Isa. 2:3; 30:29; Mic. 4:2; Zech. 8:3.

17. Exod. 3:1; 4:27; 18:5; 24:13; 1 Kings 19:8; Ezek. 28:16; Ps. 68:16.

18. Exod. ch. 3.

19. Josh. 5:15.

20. 2 Sam. ch. 6.

21. Cf. Isa. 33.14, 16; Ps. 61:5.

22. Lev. 25:23.

23. Ps. 39:13.

24. Ps. 119:19.

25. 1 Chron. 29:15.

26. Cf. Gen. 15:13, in which the future affliction is the corollary of the status of stranger.

27. Exod. 22:20; 23:9; Lev. 19:33–34; Deut. 10:19; 24:14, 17; 27:19; Jer. 7:6; 22:3; Zech. 7:10.

28. Lev. 19:34; Deut. 10:19; Mal. 3:5; cf. Job 31:32.

29. Deut. 10:18; cf. Ps. 146:9.

30. See W. Robertson Smith, *The Religion of the Semites*, 76, 269. The story of Lot and his two visitors and his attempt to protect them, as told in Gen. 19:1-11, well illustrates this code of honor. Cf. Judg. ch. 19.

31. Smith, *Religion of the Semites*, 77 notes that Arabs give the title *jar* (Heb. *ger*) *'allah* to one who resides in Mecca beside the Kaaba. In Ugaritic text 1 Aqht:153 *gr bt 'il* occurs. In Phoenician and Punic, theophoric names compounded of *gr* are abundant, e.g., *gr'smn, grb l, grmlk, grspn, grskn, grastrt*. Also of particular interest are *gr'hl, grhkl*; see I. L. Bentz, *Personal Names in the Phoenician and Punic Inscriptions* (Rome, 1982), 178, 296; cf. J. Naveh, "Unpublished Phoenician Inscriptions from Palestine," *IEJ* 37 (1987):25-26; see also *TDOT* 1:440-41; cf. M. Heltzer, *PEQ* 114 (1982):2.

32. Hebrew: *shakan*.

33. Cf. Gen. 9:27; 16:12; 35:21-22; Num. 24:2, 5; Judg. 8:11; 2 Sam. 7:5-6; Ps. 78:55, 60; 120:5; Job 11:14; 18:15. On the verb *škn*, see F. M. Cross, "The Tabernacle," *BA*, 10 (1947):66 and n. 29; Cross, *Canaanite Myth and Hebrew Epic*, 241-46.

34. Num. 16:24, 26-27; 24:5; Isa. 54:2; Jer. 30:18; Ezek. 25:4; Job 21:28; Song 1:8. See also Y. Avishur, *The Construct State of Synonyms in Biblical Rhetoric*, 11-13.

35. E.g., Heb. *mishkan ha-'edut*, in Exod. 38:21; Num. 1:53, 10:11 is interchangeable with *'ohel ha 'edut* in Num. 9:15; 17:22-23; 18:2; 2 Chron. 24:6.

36. Mowinckel, *Psalms in Israel's Worship*, 1:158, 179 counts ten demands and sees here a "decalogical tradition"; so also O. Eissfeldt, *Old Testament*, 74, who counts "exactly ten qualities." Note that the fragment of Psalms 15 and 16 discovered at Nahal Hever omits the first clause of verse 3; see Y. Yadin, "Expedition D," *IEJ*, 11 (1961):40. On the "decalogical tradition," see S. H. Weingarten, *Beth Mikra* 59 (1974): 561f.

37. Makkot 23b-24a; cf. *Mid. Tehillim*, ed. S. Buber, 119.

38. Cf. Gen. 17:1; Exod. 18:20; Lev. 18:3; 2 Kings 20:3; Isa. 38:3; Jer. 23:17; Ezek. 13:3; Mic. 2:7; 6:16; Mal. 2:6; Ps. 1:1; Prov. 28:18; Job 31:7. Akk. *alāku* features the same semantic development; see *CAD*, I, 1 *alāku* 3. Abraham ibn Ezra takes the phrase as ellipsis for "walking [in the way of the] blameless."

39. Cf. Ezek. 28:15; Ps. 101:2, 6; Prov. 11:5-20.

40. See J. Pedersen, *Israel*, 1, see index "heart."

41. Ps. 12:3.

42. Ps. 55:22.

43. Isa. 29:13.

44. Targ. and Pesh. here treat *'al* as the equivalent of the preposition *b-*; Yalon, *Pirkei Lashon*, 342, points to the similar use of *'al* in Gen. 27:40; Exod. 6:26, and the interchange of *'al* and *b-* in Lev. 12:4–5. David Kimḥi on Isa. 14:12 had already noted this usage. For a different understanding of *ragal*, see N. Bronznick, *Beth Mikra* 71 (1977):445–52. Note that Hebrew Ben Sira 4:31 has *'el* and 5:18 has *b-*.

45. Isa. 32:14; Jer. 9:4; Ps. 37:30; 39:5; Job 33:2, all with *dibber*; Ps. 35:28; 71:24; Job 27:4 with *h-g-h*, "to utter."

46. Exod. 23:1.

47. Lev. 19:16; see B. Levine, *JPS Commentary on Leviticus*, 129, for another possible interpretation.

48. Deut. 22:13–19.

49. For *'a-s-h* in the sense of "to cause," cf. 2 Kings 19:31; Isa. 9:6; 37:32; Jer. 2:17; 4:18.

50. For this sense of *ns' 'al*, cf. Jer. 15:15; Zeph. 3:18; Ps. 69:8.

51. This rendering of v.4a takes *nivzeh* as the subject of *nim'as*, so LXX and Rashi. Targ., Saad., Ibn Ezra, Kimḥi all understood the clause to express self-abasement: "He is contemptible and repugnant in his own eyes"; such an exaggerated formulation of humility seems to be unlikely.

52. Cf. Lev. 27:10, 33.

53. Cf. Lev. 5:4; so Rashi, Ibn Ezra, Kimḥi, LXX, Pesh. read *le-re'ehu*, "to his neighbor."

54. Suk. 56b.

55. Cf. Ps. 132:2 where an oath and vow are paired; see J. Milgrom, *JPS Commentary to Numbers*, Excursus 66, 488–90.

56. E.g., 1 Sam. 14:44; 2 Sam. 3:35; 1 Kings 2:23; 20:10. For the most part, the details of the imprecation are suppressed, probably for superstitious reasons.

57. Exod. 20:7; Deut. 5:11; Lev. 5:22, 24; 19:12; cf. Isa. 48:1; Jer. 5:2; 7:9; Zeph. 1:5; Zech. 5:4.

58. Lev. 5:4; 22:18; Num. ch. 30; Deut. 12:26; 23:22–24.

59. Eccl. 5:3–5; 8:2; cf. 9:2.

60. *Josephus, The Jewish War*, 135, ed. H. St.J. Thackeray, 395; cf. Tanh. *mattot* (Num. 30), ed. S. Buber, 157.

61. The Hebrew term used here for "interest" is *neshekh*. Elsewhere in the Bible this word is paired with *t/marbit*: Lev. 25:36–37; Ezek. 18:8, 13, 17; 22:12; Prov. 28:8. The difference between the two terms has long been a matter of dispute. Mish. BM 5:1 interprets *neshekh* as receiving more money or produce than was lent, whereas *t/marbit* is understood to involve increasing the amount lent by taking advantage of changes in the price of market produce. Rava in BM 60b takes the two terms to be synonymous. *Neshekh*, literally "a bite," may reflect the perspective of the borrower, and *tarbit*, literally "increase," the perspective of the lender. Other interpretations take *neshekh* to refer to advance interest, that is, interest deducted immediately from the amount of the loan; *tarbit* to accrued interest. On taking interest in the Bible, see E. Neufeld, "The Prohibition Against Loans at Interest in Ancient Hebrew Laws," *HUCA* 26 (1955): 355–412; S. E. Loewenstamm, "Neshekh and T/Marbit," JBL 88 (1969):78–80; B. Levine, *JPS Commentary on Leviticus*, 178 to Lev. 25:36.

62. So Ezek. 18:8; 22:12.

63. Tanḥ. *mishpatim* 5, 83–84; see Rashi *ad loc*.

64. Ezek. 18:8, 13, 17; 22:12.

65. Deut. 24:10.

66. Deut. v. 17.

67. Exod. 22:25–26; 24:12–13.

68. Deut. 24:6. For the rabbinic understanding of this prohibition, see Mish. BB 9:13; Tos. 10:11.

69. Deut. 15:1–2.

70. 1 Sam. 22:2.

71. 2 Kings 4:1.

72. Amos 2:8.

73. Neh. 5:13.

74. Lev. 19:2; Deut. 10:12, 17–18; 11:22; 26:17; cf. *Mekhilta de-Rabbi Ishmael, shirah* 3, ed. J. Z. Lauterbach, 25: "Abba Saul says, 'O be like Him! Just as He is gracious and merciful, so be you gracious and merciful' "; cf. Sotah 14a: "R. Hama son of R. Hanina said, What is the meaning of the scriptural text, 'you shall follow the Lord your God' (Deut. 13:5)?–to follow the attributes of the Holy One . . . blessed be He. Just as He clothes the naked (Gen. 3:21) . . . so should you . . . Just as He visited the sick (Gen. 18:1) . . . so do you . . . Just as He comforted mourners (Gen. 25:11) . . . so do you . . . Just as He buried the dead (Deut. 34:6) . . . so do you."

75. Deut. 10:17–18.

76. 2 Chron. 19:5–7.

77. 1 Sam. 12:3.

78. 1 Sam. 8:1–3.

79. The prophet here uses Heb. *kofer*, not the usual *shoḥad*. On *kofer*, see S. M. Paul, *Amos*, 174.

80. Amos 5:12.

81. Isa. 1:23.

82. Isa. 5:23.

83. Mic. 3:11.

84. Ezek. 22:12.

85. Prov. 17:23.

86. Cf. Exod. 23:8; Deut. 10:17; 16:19; 27:25; 1 Sam. 8:3; Isa. 5:23; 33:15; Ezek. 22:12; Prov. 17:23; 2 Chron. 19:7.

87. Gen. 23:10, 18.

88. Gen. 34:20, 24.

89. 2 Sam. 15:2.

90. Ruth 4:1, 11.

91. Amos 5:15.

92. Isa. 29:21.

93. Cf. Deut. 22:15; 25:7; Josh. 20:4; Prov. 2:22; Job 5:4.

94. A. Biran, "Tel Dan," *BA* 37 (1974):43–48.

95. Deut. 21:19–20; 22:15; 25:7; Prov. 31:23; Job 29:7, 12; Ruth 4:1–2, 11; Lam. 5:15.

96. Isa. 24:18–20.

97. Isa. 54:10.

98. Ps. 46:3–4.

99. Ps. 82:5.

100. Ps. 93:1; 96:10; 1 Chron. 16:30.

101. Ps. 104:5.

102. Ps. 55:23; 66:9; 112:6; 125:1; Prov. 10:30; 12:3.

Psalm 24

103. The other daily psalms are 48, 82, 94, 81, 93, 92 respectively. Aside from Tuesday's Ps. 82 and Thursday's 81, each psalm bears the appropriate

daily designation in the Greek superscription. The two omissions have not been satisfactorily explained.

104. The listing appears in an anonymous appendix to Mish. Tam. 7:4, in a *baraita* in Rosh Ha-Shanah 31a attributed to Rabbi Akiba as cited by Rabbi Judah, in AdRN 1, ed. S. Schechter, 3rd corrected ed. (New York, 1967), 5; on which see J. Goldin, *The Fathers According to Rabbi Nathan*, 11, 177, n. 48; Cf. Sof. 18:1, ed. M. Higger, 308. In our received Hebrew text, only Ps. 92 connects the composition with a day of the week.

105. On the daily Temple ritual, see S. Bialoblotzki, "Yerushalayim Be-Halakhah" in *'Alei 'Ayin. The Salman Schocken Jubilee Volume*, 25–74, esp. p. 59.

106. Cambridge ms. 73, published by W. H. Lowe under the title *Matnita' de-Talmuda' di-Venei Ma'arava'*, carries an appendix to Mish. Tam. giving the reason for the selection of Ps. 24 for Sundays: "On the first day [of Creation] the Holy One, blessed be He, created His world." Rosh Ha-Shanah 31a similarly explains, "because He took possession, and assigned [to humanity], and ruled over His world." AdRN, 1, 5, reads in the final clause, "and He will judge the world."

107. Pointed out by L. Liebreich, "The Hymns of the Levites for the Days of the Week," *Eretz-Israel* 3 (1954):171. The verb *ns'* also appears six times.

108. Heb. *tevel* means the inhabited part of the world. The term appears thirty-six times in the Bible, exclusively in poetic texts, and never with the definite article; cf. Akk. *eli tabali*, "by land," as opposed to *eli nari*, "by river/water."

109. Cf. Ps. 50:12; 89:12.

110. The use of the plural forms here may simply be "plural of intensity"; cf. Jonah 2:4 *yammim* but sing. *nahar* and the reverse in Hab. 3:8.

111. See above Psalm 8, n. 39, p. 226.

112. For the verb *'-l-h*, "to ascend," in the sense of going up to a place of worship, cf. Gen. 35:3; Exod. 34:24; Deut. 17:8; 1 Sam. 1:7, 21, 10:13; 2 Kings 19:14; 20:5, 8; 23:2; Isa. 10:13; 2 Kings 19:14; 20:5, 8; 23:2; Isa. 2:3; Mic. 4:2; Isa. 37:14; Jer. 31:5 (6); 2 Chron. 29:20; 34:30.

113. Heb. *makom*, like Arab *maqam*, frequently carries the sense of "sacred site"; cf. Gen. 12:6; 13:3, 4; 22:4; 28:11, 17, 19, 32:3, 31; 33:17; 35:7, 15; Deut. 12 *passim*; 1 Sam. 7:16 with respect to the shrines at Bethel, Gilgal, and Mitzpah, cf. LXX *ad loc*. The term also has this meaning in Isa. 26:21;

66:1; Mic. 1:2–3; Ps. 26:8; 103:22; 132:5. Most instructive is *makom* in 1 Chron. 16:27, which is replaced by *mikdash*, "temple," in the parallel Ps. 96:6. In rabbinic texts *ha-makom* is an epithet of God; see Marmorstein, *The Old Rabbinic Doctrine of God*, 1:92–93.

114. Lit. "what is merited." For *tsedakah* in this sense, cf. Gen. 15:6; Ps. 106:31. The word means success in Isa. 41:2; 46:13; 48:18; 51:5; 54:17; 61:10; Prov. 8:18; 21:21.

115. This meaning of *dor* also appears in Ps. 14:5; 75:15, and in Phoenician-Punic, as evidenced by Karatepe III.19; *KAI*, 26A III.19, and in Ugaritic, see *UT* 19.697.

116. The Hebrew phrase *ns'nefesh*, with the sole uncertain exception of 2 Sam. 14:14, invariably means "to long for, aspire to"; cf. Deut. 24:15; Hos. 4:8; Ps. 25:1; 86:4; 143:8; Prov. 19:18. Note that LXX, Pesh., and Targ. all presuppose the reading *nafsho*. The critical masoretic commentary, *minhat shai*, by Jedidiah Solomon of Norzi (sixteenth–seventeenth cents.) concludes that the correct reading is *nafsho*, the supposed *Qre* reading *nafshi* being an error: the final *vav* is *qetia'*, "cut short."

117. Deut. 4:29; Judg. 6:29; Isa. 65:1; Jer. 29:13; Zeph. 1:6; Ps. 105:4; 1 Chron. 16:11; 2 Chron. 20:3–4.

118. The distinction is clear from the fact that whereas one finds *bakkesh penei YHVH*, "to seek the Presence of the Lord" (2 Sam. 12:16; 21:1; Hos. 5:15; Ps. 27:8; 105:4; 1 Chron. 16:11; 2 Chron. 7:14), the verb *darash* never takes *panim* as its object. For this reason, the hypothetical restoration of F. M. Cross, "The Divine Warrior in Israel's Early Cult," in *Biblical Motifs: Origins and Transformations*, 1966:20, is implausible.

119. Cf. e.g., Gen. 25:22; Exod. 18:15; Deut. 4:29; Isa. 9:12; Hos. 10:12; Amos 5:4, 6; Ps. 9:11; 22:27; 34:5, 11, etc.

120. 1 Kings 7:7.

121. Gen. 44:23, cf. v. 6.

122. Exod. 10:28, cf. v. 29.

123. 2 Sam. 14:24, 28; cf. v. 32.

124. Cf. 2 Sam. 3:3; 1 Kings 10:24; 2 Chron. 9:23; 2 Kings 25:19; Jer. 52:25; Hos. 3:5; Esth. 1:14; cf. Prov. 29:26.

125. See M. Z. Brettler, *God Is King: Understanding an Israelite Metaphor*, for a thorough study of the phenomenon.

126. Cf. 2 Sam. 12:16; 21:1; Hos. 5:15.

127. Ps. 27:8 9, cf. v. 4; 105:4; 1 Chron. 16:11, cf. v. 1. Note that "to

see the face of the Lord" always appears in the Hebrew Bible with the verb in the *nif'al* form: Exod. 23:15, 17; 34:20, 23, 24; Deut. 16:16; 31:11; 1 Sam. 1:22; Isa. 1:2; Ps. 42:3. The most plausible explanation for this peculiarity is that of A. Geiger, *Urschrift und Übersetzungen der Bible*, 336, 341; 2nd ed.; 237f., Hebrew translation by J. L. Baruch, *Ha-Mikra' Ve-Targumav*, 218–19, 337–40, that pious scribes changed the vowels of the theologized phrase in order to avoid the anthropomorphism.

128. Exod. 16:7, 10; 19:16–21; 24:16; 40:34–37; Num. 10:34; 17:7; cf. 1 Kings 8:10–11.

129. Exod. 3:2; 19:18; 24:17; Lev. 9:6, 23:24; Deut. 4:12, 15, 24, 33, 36; 5:4, 5, 21, 23; 9:3; 10:4; 18:16; cf. Isa. 30:27; 33:14; 66:15–16; Ezek. 8:2; 2 Chron. 7:1–3.

130. Exod. 13:21–22; 14:24; 24:16–17; 40:38; Num. 9:15–16; 14:14; Deut. 1:33; 5:19; Neh. 9:12, 19; cf. Ezek. 1:4, 27–28.

131. Exod. 25:21–22.

132. Num. 7:89.

133. 1 Sam. 4:4; 2 Sam. 6:2; 2 Kings 19:15; Isa. 37:16; Ps. 80:2; 99:1; 1 Chron. 13:6; cf. Jer. 3:16–17.

134. Jer. 14:21; 17:12; cf. Ezek. 43:7.

135. 1 Sam. 4:4, 11, 19–22.

136. This legend appears in several versions. The fullest is in *Mid. Tehillim* 24:10, 207–8; Tanḥuma, ed. S. Buber, 2:6, 21f. (*va'era'*); cf. Shab. 30a; Sanh. 107b.

137. 1 Kings 5:11.

138. 2 Sam. 5:7, 9; 1 Chron. 11:5, 7.

139. Cross, *Canaanite Myth and Hebrew Epic*, 93, accepts that "The portion of the psalm in verses 7–10 had its origin in the procession of the Ark to the sanctuary at its founding, celebrated annually in the cult of Solomon and perhaps even of David." In contrast, M. Treves, "The Date of Psalm XXIV," VT 10 (1960): 428–34, places the psalm in Maccabean times.

140. Cf. Ps. 68:2.

141. Josh. 6:6–13.

142. 1 Sam. 4:3–7.

143. Cf. also Num. 14:42–45; Josh. 3:5–7, 10–11.

144. 2 Chron. 20:27–28.

145. Cross, *Canaanite Myth and Hebrew Epic*, postulates an annual cultic celebration of the founding of the sanctuary.

146. Exod. 7:4; 12:41, cf. v. 51.

147. Exod. 14:14; cf. Deut. 20:4.

148. Exod. 15:3; cf. Isa. 42:13.

149. Exod. 17:16.

150. Judg. 5:20.

151. Gen. 2:1; cf. 1 Kings 17:16; 23:14, etc.

152. Josh. 5:14f; 1 Kings 22:19.

153. Exod. 23:22; Judg. 5:31; 1 Sam. 30:26.

154. Exod. 17:16; 1 Sam. 18:17; 25:28; 2 Chron. 20:29.

155. For the supposed concept of "holy war," see G. Von Rad, *Der heilige Krieg im alten Israel* (Zurich, 1951). The phrase, as such, is never found in the Hebrew Bible. On the divine warrior, see Cross in *Biblical Motifs*, 11–63; Cross, *Canaanite Myth and Hebrew Epic*, 91–111; P. D. Miller, *The Divine Warrior in Early Israel*.

156. Ezek. 43:1 3.

157. Ezek. 44:1–2.

158. Yoma 21b, 52b, Horayot 12a, P. Shekalim 6:1 (49c); see M. Haran, "The Disappearance of the Ark," *IEJ* 13 (1963):46–58.

159. Gen. 28:17.

160. 1 Kings 8:39; 22:19; Isa. 6:1; 18:4; 63:15 (cf. 1 Kings 8:13); Mic. 1:2–3; Hab. 2:20; Ps. 11:4; and possibly also Amos 9:1; Ps. 18:7; 2 Sam. 22:7; Ps. 29:9. See A. Aptowitzer, "The Upper Temple" [Hebrew], *Tarbiz* 2 (1931): 137–53; 257–87; R. Patai, *Man and Temple*, 130–39; J. Strugnell, "The Angelic Liturgy at Qumran—4Q Serek Širot ʿOlat Haššabat," *VT Sup.* 7 (1960):318–45.

161. N. M. Sarna, *Exploring Exodus*, 200–203; Sarna, *JPS Commentary on Exodus*, 156, 255 n. 2; M. Eliade, *Cosmos and History*, 3–11; A. S. Kapelrud, "Temple Building, A Task for Gods and Men," *Orientalia* 32 (1963):56–62; *Mid. Tehillim*, ed. Buber, p. 233 (to Ps. 30), cf. *Yalk. Ha-Makhiri*, ed. Buber, 192 (to Ps. 30), which specifically has the celestial Temple exactly situated above the terrestrial one.

162. See Mowinckel, *Psalms in Israel's Worship*, 1:5–6, 115, 177–78. A. Cooper, "Ps. 24:7, Mythology and Exegesis," *JBL* 102 (1983):37–60 thinks that vv. 7 and 9 refer to God's descent into the netherworld and His re-emergence from it.

163. Lev. 23:23–25; Num. 29:1–6.

CHAPTER FIVE: PSALM 30

1. For prayers for recovery from illness, cf. Num. 12:13; Isa. 38:2–3; Jer. 17:14; Pss. 6:2–3; 40:4–5; 41:5.

2. Cf. Exod. 15:2; Isa. 25:1; Pss. 99:5, 9; 107:32; 118:28; 145:1.

3. H. L. Ginsberg, "Psalms and Inscriptions of Petition and Acknowledgement," in *Louis Ginzberg Jubilee Volume*, 166–68; S. Mowinckel, *The Psalms in Israel's Worship*, 2:185–87. For the text of the Egyptian hymn, see *ANET*, 380; M. Lichtheim, *Ancient Egyptian Literature*, 2:104–7.

4. The same is true in several other, unrelated languages; see next note.

5. C. Westermann, *Praise and Lament in the Psalms*, 25–35, has persuasively demonstrated this phenomenon. The primary meaning of the Hebrew verb *hodah* and the noun *todah* is "praise." All forms of this vocable, with the inexplicable exception of Gen. 49:8, are directed to God. Note that Ps. 49:19 is problematical, and in Job 40:14 it is God who is the subject of the verb.

6. English "exalted," from Latin *ex-altere*, also originally meant "to raise to a height."

7. Cf. Exod. 2:16, 19; Prov. 20:5, and Heb. *dli*, "a bucket," Num. 24:7; Isa. 40:15; so Akk. *dalû*, "to draw water from a well," and *dālu*, "a bucket" (*CAD* 3:56). The meaning "to save" is secondary.

8. Cf. Gen. 37:22, 24, 28; Jer. 38:6, 9–13; Ps. 40:3; Lam. 3:53–55.

9. The name occurs in Jer. 36:12, 25; Neh. 6:10; 7:62; 1 Chron. 3:24; 24:18, and at Elephantine and in the latter also in the hypocoristic form *dalah*; see A. Cowley, *Aramaic Papyri of the Fifth Century B.C.*, Nos. 30:29, p. 113; 41:4, p. 140; E. G. Kraeling, *The Brooklyn Museum Aramaic Papyri*, no. 5:17, pp. 180, 187. The cognate Aram. proper names *byt'ldlny*, "[The god] Bethel rescued me," and *šmšdlh*, "[The god] Shamash rescued" have also been preserved; see *KAI* nos. 227, RS 24, 236, RS 7; cf. also the Phoen. town name *âl Da-La-I/Emme*, "[The sun-god] Ḥammu rescued": see J. Lewy, *HUCA* 18 (1944): 475f., n. 248.

10. For similar malicious rejoicing, cf. Pss. 13:5; 35:19, 24, 26; 38:17; 41:6, 12; 89:43; cf. Isa. 14:29; Mic. 7:8; Prov. 24:17; Lam. 2:17.

11. The same phrase occurs in "The Poem of the Righteous Sufferer"; see W. G. Lambert, *Babylonian Wisdom Literature*, 46, lines 116–18.

12. Pss. 5:3; 18:17, 42; 22:25; 28:2; 31:24; 72:12; 88:14; 119:147; cf. the use of the noun *shav'ah* in Pss. 18:7; 34:16; 39:13; 40:2; 102:2; 145:19.

13. Job 26:6; cf. Hos. 13:14.

14. Deut. 32:22; Isa. 5:14; 14:9; 38:18; Ps. 86:13; Prov. 27:20; Song 8:6.

15. On Sheol, see Y. Kaufmann, *Toledot Ha-'Emunah Ha-Yisre'elit*, 2:544–56; Y. Kaufmann, *The Religion of Israel*, 311–16; N. J. Tromp, *Primitive Conceptions of Death and the Netherworld in the Old Testament*; H. C. Brichto, "Kith, Cult, Land and Afterlife—A Biblical Complex," *HUCA* 44(1973):1–54.

16. See A. J. Spenser, *Death in Ancient Egypt*.

17. Num. 16:30; Deut. 32:22; Isa. 7:11; 14:9, 15; Ezek. 31:14–18; cf. Pss. 63:10; 88:4–7.

18. Ps. 88:7; 143:3; Lam. 3:6; Job 17:13; 38:17.

19. Job 30:23.

20. Job 3:13–19.

21. Isa. 38:10; Pss. 9:14; 107:18; Prov. 7:27; Job 38:17.

22. Prov. 7:27.

23. Isa. 14:15, 19; 38:18; Ezek. 26:20; 31:14, 16; 32:18, 23, 24, 25, 29, 30; Pss. 28:1; 88:5, 7; 143:7; Prov. 1:12.

24. On the Mesopotamian notions, see S. G. F. Brandon, *The Judgment of the Dead* (New York, 1967), 49–55; B. Bayliss, "The Cult of the Dead in Assyria and Babylonia," *Iraq* 25 (1973):115–25; B. Alster, ed., *Death in Mesopotamia*.

25. Cf. Akk. *bît ikleti*, CAD 7:61, 2.

26. Cf. Akk. *erṣet la târi*, CAD, 4:310–11; cf. Prov. 2:18–19; Job 7:9–10; 10:21.

27. Cf. the Sumerian myth "Inanna's Descent to the Netherworld," *ANET*, 52–57; "The Descent of Ishtar to the Nether World," *ANET*, 106–9.

28. Lev. 19:31; 20:6, 27; Deut. 18:11; 2 Kings 23:24; Isa. 8:19; 29:4.

29. Deut. 26:14; Ps. 106:28; 2 Chron. 34:4.

30. The Kethib *mi-yordei* corresponds to the Hebrew text that underlies the Greek, Theodotian, Vulgate, and Syriac: "from those who go down"; cf. Isa. 38:18; Ezek. 26:20; 31:14, 16; 32:18, 24, 25, 29, 30; Pss. 28:1; 85:5; 143:7; Prov. 1:12; the Qre *mi-yordi* (instead of the usual *me-rideti*) means "that I do not go down," the preposition having negative, privative force, so Rashi, Kimḥi; cf. Gen. 27:1; 1 Sam. 15:23, 26; 1 Kings 15:13; Isa. 7:8; 17:9; 23:1; 22:3; Jer. 48:42, 45; Mic. 3:6; Ps. 83:5; Job 11:15; 19:26; 21:9.

31. Cf. 1 Sam. 2:6; Jonah 2:3–4; Pss. 9:14; 16:10; 49:16; 71:20; 86:13; 88:4–7; 107:18; 116:3.

32. See A. Heidel, *The Gilgamesh Epic and Old Testament Parallels*, 208; *CAD* 2:58; K. Tallqvist, *Akkadische Götterepitheta*, 67f.; Lambert, *Babylonian Wisdom Literature*, 59, Tablet iv, lines 4–6, 29, 33, 35.

33. For *zekher* as "name," cf. Exod. 3:15; Isa. 26:8; Pss. 135:13; Prov. 10:7; Job 18:17 all in parallel with *shem*; in Hos. 12:6; Pss. 97:12; 102:13, *zekher* appears alone.

34. Cf. Isa. 54:7. The same sentiment appears in the Mesopotamian poem, Lambert, *Babylonian Wisdom Literature*, 41, tablet II, lines 39–42.

35. As Ibn Ezra notes, Heb. *bekhi* is here ellipsis for *be-bekhi*; cf. Gen. 14:4; Exod. 6:3; 20:11; 2 Kings 12:1; Ps. 18:34. For the preposition after the verb *li/un*; cf. Ps. 25:13; Job 41:14.

36. On Heb. *rinnah*, see N. E. Wagner, "*Rinnah* in the Psalter," *VT* 10 (1960):435–41.

37. On the Heb. root *ḥ-s-d*, see A. R. Johnson, "ḤESED and ḤĀSÎD" in *Festschrift S. Mowinckel* (Norsk Teologisk Tidsskrift) 56 (1955):100–112; L. Jacobs, "The Concept Ḥasid in Biblical and Rabbinic Literatures," *JJS* 8 (1957):143–54; N. Glueck, *Ḥesed in the Bible*; K. D. Sakenfeld, *The Meaning of Ḥesed in the Hebrew Bible*.

38. On the use of music in ancient Israelite worship, see R. de Vaux, *Ancient Israel: Its Life and Institutions*, 382–85, 390–94, 457–58.

39. Pss. 71:22; 98:5; 147:7; 149:3.

40. Ps. 144:9.

41. Ps. 149:3.

42. Ps. 92:3.

43. 1 Sam. 10:5; 1 Kings 1:40; Isa. 5:12; 30:29.

44. Heb. *shalvi* presupposes a masc. noun *shelev*; otherwise the fem. form *shalvah* appears: Jer. 22:21; Ezek. 16:49; Ps. 120:7; Prov. 1:32; 17:1; Dan. 8:25; 11:21, 24; cf. Ps. 5:3 *shav'i* from a putative form *sheva'*; cf. similar masc. forms *tevun* for *tevunah* in Hos. 13:2; *tsur* for *tsurah* in Ps. 49:15; '*orem* for '*ormah* in Job 5:13; cf. the frequent *tsedek* and *tsedakah*.

45. For this formula introducing an erroneous assumption, cf. 1 Sam. 2:30; Isa. 38:10f.; 49:4; Jer. 3:19–20; Jonah 2:5; Zeph. 3:7–8; Pss. 31:23; 82:6; 116:11; Job 7:13–14. M. Tsevat, *A Study of the Language of the Biblical Psalms*, 49, 132 n. 390, points out that a similar use of the phrase "I thought" appears in the Akkadian of the El-Amarna letters as *anaku aqabbi*, apparently a Canaanism. See also C. J. Labuschagne, *New Light on Some Old Testament Problems*, 27–33.

46. For this rendering, see Moses ibn Chiquitilla (d.c. 1080), as cited by Ibn Ezra *ad loc.*

47. Pss. 10:11; 13:2; 22:25; 27:9; 44:25; 69:18; 88:15; 102:3; 104:29; 143:7. The same is expressed elsewhere in the Bible where it is invariably in a context of divine response to sin: Deut. 31:17, 18; 32:20; Isa. 8:17; 54:8; 59:2; 64:6; Jer. 33:5; Ezek. 39:23, 24, 29; Mic. 3:4; Job 13:24; 34:29.

48. Heb. *shahat*, lit. "a ditch" (in v. 4 the Hebrew for the same "Pit" is *bor*). For this figurative use, cf. Isa. 38:17; 51:14; Ezek. 28:8; Jonah 2:7; Pss. 16:10; 49:10; 103:4; Job 17:14; 33:18, 22, 24, 28, 30.

49. "Dust" refers to the dead who "return to dust"; cf. Gen. 3:19; Ps. 104:29; Job 10:9; Eccl. 3:20; 12:7.

50. For a similar sentiment, cf. Isa. 38:18.

51. For this rhetorical question, cf. Gen. 37:26; Mal. 3:14; also Job 22:3. The translation of *dam*, lit. "blood" as "demise" is based on the understanding of an ellipsis for "spilling blood," as in Lev. 19:16; Deut. 17:8. A. B. Ehrlich, *Die Psalmen*, 64 and N. H. Tur-Sinai, *The Book of Job*, 163, fn. to 16:8, emend to *dummi*, "if I am silenced," a euphemism for death. It is to be noted that various forms of the root *dm* appear in contexts of death: 1 Sam. 2:9; Isa. 38:10; Pss. 31:18; 94:17; 115:17. In the present instance, there may be a wordplay with *yiddom*, v. 13.

52. For this kind of reversal of fortune, cf. Jer. 31:12(13); Amos 8:10; Lam. 5:15; Esth. 9:22; cf. also Eccl. 3:4.

53. H. L. Ginsberg, *Koheleth*, 73 to 3:4, points out that Syr. *sfd* means "to dance" as a mourning ritual; cf. Isa. 32:12, which indicates beating the breast to a certain rhythm; cf. Akk. *sapadu*, "to mourn, to beat the breast to a certain beat"; *CAD* 15:150f.; cf. Tos. Moed Katan 2:17, ed. Zuckermandel, 231.

54. In Ps. 100:1 *le-todah* more likely means "for thanksgiving" than "for the thanksgiving offering." In any case, the preposition is attached.

55. These are Pss. 65, 68, 75, 76, 87.

56. *Shir* in Ps. 33:3 and 40:4 are not titles.

57. Note that the preposition "for" is absent, probably because the psalm was not originally composed for that occasion, only adapted to it.

58. Cf. 1 Esdras 7:5–9.

59. On this passage, see J. Goldstein, *I Maccabees*, AB, 1976, 272–88; cf. II Macc. 10:1–8.

60. *Massekhet Soferim* 18:3, ed. M. Higger, 313.

61. Cf. Tos. Bik. 2:10, ed. Zuckermandel, p. 102, on which see S. Lieberman, *Tosefta Ki-fshutah (Order Zeraim)* part 2, 850 n. 79.

62. For the biblical sources on the first fruits, see Exod. 23:19–23; 34:26; Lev. 23:16–17; Num. 15:17–21; 18:12–13; 28:26–31; Deut. 26:1–11.

63. See S. Lieberman, *Hellenism in Jewish Palestine*, 140, n. 11. On the place of Psalm 30 in the Jewish liturgy, see Y. P. Merhaviah, *Sinai* 40 (1957):182–85.

CHAPTER SIX: PSALM 48

1. E.g., Pss. 46, 48, 76, 84, 87, 122.

2. Ps. 2:6; 3:5; 43:3; 48:2; 87:1; 99:9.

3. Ps. 78:68; 132:13.

4. Ps. 132:13.

5. Ps. 78:68; 87:2.

6. Ps. 74:2; 76:3; 132:13–14; 135:21.

7. Ps. 9:12; 110:2; 146:10.

8. Ps. 14:7; 53:7; 20:3; 69:36; 102:14; 128:5; 134:3.

9. Ps. 125:1.

10. Ps. 48:3; 50:2.

11. For the role of Zion in biblical religion and especially in this psalm, see J. D. Levenson, *Sinai and Zion*, esp. 89–184.

12. J. J. M. Roberts, "The Davidic Origin of the Zion Tradition," *JBL* 92 (1973):329–44; "Zion in the Theology of the Davidic-Solomonic Empire," in *Studies in the Period of David and Solomon and Other Essays*, ed. T. Ishida, 93–108; M. Weinfeld, "Zion and Jerusalem as Religious and Political Capital: Ideology and Utopia," in *The Poet and the Historian*, ed. R. E. Friedman, 75–115.

13. Cf. Heb. *tsiyyah*, Isa. 35:1; Jer. 2:6; Hos. 2:5; and *tsayon*, Isa. 25:5; 32:2.

14. Cf. *tsiyyun*, "a stone or heap of stones as a grave marker," 2 Kings 23:17; Jer. 31:20 (21); Ezek. 39:15; see H. Bar-Deroma, "Kadesh-Barnea," *PEQ* 96 (1964):107.

15. 2 Sam. 5:7; 1 Chron. 11:5.

16. 2 Sam. 5:7, 9; 1 Chron. 11:5, 7; 1 Kings 8:1; 2 Chron. 5:2.

17. Isa. 18:7; 24:23; Jer. 31:5(6); Joel 4:17; Mic. 4:7.

18. 2 Kings 19:21; Isa. 2:3; 3:16–17; 4:3; 10:24; 33:14; 52:1; 60:14; Ps.

48:3, 13; 69:35; 133:3. It even refers to the people of Israel in Isa. 51:16, a peculiarity noted in P. Taan. 4:2 (68a); P. Meg. 3:7 (74b).

19. Ps. 125:2; see Y. Karmon, "The Mountains Round About Jerusalem," in *Jerusalem Throughout the Ages*, 96–108.

20. Josh. 15:63; Judg. 1:21.

21. Judg. 1:8.

22. Judg. 19:10–12.

23. Deut. 33:7.

24. 2 Sam. 2:11; 5:2–6; 1 Chron. 3:4; 11:1–3.

25. 2 Sam. 5:6.

26. Cf. 1 Chron. 11:4–7.

27. On this topic, see John H. Hayes, "The Tradition of Zion's Inviolability," *JBL* 82 (1963):419–26.

28. N. Avigad, *Qadmoniot* 24(1991):61 points out that following the building of Solomon's Temple, no other place of worship is ever referred to as the "House of the Lord," despite the existence of provincial shrines.

29. Vv. 2, 11, 15.

30. This liturgical line is found also in Pss. 96:4; 145:3.

31. See above, n. 2, and Isa. 11:9; 27:13; 66:20; Jer. 31:23; Ezek. 28:14; Joel 2:1; 4:17; Zech. 8:3; Dan. 9:16, 20.

32. Heb. *nof* is unique in biblical Hebrew; cf. Arab. *nāfa*, "high, lofty." In tannaitic Hebrew *nof* refers to the summit of a tree; cf. M. Shev. 2:4; M. Maas. 3:10; M. Eruv. 10:8; M. Makk. 2:7. F. M. Cross, "An Aramaic Inscription from Daskylion," *BASOR* 184 (1966):8 and fn. 17, notes that the second element of the pr. n. *Elnap* appears in Arabic and OSA names, meaning "to be exalted, high."

33. For the *nif'al* of the root *y-d-'* in the sense of God manifesting His Presence, cf. Exod. 6:3; Isa. 19:21; 66:14; Ezek. 20:5, 9; Ps. 9:17; 76:2. The preposition *l-* can hardly be the dative, and is probably an emphatic, "a veritable haven." On this usage of *l-*, see F. Notscher, "Zum emphatischen Lamed," *VT* 3(1953):372–80; C. H. Gordon, *Ugaritic Textbook*, 76, 9.16; M. Dahood, *Psalms*, AB, 3, 406.

34. See R. J. Clifford, *The Cosmic Mountain in Canaan and the Old Testament*, esp. 98–181.

35. Gen. 28:12ff.

36. Cf. Isa. 2:2; on this see B. Childs, *Myth and Reality in the Old Testament*, 87.

37. Isa. 14:13.

38. On Zaphon, see O. Eissfeldt, *Baal Zephon, Zeus Kasios und der Durchzug der Israeliten durchs Meer*; A. Lauha, *Zaphon, der Norden und die Nordvölker im Alten Testament*; W. R. Albright, "Baal Zaphon," in *Festschrift Alfred Bertholet zum 80 Geburtstag*, ed. W. Baumgartner, 1–14; A. Robinson, "Zion and Saphon in Psalm XLVIII 3," *VT* 24 (1974):118–23; N. M. Sarna, "Ṣaphon," in *Encyclopaedia Mikra'it* 6:747–51.

39. *KAI*, 12, no. 50, lines 2–3; Beyerlin, *Near Eastern Texts Relating to the Old Testament*, 253–54.

40. See Childs, *Myth and Reality*, 83–93.

41. Heb. *melekh rab* appears as a divine epithet in Ugaritic texts 118.13, 26; 1018.2, 17; see *UT* 19.2297; in Aramaic in the Sefira inscription B line 7; see J. A. Fitzmyer, "The Aramaic Inscriptions of Sefire I and II," *JAOS* 81(1961):178–222, esp. 182, 186, 202; *KAI* 1, no. 222, 2:253; and Akkadian *šarru rabû*. For this qualitative sense of *rab*, cf. Exod. 23:2; Isa. 51:10; Amos 7:4; Ps. 36:7. See also J. C. Greenfield, "Some Aspects of Treaty Terminology in the Bible," *Fourth World Congress of Jewish Studies Proceedings*, 1:118–19.

42. Mal. 1:14; Pss. 47:3; 95:3. In 2 Kings 18:19, 28; Isa. 36:4, 13; Jer. 25:14; 27:7; Ps. 136:17; Eccl. 9:14 the references are to foreign enemy potentates who are described by the honorifics they assign to themselves. The same applies to Hos. 5:13; 10:6 where the text has long been recognized as being really *malk(i) rab*.

43. For this military usage, cf. Josh. 11:5.

44. For the verb '-*v*-*r* in a military context, cf. Judg. 11:29; 12:1; 2 Kings 8:21.

45. For the verb *ḥ*-*f*-*z* in the sense of precipitate flight, cf. 2 Sam. 4:4; 2 Kings 7:15; Ps. 104:7.

46. So Saadia (on v. 5), Rashi (on vv. 2, 5) Kimḥi (on vv. 1, 5, 9), cf. Ibn Ezra (on v. 13), H. Gunkel, *Die Psalmen, ad loc.*

47. Dahood, *Psalms*, AB, 1, 291 (to v. 5) calls the reference "mere literary foils."

48. See W. T. Davison, *The Psalms*, 245; A. F. Kirkpatrick, *The Book of Psalms*, 262. M. Buttenwieser, *The Psalms*, 103–5, has made a convincing case for this historical background to the psalm; see also L. Krinetzki, "Zur Poetie und Exegesis von Ps. 48," *BZ* 9 (1960):79–97.

49. 2 Kings 16:9; Isa. 10:9f; 17:1; Amos 1:4f.

50. 2 Kings 17:3–6.

51. 2 Kings vv. 6, 23f., 18:9–11.

52. 2 Kings 18:1–6, 22; 2 Chron. 29:1–30:21; 31:1. Archaeological proof for Hezekiah's centralization of worship is now provided by the excavations at Arad; see Y. Aharoni, "Arad: Its Inscriptions and Temple," *BA* 31 (1968):26.

53. Isa. 2:1–4; cf. Mic. 4:1–4.

54. B. Mazar, in *Jerusalem Through the Ages*, 8.

55. 2 Chron. 32:5.

56. 2 Kings 20:20; Isa. 22:9–11; 2 Chron. 32:2–4, 30; cf. Ben Sira 48:17; M. Pes. 4:9; b. Pes. 56a; M. Ber. 10:6; see L. Ginzberg, *The Legends of the Jews*, 6:369 n. 69. Hezekiah's feat is apparently recorded on the "Siloam Inscription," for which see, *KAI* 1 no. 189; *ANET*, 321; *NSI*, 15ff.

57. For the events of this period, see J. Bright, *A History of Israel*, 3rd ed., 269–88; B. Oded, in *Israelite and Judaean History*, eds. J. H. Hayes and J. Maxwell Miller, 435–51; I. Eph'al, "Assyrian Dominion in Palestine," in *The World History of the Jewish People*, 4:i, 276–89; H. Tadmor, "Sennacherib's Campaign in Judah—Historical and Historiographical Considerations," *Zion* 50 (1985):65–80.

58. See B. S. Childs, *Isaiah and the Assyrian Crisis*.

59. 2 Kings 19:32–34; Isa. 37:33–35; 2 Chron. 32:21.

60. 2 Kings 19:35f., Isa. 37:36f.

61. *ANET*, 287f.

62. Herodotus, *Histories* 2, 141 tells that a multitude of field mice invaded the Assyrian camp at night and devastated their armaments. Next morning the enemy commenced their flight and great multitudes fell. However, Herodotus reports this in connection with Sennacherib's invasion of Egypt, not Jerusalem.

63. Jer. chs. 7 and 26.

64. *ANET*, 288, col. III:31–34; cf. the role of the Edomites at the time of the Babylonian invasion of Judea: Ezek. 25:12–14; 35:2–15; Ob. 10–14; Ps. 137:7; Lam. 4:21.

65. Jer. 6:24; 22:23; 50:43; Mic. 4:9; cf. Exod. 15:14; Isa. 13:8; 21:3; 26:17; Jer. 30:6.

66. Gen. 41:6, 23, 27; Exod. 10:13; 14:21; Isa. 27:8; Jer. 18:19; Ezek. 17:10; 19:12; 27:26; Hos. 13:15; Job 27:21.

67. The Greek translation always avoids rendering *kadim* by "east." See M. Harel, *The Sinai Journeys*, 199.

68. 1 Kings 20:49; cf. 2 Chron. 20:36f.

69. Ezek. 27:25f.

70. Gen. 10:5; cf. Isa. 66:19.

71. So Targs. Jon. and Yerushalmi.

72. So 1 Chron. 1:7, LXX, and Sam versions, and several Heb. mss.

73. Jonah 1:3.

74. 1 Kings 10:22; Isa. 23:1, 6, 10, 14; Ezek. 27:12, 25.

75. ANET, 290.

76. KAI, 1 no. 46, see F. M. Cross, "An Interpretation of the Nora Stone," BASOR 208 (1972):13–19.

77. S. B. Hoenig, "Tarshish," JQR 69 (1979):181f.

78. C. Torr, Ancient Ships; R. D. Barnett, "Early Shipping in the Near East," Antiquity 32 (1958):220–30.

79. Exod. 28:20; 39:13; Ezek. 1:16; 10:9; 28:13; Song 5:14; Dan. 10:6.

80. Judg. 9:13; Isa. 24:7; 65:8; Hos. 4:11; Joel 2:24; Mic. 6:15; Prov. 3:10 et al.

81. C. H. Gordon, "The Wine-Dark Sea," JNES 37 (1978):51f.

82. 1 Kings 22:49; Isa. 60:9; Jer. 10:9; Ezek. 27:12; 38:13.

83. W. F. Albright, "New Light on the Early History of Phoenician Colonization," BASOR 83 (1941):21f.; Albright, "The Role of the Canaanites in the History of Civilization," in The Bible and the Ancient Near East, 346f., 360 n. 96; 361 n. 103.

84. Eli Schulman pointed out to me that v. 9 must belong to the following stanza, spoken by Judeans. An enemy would not refer to God as "Lord of Hosts" and "our God."

85. This rendering of the unique Heb. verb pasgu is based on the meaning of the root in Aramaic and postbiblical Hebrew, "to cut, divide"; cf. the Gk. translation katadielesthe, Vulg. distribuite. J. C. Greenfield points out that such verbs often have the semantic development, "to cut one's way through, to pass through"; so BDB:819, "pass between." Rashi, Ibn Ezra, Kimhi all connect with the noun pisgah (Num. 21:20; 23:14; Deut. 3:27; 34:1), and take the verb to mean "to be high." See N. H. Tur-Sinai, Ha-Lashon Ve-Ha-Sefer II, vol. Ha-Sefer, 431; and his n. 3 on p. 5014 to E. Ben-Yehudah, Thesaurus, 10.

86. T. H. Gaster, Myth, Legend and Custom in the Old Testament, 2:411f.; Gaster, The New Golden Bough, 78[55]; H. Frankfort, Kingship and the Gods, 104, 124; CAH 1, 2:16f., 36.

87. That Heb. sabbotem with hakkef in Josh. 6:3 means "to circuit," not "surround" as the Greek, is proven by the combination of the same two verbs

in the present psalm; cf. Ps. 26:6 where the verb *s-v-v* alone can only mean "to circuit."

88. M. Suk. 4:5.

89. Maimonides, *Hilkhot Sukkah* 7:23.

90. Cf. Jubilees 16:31.

91. Dr. Linda Gordon Kuzmack suggested this analogy to me.

92. Gaster, *Myth, Legend and Custom*, 2:12.

93. See G. E. von Grunebaum, *Muhammadan Festivals*, 29f.

94. Gilgamesh, Tablet I, *ANET*, 73; tablet XI, *ANET*, 97. See Oppenheim, *Ancient Mesopotamia*, 257, cf. p. 128.

95. Isa. 33:18.

96. This objective is emphasized numerous times in the Bible: Exod. 12:26f; 13:8–10, 14–16; Deut. 4:9f; 6:7, 20–25; 11:19; 31:10–13; 32:7, 46; Josh. 4:21–24; Judg. 3:2; cf. Deut. 26:5–9; 1 Sam. 12:6–11; Pss. 44:2–3; 78 *passim*; 106:7ff.

97. Heb. biblical manuscripts disagree as to whether '*l mwt* or '*lmwt*, one or two words, are to be read. This is listed as one of the differences between the masoretic traditions of the schools of Ben Asher and Ben Naphtali; see L. Lipschütz, "Mishael b. Uzziel's Treatise on Differences Between Ben Asher and Ben Naphtali" [Hebrew] *Textus* II (1962):46. Clearly, the exegesis of P. Moed Katan 3:7 (83b) favors reading '*lmt*, though one explanation does imply two words. The Targum "as in the days of our youth," so Saadia, indicate a single word, as do LXX A and Symm.; Rashi and Ibn Ezra treat as one word, although the latter notes that the masorah has two. Kimḥi appears to prefer a meaning "unto death" but observes that an alternative "as in the days of our youth" is also possible. He cites Isa. 61:1, Jer. 46:20, and Ps. 123:4 as other examples of masoretic orthographic bisections ignored in interpretation. Syr. *l'al min mauta'* and Jerome *in mortem* both reflect a two word tradition; cf. Ps. 9:1. A reading '*lmwt-'alamot*, "maidens" may be a technical musical term, "high pitched," "soprano," "falsetto"; cf. Pss. 46:1; 68:26; 1 Chron. 15:20. It may belong to Ps. 49:1.

CHAPTER SEVEN: PSALM 82

1. See above p. 240, Psalm 24, n. 104, for the sources.

2. On this psalm, see J. Morgenstern, "The Mythological Background of

Psalm 82," *HUCA* 14 (1939):29–126; G. E. Wright, *The Old Testament Against Its Environment*, 30:41; M. Tsevat, "God and the Gods in Assembly"; *HUCA* 40–41 (1969–70):123–37; M. Z. Brettler, *God Is King: Understanding an Israelite Metaphor*, 125–68.

3. Note the interchange of *'elohim* with *mal'akh*, "angel," in Gen. 16:7, 9, 11 and v. 13; 22:11, 15 and vv. 16–18; 28:12 and 35:7; Exod. 3:2 and v. 4, "the Lord"; Judg. 6:11 and v. 14 et al., ch. 13 *passim*, "angel," and v. 22; Hos 12:4 and v. 5. *Mid. Tehillim*, ed. S. Buber, 368 to Ps. 82:1 takes the second *'elohim* in that verse to mean "judges," based on the rabbinic understanding of Exod. 21:6; 22:8 on which see Sarna, *JPS Commentary on Exodus*, 120, 252 n. 16.

4. YHṼH occurs only 45 times in the Elohistic Psalter, while *'elohim* appears 210 times. In the rest of the Psalter, *'elohim* occurs only 94 times, while YHṼH appears 584 times. On this phenomenon, see M. H. Segal, "El, Elohim and YHWH in the Bible," *JQR* 46 (1955):89–115, esp. 104–6; R. G. Boling, "Synonymous Parallelism in the Psalms" *JSS* 5 (1960):221–55; W. F. Albright, *Yahweh and the Gods of Canaan*, 30–34. See also *Massekhet Soferim*, ed. M. Higger, 4:2, p. 147.

5. UT 128:II:7, 11 *'dt 'lm* corresponds exactly to Heb. *'adat 'el*.

6. See R. T. O'Callaghan, "A Note on the Canaanite Background of Psalm 82," *CBQ* 15 (1953):311–14.

7. The synonymous terms *phr*, *mphrt*, *dr* are fairly common in Ugaritic and Phoenician; for the former cf. *UT* 1:7; 2:17, 34; 107:2–3; for the last, see *KAI*, 1, No. 4, line 4; 6, No. 26, A III, line 19; No. 27, lines 11–12, and possibly p. 7, No. 30, line 5 on which fragmentary text see P. Kyle McCarter, "The Early Diffusion of the Alphabet," *BA* 37 (1974):66. For Akk. *puhru*, see *AHW*:876. On the divine assembly, see E. Theodore Mullen, *The Assembly of the Gods: The Divine Council in Canaanite and Hebrew Literature*. For the rabbinic counterpart, see E. E. Urbach, *The Sages: Their Concepts and Beliefs*, 115–63; Eng. trans., 135–83.

8. Job 1:6–12; 2:1–6.

9. Job 15:8 though the synonym *sod* is used for "council" as in Gen. 49:6; Jer. 6:11; Pss. 89:8; 111:1.

10. Jer. 23:18.

11. Exod. 18:13.

12. Judg. 4:5.

13. Joel 4:12.

14. Pss. 9:5, 8; 122:5.

15. Prov. 20:8; cf. Job 29:7, 12–18; Dan 7:9–10.

16. So Num. 10:35; Isa. 3:13; Jer. 2:29; Pss. 3:8; 7:7; 9:20; 10:12; 12:6; 17:13; 35:2; 44:27; 68:2; 74:22; 76;10.

17. For the Heb. *shafaṭ* in the sense of executing justice, not just adjudicating, see *BDB*, 1047, col. b, 3.

18. The principal eighth century B.C.E. prophetical texts are Isa. 1:27, 21–23; 2:7, 16; 3:14–15, 16–23; 5:7–8, 11–12, 22–23; 10:1–2; 28:3, 7–8; 30:12; 32:7; 33:15; Hos. 4:2, 11; 5:11; 7:1; 12:8; Amos 2:6–8; 3:10, 15; 4:1; 5:7, 11–12; 6:4–6, 12; 8:4–6; Mic. 2:1–2, 8–9; 3:1–3, 5, 9–11; 6–8, 10–12.

19. The same concept is projected in Deut. 29:25. In Deut. 32:8, the LXX renders *bnei yisra'el* by *angelōn theou*, which presupposes an underlying Heb. *bnei 'elohim*. This reading has now turned up in a fragment from the Song of Moses from Qumran Cave IV; P. Skehan, *BASOR* 136 (1954):12; *JBL* 78 (1959):21. Cf. Ben Sira 17:17, ed. R. H. Charles, *The Apocrypha and Pseudepigrapha of the Old Testament in English*, 1:376 and note *ad loc.*, Jubilees 15:31–32, 2:37; Targ. Jon. to Gen. 11:7–8; Mechilta, Beshalaḥ, Shirah 2, eds. Horovitz-Rabin, 2nd ed., 124–25.

20. Ps. 58:2 most likely expresses the same idea that divine beings pervert justice. On the reading *'elim*, "gods," for the enigmatic MT *'elem*, see O. Eissfeldt, *The Old Testament*, 111; M. Dahood, *Psalms*, AB, 2:57.

21. For this mode of expressing a supposition disproved by reality, cf. Isa. 49:4; Jer. 3:19–20; Zeph. 3:7; Ps. 31:23; Job 32:7–8; cf. also Ps. 30:7.

22. This expression is unparalleled. If *'elyon* is here an epithet of God, it may correspond to *bnei 'elim* in Pss. 29:1; 89:7, and to *bnei (ha-) 'elohim* in Gen. 6:24; Job 1:6; 2:1; cf. also *bnei 'el ḥai* in Hos. 2:1. It would thus be synonymous with *'adat 'el* in v. 1. Targ., Rashi, and Ibn Ezra all take the phrase as referring to angels. E. Z. Melammed, *Sefer Segal*, 189–90 takes the binary verse as an instance of the break-up of a stereotype phrase *bnei 'elohim 'elyon*, "sons of the Most High God"; cf. Ps. 78:56. It is also possible that *'elyon* is here employed in the secular sense of "superior," as in Deut. 26:19; 28:1; 1 Kings 9:8; Ps. 89:28; 2 Chron. 7:21.

23. For this comparison, cf. Num. 16:29; Judg. 16:7, 11, 17; Isa. 14:10–15; 41:23. R. Gordis, "The Knowledge of Good and Evil in the Old Testament and Qumran," *JBL* 76 (1957):127f., and n. 16 takes *ke-'adam* to mean "like Adam," so Hos. 6:7; Job 31:31. This understanding of our verse is found in *Mid. Tehillim*, 369, 30, and is followed by Rashi. For a possible Ugaritic analogy, see *UT* 125:17–23 (*ANET*, 147–48).

24. It is noteworthy that where *n-f-l* and *m-w-t* occur together, the usual

sequence is "fall . . . die"; cf. Judg. 3:25; 4:22; 2 Sam. 2:23. Our v. 7 may well be an instance of *hysteron proteron* in order to place the emphasis on the deprivation of celestial status. It is unclear whether *n-f-l* here is to be taken literally, that is, to suffer a violent death, as in Judg. 5:27; 1 Sam. 4:10; 14:13; 2 Sam. 11:17; 21:9, or figuratively, as in Amos 5:2; 8:14; cf. Esth. 6:13.

25. Cf. Judg. 16:7, 11 *ke-'aḥad ha-'adam*; v. 17 *ke-khol ha-'adam*.

26. Heb. *sar* is a term for a prince or an officer of the realm. In several texts the *sar* is mentioned together with the judge or in a judicial capacity; cf. Exod. 2:14; 18:21–23; Isa. 1:23, cf. v. 26; 32:1; Jer. 26:10–16; Hos. 13:10; Amos 2:3; Mic. 7:3; Zeph. 3:3; Ps. 148:11; Prov. 8:16. In the seventh century B.C.E. Hebrew inscription from Yavne-Yam, *KAI*, 36, No. 200 (*ANET*, 568), a *sar* is appealed to for a judicial hearing. According to A. S. Yahuda, *The Language of the Pentateuch in Its Relation to Egyptian*, 35f., *sr* appears frequently in New Kingdom texts, notably in reference to judges in high positions.

27. On these myths, see L. Jung, *Fallen Angels in Jewish, Christian and Mohammedan Literature*; B. J. Bamberger, *Fallen Angels*; A. Rofé, *Israelite Belief in Angels in the Pre-exilic Period as Evidenced by Biblical Traditions*, 108–11.

28. So Morgenstern, "The Mythological Background of Psalm 82," 29ff.; S. Mowinckel, *The Psalms in Israel's Worship*, 2:249. On this topic, see below, pp. 180–82 to Ps. 93.

CHAPTER EIGHT: PSALM 93

1. See above p. 240, n. 104.

2. Rosh Ha-Shanah 31a.

3. These correspondences were pointed out by L. Liebreich, "The Hymns of the Levites for the Days of the Week" [Heb.], *Eretz-Israel* 3 (1954): 170–73.

4. With Ps. 93:1 cf. 24:7–10.

5. With 93:3–4 cf. 24:2.

6. With 93:1 cf. 24:8.

7. With 93:5 cf. 24:3.

8. Verse 18.

9. My attention was drawn to this extraordinary fact by Joel R. Leeman.

For the covenant pattern, see my *Exploring Exodus*, 134–37, and the literature cited thereon p. 235, nn. 15–24.

10. See J. H. Tigay, *You Shall Have No Other Gods: Israelite Religion in the Light of Hebrew Inscriptions*, 1986; J. D. Fowler, *Theophoric Personal Names in Ancient Hebrew. A Comparative Study.*

11. Gen. 46:17; Num. 26:25; 1 Chron. 7:31.

12. Judg. 8:31; ch. 9 *passim*.

13. Ruth 1:2, etc.

14. The Akkadian and Ugaritic equivalents are given in the respective entries for each name in the *Encyclopaedia Mikra'it.*

15. The classic work on the subject is H. Frankfort, *Kingship and the Gods.*

16. *ANET*, 265.

17. Y. Kaufmann, *Toledot Ha-'Emunah Ha-Yisre'elit*, 1:655–57; Kaufmann, *The Biblical Account of the Conquest of Palestine*, 90, strongly draws attention to this important fact, which has been largely ignored by later scholars.

18. Deut. 17:14 (cf. 28:26) envisages the possible emergence of a monarchy in Israel, but it is presented as being in imitation of the surrounding kingdoms; cf. 1 Sam. 8:5.

19. Judg. 8:22–23.

20. Judg. ch. 9; cf. 2 Sam. 11:21.

21. 1 Sam. ch. 4.

22. 1 Sam. 8:6.

23. E.g., Pss. 24, 47, 95–99.

24. On the "Enthronement Psalms," see S. Mowinckel, *The Psalms in Israel's Worship*, 1:106–92; 2:222–24. Additional Note 6; J. H. Eaton, *Kingship and the Psalms*; M. Z. Brettler, *God Is King: Understanding an Israelite Metaphor*, 145–58.

25. 2 Sam. 15:10.

26. 2 Kings 9:13; cf. 1 Kings 1:11, 13, 18.

27. Ps. 47:3, 7, 8, 9.

28. Mowinckel, *Psalms in Israel's Worship*, n. 24.

29. Pss. 96:13; 98:9.

30. Lev. 23:24; Num. 29:1–6.

31. Exod. 23:16; 34:22.

32. *KAI*, 34, No. 182; *ANET*, 320.

33. Neh. 8:1–11.

34. On the Rosh Ha-Shanah festival, see W. O. E. Oesterley and G. H. Box, *The Religion and Worship of the Synagogue*, 381–91; M. Friedlander, *The Jewish Religion*, 400–405; N. H. Snaith, *The Jewish New Year Festival*; T. H. Gaster, *Festivals of the Jewish Year*, 107–23; "Rosh Ha-Shanah," *Encyclopaedia Judaica*, 14:305–10.

35. See S. A. Pallis, *The Babylonian Akitu Festival*; S. H. Hooke, *Babylonian and Assyrian Religion*, 48ff., 101–23; H. and H. A. Frankfort and T. Jacobsen, in *The Intellectual Adventure of Ancient Man*, 7f., 24f. 200, 236, 364, 366.

36. *ANET*, 60–72; A. Heidel, *The Babylonian Genesis*.

37. M. H. Segal, *Mevo' Ha-Mikra'*, 3:565 n. 14, entertains the possibility that the psalms which hail God as King were recited in the Temple on Rosh Ha-shanah. Kaufmann, *Toledot*, 2:496–97, concedes the same possibility but refers to "popular religion," not part of the "priestly cult"; see the English abridgement by M. Greenberg, *The Religion of Israel* (Chicago 1960), 117–20, 306–9.

38. See Snaith, *Jewish New Year Festival*, 195–203; M. Buttenwieser, *The Psalms*, 320–43; N. M. Sarna, "Prolegomenon," repr. 1969: XXI–XXVII; Kaufmann, *Toledot*, 1:580–83.

39. I have borrowed this felicitous term from G. E. Wright, *The Old Testament Against Its Environment*, 38, fn., who attributes its coinage to Edmund Perry.

40. See Brettler, *God Is King*, 79–87.

41. So Isa. 51:9; 52:1; 59:17; 61:10; Ps. 104:1; Job 40:10. For the same figurative usage with respect to human beings, cf. Ps. 132:9, 16, 18; Job 8:22; 2 Chron. 6:41.

42. *CAD* 9, 18f., b) 3', cf. c) 2'.

43. Iliad 9:372, 231, pointed out by C. H. Gordon, "Homer and the Bible," *HUCA* 26 (1955):104, 169.

44. Cf. Exod. 12:11; 1 Kings 18:46.

45. Deut. 1:41; Judg. 18:11; 1 Sam. 17:39; 25:13; 2 Sam. 20:8; 2 Kings 3:21; Isa. 5:27; Ps. 18:40 (cf. 2 Sam. 22:40); 45:4.

46. C. H. Gordon, "Belt-Wrestling in the Bible World," *HUCA* 23:1 (1950–51):131–36, points out that a widespread sport in the ancient world was belt-wrestling, in which the winner was the one who was able to wrest the belt of his opponent.

47. Cf. Ps. 96:10; 104:5.

48. Cf. Ps. 9:5; 122:5.

49. Cf. Heb. *me'az* in Prov. 8:22–23; 45:21; 48:7.

50. Heb. *dokhyam* has not been satisfactorily explained. The ancient versions had no secure tradition as to its meaning. The colon is missing in several recensions of the Greek. The Codex Alexandrians (fifth cent. C.E.) renders the word "waves," which is the understanding of Ibn Ezra and Kimḥi. Aquila has "depths," so Rashi. Pesh. "in purity" is based on the Aramaic root *dky*. Ugaritic *dkym* (49, v. 3) is itself uncertain, *pace* M. Dahood, *Psalms*, AB, 341. The present translation is based on Heb. root *dkh*, "to crush."

51. On this phrase, see H. G. May, "Some Cosmic Connotations of *mayim rabbim*, 'many waters,'" *JBL* 74 (1955):9–21.

52. Following Kimḥi who apparently carries over the comparative *min* of the first colon into the second.

53. See above pp. 56–60, 121–22.

54. So Kimḥi, who takes *me'od* in the sense of "indubitably."

55. See above p. 83f. on Ps. 19:8.

56. On the celestial temple, see above p. 132f. *re* Ps. 24:7, and n. 59 thereon.

CHAPTER NINE: PSALM 94

1. See above p. 242, n. 104.

2. On this literary device in biblical Hebrew poetry, noted by RaShBam in his comment to Exod. 15:6, see S. E. Loewenstamm, *Comparative Studies in Biblical and Ancient Oriental Literatures*, 281–309, 496–502; J. L. Kugel, *The Idea of Biblical Poetry*, 1–2, 35. Other biblical instances of anadiplosis are Gen. 49:22; Exod. 15:6, 11, 16; Judg. 5:7; Hab. 3:8; Pss. 29:1–2; 67:4, 6;77:17; 92:10; 93:3; Prov. 31:4; Song 4:1, 8; 5:9; 7:1; Eccl. 1:2.

3. For the construction, cf. Deut. 32:4; 1 Sam. 2:3; Jer. 51:56; Pss. 29:3; 31:6. The plural form of the attribute signifies intensity; see *GKC* §124e.

4. For this epithet, cf. Gen. 18:24; Isa. 33:22; Ps. 58:12.

5. For the meaning of the biblical Heb. stem *n-k-m*, see G. E. Mendenhall, *The Tenth Generation*, 69:104; E. P. Campbell, "Two Amarna Notes," in *Magnalia Dei. Essays in Honor of George Ernest Wright*, 48–49, eds. F. M. Cross et al.; W. T. Pitard, "Amarna *ekemu* and Hebrew *naqam*," *Maariv* 3 (1982):5–25.

6. For this verb, cf. Deut. 33:2; Pss. 50:2; 80:2; Job 3:4; 10:3, 22; 37:15; cf. the noun form *yif'ah* in Ezek. 28:7, 17.

7. See above, p. 168.

8. Heb. *'atak* is always associated with speech; cf. 1 Sam. 2:3; Pss. 31:19; 75:6.

9. This point has been stressed by Y. Kaufmann, *Toledot Ha-'Emunah Ha-Yisre'elit*, 2:521.

10. For the question addressed to God, cf. Isa. 6:11; Jer. 12:24; Zech. 1:12; Pss. 6:4; 74:10; 80:5; 90:13; cf. the variant Heb. form in Hab. 1:2; Ps. 13:2–3.

11. These verses are known in Jewish tradition as "The Thirteen Attributes of God." How this enumeration is arrived at is a matter of dispute; see S. D. Luzatto, *Commentary to the Pentateuch* [Heb.] (repr. Tel Aviv, 1965), 386–87; cf. the discussion to Psalm 93 in *Mid. Tehillim*, ed. Buber, 416; see also the remarks of Tosafot to RH 17b.

12. The liturgical application of the declaration is clear from the frequency of citation; cf. Num. 14:18; Joel 2:13; Jonah 4:2; Nah. 1:3; Pss. 86:15; 103:8; 145:8; Neh. 9:17; cf. also Pss. 111:4; 112:4; 116:5; Neh. 9:31; 2 Chron. 30:9.

13. For the combination *'am* and *nahalah*, cf. Deut. 4:20; 9:26, 29; 1 Kings 8:36, 51; Isa. 47:6; Joel 4:2; Mic. 7:14.

14. 2 Kings 24:11–16.

15. 2 Kings 25:11–12, 18–22; Jer. 29:1–2.

16. Cf. "My people" in Isa. 3:15; Mic. 2:9; 3:3; Ps. 14:4. See G. W. Anderson: "Israel: Amphictyony: *'Am, Ḳāhāl, 'Edah*" in *Translating and Understanding the Old Testament. Essays in Honor of H. G. May*, 135ff., eds. H. T. Frank and W. L. Reed.

17. The prophetic social protest is to be found in Isa. chs. 1, 3 (esp. vv. 13–15); 5:8, 20, 23; 10:1–2; Jer. 5:26–28; 7:5–6; 21:11; 22:3, 13–17; Amos 1:6–8; 3:9, 10, 15; 4:1; 5:7, 10–12, 15, 24; 6:6, 12; 8:4–6; Mic. 2:1–2; 3:1–3, 5, 9–11; 6:10–12; 7:2–3; Hab. 1:2–4; 2:12; Zeph. 1:9.

18. Jer. 7:6–9; 19:4; 22:3, 17; Ezek. 7:23; 9:9; 11:6; 16:38; 22:2–4, 6, 9, 12, 13, 25, 27; 23:37, 45; 24:6, 7, 9; 33:25; 36:18; cf. Hos. 4:2; Mic. 3:10; 7:2; Hab. 2:11.

19. Cf. Jer. 15:4.

20. Cf. Ps. 53.

21. Cf. Ps. 73:11; Ezek. 8:12; Job 21:14–16.

22. As to whether true atheism existed in the ancient world, see A. B. Drachman, *Atheism in Pagan Antiquity*.

23. This is a unique phrase, probably deriving from a conception of the ear

as a discrete entity implanted in the head. For a different notion, cf. Ps. 40:7.

24. Heb. *be'ir*, "a beast," occurs in Gen. 45:17; Exod. 22:4; Num. 20:4, 8, 11; Ps. 78:48. For the abstract noun *ba'ar* "brutishness," cf. Ps. 49:11; 73:22; 92:7; Prov. 12:1; 30:2. The verbal forms occur in Isa. 19:11; Jer. 10:8, 14 (51:17), 21; Ezek. 21:36.

25. For "folly" and "fool" as the antitheses of "wisdom" and "the wise," cf. Prov. 3:35; 10:8, 23; 12:15; 13:16, 20; 14:3, 8, 16, 24; 15:2, 7, 14, 20; 16:22; 17:10, 16, 24; 21:20; 26:12; 29:9, 11; Eccl. 2:13, 14–16; 4:13; 6:8; 7:4–5; 9:17; 10:12. See T. D. Donald, "The Semantic Field of 'Folly,' " 285–92.

26. Prov. 1:7, 22.

27. Prov. 12:15.

28. Prov. 12:15.

29. Prov. 8:5.

30. Prov. 7:22; 19:29; 26:3.

31. Prov. 27:22.

32. Cf. Exod. 4:11; Prov. 20:12.

33. So Ibn Ezra, Kimḥi.

34. Cf. Isa. 7:4; 30:15; 32:17.

35. For this figurative term for death or the underworld, cf. Isa. 38:17; 51:14; Ezek. 28:8; Jonah 2:7; Pss. 16:10; 30:10; 49:10; 55:24; 103:4; Job 33:18, 22, 24, 28, 30.

36. With this clause, cf. 1 Sam. 12:22.

37. On the two Heb. words *tsedek* and *mishpat*, see M. Weinfeld, *Justice and Righteousness in Israel and the Nations*.

38. Cf. Deut. 4:6.

39. On Heb. *dumah*, see above p. 249, and n. 51 *re* Ps. 30:10; cf. Ps. 115:17.

BIBLIOGRAPHY

Aharoni, Y. "Arad: Its Inscriptions and Temple," *BA* 31 (1968):2–32.

Albright, W. F. "New Light on the Early History of Phoenician Colonization," *BASOR* 83 (1941):14–22.

———. "Baal Zaphon," in *Festschrift Alfred Bertholet zum 80 Geburtstag*, ed. W. Baumgartner. Tübingen, 1950:1–14.

———. "The Role of the Canaanites in the History of Civilization," in *The Bible and the Ancient Near East*, ed. G. E. Wright. New York. 1961: 328–62.

———. *Yahweh and the Gods of Canaan: A Historical Analysis of Two Contrasting Faiths*. Garden City, NY, 1968.

———. *Archaeology and the Religion of Israel*. 5th ed. Garden City, NY, 1969.

Allegro, J. M. "Fragments of a Qumran Scroll of Eschatological Midrashim." *JBL* 77 (1958):350–54.

Allen, T. G. *The Egyptian Book of the Dead*. Chicago, 1974.

Alliot, R. *Le culte d'Horus à Edfou*, I. Cairo, 1949.

Alster, B., ed. *Death in Mesopotamia*. Copenhagen, 1980.

Anderson, G. W. "Israel: Amphictyony: 'Am, Ḳāhāl, 'Edah," in *Translating and Understanding the Old Testament. Essays in Honor of H. G. May*, eds. H. T. Frank and W. L. Reed. Nashville, TN, 1970.

Aptowitzer, A. "The Upper Temple," *Tarbiz* 2 (1931):137–53, 257–87 [Hebrew].

Asher, A. A. *Itinerary of Benjamin of Tudela*. London, 1840; reprint, 1927.

Avery, C. B., ed. *The New Century Classical Handbook*. New York, 1962.

Avigad, N. "It Is Indeed a Pomegranate from the 'House of the Lord,' " *Qadmoniot* 24 (1991):60–61 [Hebrew].

Avishur, Y. *The Construct State of Synonyms in Biblical Rhetoric*. Jerusalem, 1977 [Hebrew].

Baly, D. *The Geography of the Bible*. New York, 1957.

Bamberger, B. J. *Fallen Angels*. Philadelphia, PA, 1952.

Barnett, R. D. "Early Shipping in the Near East," *Antiquity* 32 (1958):220–30.

Bayliss, B. "The Cult of the Dead in Assyria and Babylonia," *Iraq* 25 (1973):115–25.

Becker, J. *Gottesfurcht im Alten Testament*. Rome, 1965.

Bentz, I. L. *Personal Names in the Phoenician and Punic Inscriptions*. Rome, 1982.

Berlin, A. *Poetics and Interpretation of Biblical Narrative*. Sheffield, 1983.

———. *The Dynamics of Biblical Parallelism*. Bloomington, IN, 1985.

Beyerlin, W. *Near Eastern Texts Relating to the Old Testament*, trans. J. Bowden. Philadelphia, PA, 1978.

Bialoblotzki, S. "Yerushalayim Be-Halakhah," in *'Alei 'Ayin. The Salman Schocken Jubilee Volume*. Jerusalem, 1952:25–74 [Hebrew].

Biran, A. "Tel Dan," *BA* 37 (1974):43–48.

Boling, R. G. "Synonymous Parallelism in the Psalms," *JSS* 5 (1960): 221–55.

Bram, J. R. "Sun," *Encyclopaedia of Religion*, 14:132–43.

Brandon, S. G. F. *The Judgment of the Dead*. New York, 1967.

Brettler, M. Z. *God Is King: Understanding an Israelite Metaphor*. Sheffield, 1989.

Brichto, H. C. "Kith, Cult, Land and Afterlife—A Biblical Complex," *HUCA* 44 (1973):1–54.

Briggs, C. A. *The Book of Psalms* [International Critical Commentary]. Edinburgh, 1906.

Bright, J. A *History of Israel*, 3rd ed. Philadelphia, PA, 1973.

Bronznick, N. M. "Psalm 15:3," *Beth Mikra* 71 (1977):445–52.

Buber, M. *Good and Evil*. New York, 1952.

Buber, S., ed. *Tanḥuma*. 2 vols. Vilna, 1885.

———. *Midrash Tehillim*. Vilna, 1891; reprint, 1966.

————, ed. *Yalkut Ha-Makhiri*. Berdichev, 1900; reprint, Jerusalem, 1964.

Budge, E. A. Wallis. *The Book of the Dead*. London 1898; reprint, 1960.

Buhl, F. "Die Bedeutung des Stammes *lwṣ* oder *lyṣ* im Hebräischen," *BZAW* 27 (1914):81–86.

Buttenwieser, M. *The Psalms*. Chicago, 1938; reprint, 1969.

Campbell, E. P. "Two Amarna Notes: The Shechem City-State and Amarna Administrative Terminology," in *Magnalia Dei. Essays in Honor of George Ernest Wright*, eds. F. M. Cross et al. New York, 1975:39–54.

Cassin, E. *La splendeur divine. Introduction à l'étude de la mentalité mesopotamienne*. Paris, 1968.

Cassuto, U. *The Goddess Anath*, trans. I. Abrahams. Jerusalem, 1971.

————. *Biblical and Canaanite Literatures*. 2 vols. Jerusalem, 1972, 1979 [Hebrew].

Cazelles, H. " *'ashrê*," in *Theological Dictionary of the Old Testament*, eds. C. J. Botterwick and H. Ringgren, trans. J. T. Willis. Grand Rapids, MI, 1974. Vol. 1:445–48.

Charles, R. H. ed. *The Apocrypha and Pseudepigrapha of the Old Testament*. 2 vols. Oxford, 1913.

Childs, B. S. *Myth and Reality in the Old Testament*. Naperville, IL, 1960.

————. *Isaiah and the Assyrian Crisis*. London, 1967.

Cirlot, J. E. *A Dictionary of Symbols*. 2d. ed. New York, 1971.

Clifford, R. J. *The Cosmic Mountain in Canaan and the Old Testament*. Cambridge, MA, 1972.

Coates, G. W. "Self-abasement and Insult Formulas," *JBL* 89 (1970): 14–26.

Cogan, M. *Imperialism and Religion: Assyria, Judah and Israel in the Eighth and Seventh Centuries B.C.E.* Missoula, MT, 1974.

Cooke, C. A. *A Text-Book of North-Semitic Inscriptions*. Oxford, 1903.

Cooper, A. "The Life and Times of King David According to the Book of Psalms," in R. E. Friedman, ed., *The Poet and the Historian. Essays in Literary and Historical Criticism*. Chico, CA, 1983:117–31.

————. "Ps. 24:7, Mythology and Exegesis," *JBL* 102 (1983):37–60.

Cowley, A. *Aramaic Papyri of the Fifth Century B.C.* Oxford, 1923.

Cross, F. M. "The Tabernacle: A Study from an Archaeological and Historical Approach," *BA* 10 (1949):45–88; reprinted and slightly revised as

"The Priestly Tabernacle," in *Biblical Archaeological Reader*, eds. G. E. Wright and D. N. Freedman, New York, 1961:201–28.

———. "An Aramaic Inscription from Daskylion," *BASOR* 184 (1966):7–10.

———. "The Divine Warrior in Israel's Early Cult," in A. Altmann, *Biblical Motifs: Origins and Transformations*. Cambridge, MA, 1966:11–30.

———. "An Interpretation of the Nora Stone," *BASOR* 208 (1972): 13–19.

———. *Canaanite Myth and Hebrew Epic*. Cambridge, MA, 1973.

———. " *'el*" in *TDOT* 1: 242–81.

Dahood, M. *Psalms* [Anchor Bible], 3 vols. Garden City, NY, 1966–70.

Davison, W. T. *The Psalms*. Edinburgh, n.d.

Donald, T. D. "The Semantic Field of 'Folly' in Proverbs, Job, Psalms, and Ecclesiastes," *VT* 13 (1963):285–92.

Donner. H. and Röllig, W. *Kanaanänische und Aramäische Inschriften*. Wiesbaden, 1964.

Drachman, A. B. *Atheism in Pagan Antiquity*. Copenhagen, 1922; reprint, Chicago, IL, 1977.

Driver, G. R. and Miles, J. C. *The Babylonian Laws*. 2 vols. Oxford, 1955.

Duerr, L. *Sellin Festschrift*. Leipzig, 1927:37–48.

Eaton, J. H. *Kingship and the Psalms*. Naperville, IL, 1976.

Edzard, D. O. *Wörterbuch der Mythologie*, ed. H. W. Haussig. Stuttgart, n.d.

Ehrlich, A. B. *Die Psalmen*. Berlin, 1905.

Eissfeldt, O. *Baal Zephon, Zeus Kasios und der Durchzug der Israeliten durchs Meer*. Halle, 1932.

———. *The Old Testament: An Introduction*, trans. P. R. Ackroyd. New York, 1965.

Eliade, M. *The Forge and the Crucible*. New York, 1956.

———. *Cosmos and History*. New York, 1959.

Elioenai, M. "On the Meaning of the Verb *s-w-s/s-y-s*," *Beth Mikra* 42 (1960):323–26 [Hebrew].

Emerton, J. "A Consideration of Some Alleged Meanings of ידע in Hebrew," *JSS* 15 (1970):145–80.

Engnell, I. "Planted by Streams of Water," in *Studia Orientalia Joanni Pedersen Dicata*. Hauniae, 1953:85–96.

Eph'al, I. "Assyrian Dominion in Palestine," in *The World History of the Jewish People*, ed. A. Malamat. Vol. 4. 1979:276–89.

Fairman, H. W. "Worship and Festivals in an Egyptian Temple," *BJRL* 37 (1954):165–203.

Feliks, J. *Agriculture in Palestine in the Period of the Mishna and Talmud*. Jerusalem, 1963 [Hebrew].

Finley, M. I. *The World of Odysseus*. New York, 1959.

Fitzmyer, J. A. "The Aramaic Inscriptions of Sefire I and II," *JAOS* 81 (1961):178–222.

Fowler, J. D. *Theophoric Personal Names in Ancient Hebrew. A Comparative Study*. Sheffield, 1986.

Frankfort, H. *Kingship and the Gods*. Chicago, 1948; reprint, 1978.

––––––. *Ancient Egyptian Religion*. New York, 1961.

––––––, and Frankfort, H. A., and Jacobsen, T. *The Intellectual Adventure of Ancient Man*. Chicago, 1977.

Freedman, D. N. "But Did David Invent Musical Instruments?" *Bible Review* I (1965):49–51.

Friedlander, M. *The Jewish Religion*. London, 1935.

Friedman, M. *Pesikta' Rabbati*. Vienna, 1880; reprint, Tel Aviv, 1963.

Gandz, S. "Oral Tradition in the Bible," in *Jewish Studies in Memory of George Kohut*, eds. S. W. Baron and A. Marx. New York, 1935:248–69.

Gaster, T. H. "Ezekiel and the Mysteries," *JBL* 60 (1941):289–310.

––––––. *Festivals of the Jewish Year*. New York, 1952.

––––––. *The New Golden Bough*. Garden City, NY, 1961.

––––––. *Myth, Legend and Custom in the Old Testament*. New York, 1969.

Geiger, A. *Urschrift und Übersetzungen der Bible*. Breslau, 1857, 2d ed. Frankfort am Main, 1928; Hebrew translation J. L. Baruch, Jerusalem, 1949.

Gelling, P. and Davidson, H. R. Ellis. *The Chariot of the Sun*. New York, 1969.

Gerhardsson, B. *Memory and Manuscript*. Copenhagen, 1961.

Gilbert, M. *Shcharansky, Hero of Our Time*. New York-Philadelphia, 1986.

Ginsberg, C. D. *Introduction to the Massoretico-Critical Edition of the Hebrew Bible*. London, 1897; reprint, New York, 1966.

Ginsberg, H. L. *The Ugaritic Texts*. Jerusalem, 1936.

––––––. "Ugaritic Studies and the Bible," *BA* 8 (1945):41–58.

————. "Psalms and Inscriptions of Petition and Acknowledgement," in *Louis Ginzberg Jubilee Volume*, New York, 1945:166–68.

————. "Some Emendations in Psalms," *HUCA* 23, 1 (1950–51):97–104.

————. *Koheleth*. Tel Aviv-Jerusalem, 1961 [Hebrew].

————. "Heart," *Encyclopaedia Judaica*, 8:7.

Ginzberg, L. *The Legends of the Jews*. 7 vols. Philadelphia, PA, 1909–38.

Glueck, N. *Ḥesed in the Bible*. Cincinnati, 1967.

Goldin, J. *The Fathers According to Rabbi Nathan*. New Haven, CT, 1955.

Goldstein, J. *I Maccabees* [Anchor Bible]. Garden City, NY, 1976; *II Maccabees*, 1983.

Gordis, R. "The Knowledge of Good and Evil in the Old Testament and Qumran," *JBL* 76 (1957):123–38.

Gordon, C. H. *Ugaritic Literature*. Rome, 1949.

————. *Ugaritic Textbook*. Rome, 1965.

————. "The Wine-Dark Sea," *JNES* 37 (1978):51–52.

Goshen-Gottstein, M. "Sepher Hagu—The End of a Puzzle," *VT* 8 (1958):286–88.

Graves, R. *The Greek Myths*. New York, 1955.

Greenberg, M. *Ezekiel 1–20* [Anchor Bible], Garden City, NY, 1983.

Greenfield, J. C. "Lexicographical Notes II," *HUCA* 30 (1959):141–51.

————. "Some Aspects of Treaty Terminology in the Bible," *Fourth World Congress of Jewish Studies Proceedings*. Jerusalem, 1967 1:117–19.

Grunebaum von, G. E. *Muhammadan Festivals*. New York, 1951.

Gunkel, H. "Psalm 8: An Interpretation," *The Biblical World* 21 (1903):206–9.

————. *Die Psalmen*. Göttingen, 1926.

————. *Einleitung in die Psalmen*, ed. J. Begrich. Göttingen, 1933; reprint, 1975.

————. *The Psalms. A Form-Critical Introduction*, trans. Th. M. Horner. Philadelphia, PA, 1967.

Güterbock, H. G. "The Composition of Hittite Prayers to the Sun," *JAOS* 78 (1958):237–45.

Guthrie, M. K. C. *The Greeks and Their Gods*. Boston, 1955.

Haberman, A. *Megilloth Midbar Yehuda*. Jerusalem, 1959.

Hadas, M. *Ancilla to Classical Reading*. New York, 1954.

Halsberghe, G. H. *The Cult of Sol Invictus*. Leiden, 1972.

Hallo, W. W. "The Cultic Setting of Sumerian Poetry," *Actes de la XVII*ᵉ *Rencontre Assyriologique Internationale*, 1969:116–34.

Haran, M. "The Disappearance of the Ark," *IEJ* 13 (1963):46–58.

———. "The Priestly Image of the Tabernacle," *HUCA* 36 (1965):191–226.

———. "The Four Blessings and the Five 'Books' in the Book of Psalms," *Proceedings of the Israel National Academy of Sciences* 8, 1 (1989):1–32 [Hebrew].

Harel, M. *The Sinai Journeys*. Tel Aviv, 1973 [Hebrew].

Harrison, J. E. *Epilegomena to the Study of Greek Religion*. Cambridge, 1921.

Haupt, P. "The Harmony of the Spheres," *JBL* 38 (1919):180–83.

Haussig, H. W. *Wörterbuch der Mythologie*. Stuttgart, s.d.

Hawkes, J. *Man and Sun*. New York, 1962.

Hayes, J. H. "The Tradition of Zion's Inviolability," *JBL* 82 (1963): 419–26.

———. *Understanding the Psalms*. Valley Forge, PA, 1976.

Hayes, W. C. "The Middle Kingdom in Egypt," Cambridge Ancient History, 3rd ed. Cambridge, 1971, vol. 1,2:464–531.

Heidel, A. *The Gilgamesh Epic and Old Testament Parallels*. Chicago, 1949.

———. *The Babylonian Genesis*. Chicago and London, 1963.

Heinemann, J. "The Triennial Cycle and the Calendar," *Tarbiz* 33 (1964):362–68 [Hebrew].

Heltzer, M. "The Inscription on the Nimrud Bronze Bowl No. 5 (BM91303)," *PEQ* 114 (1982):1–6.

Hendrickson, L. "Ancient Reading," *Classical Journal* 25 (1929):182–96.

Herford, R. T. *The Ethics of the Talmud: Sayings of the Fathers*. New York, 1945.

Heschel, A. J. *The Prophets*. Philadelphia, PA, 1955.

Higger, M. *Massekhet Soferim*. New York, 1937.

Hillers, D. R. *Covenant: The History of a Biblical Idea*. Baltimore, 1969.

Hoenig, S. B. "Tarshish," *JQR* 69 (1979):181–82.

Hoftijzer, J. and Vander Kooij, *Aramaic Texts from Deir 'Alla*. Leiden, 1976.

Hollis, F. I. "The Sun-cult in Jerusalem," in *Myth and Ritual*, ed. S. H. Hooke. London, 1933:87–110.

Hooke, S. H. *Babylonian and Assyrian Religion*. Oxford, 1962.

Horovitz, H. S. and Rabin, I. A. *Mechilta D'Rabbi Ismael*. Jerusalem, 1960.

Horovitz, H. S. and Finkelstein, L., eds. *Sifrei to Deuteronomy*. Berlin, 1939; reprint, New York, 1969.

Huffmon, H. B. "The Treaty Background of Hebrew *yada'*," *BASOR* 181 (1966):31–37.

——— and Parker, B. "A Further Note on the Treaty Background of Hebrew *yada'*," *BASOR* 184 (1966):36–38.

Jacobs, L. "The Concept *Ḥasid* in Biblical and Rabbinic Literatures," *JJS* 8 (1957):143–54.

James, E. O. *Ancient Gods*. London, 1960.

Jansen, W. " 'Ašrê in the Old Testament," *HTR* 57 (1965):215–26.

Jeremias, A. *Handbuch der Altorientalischen Geistkultur*. Leipzig, 1913.

Joel, I. "The *sedarim* in the Torah," *Kirjath Sefer* 38 (1962):126–32.

Johnson, A. R. "*ḤESED* and *ḤĀSÎD*," in *Festschrift S. Mowinckel* (Norsk Teologisk Tidsskift) 56 (1955):100–112.

Jung, L. *Fallen Angels in Jewish, Christian and Mohammedan Literature*. Philadelphia, PA, 1926; reprint, New York, 1974.

Kadushin, M. *Worship and Ethics*. Evanston, IL, 1964.

Kapelrud, S. "Temple Building, A Task for Gods and Men," *Orientalia* 32 (1963):56–62.

Karmon, Y. "The Mountains Round About Jerusalem," in *Jerusalem Through the Ages*, ed. J. Abiram. Jerusalem, 1968:96–108 [Hebrew].

Kaufmann, Y. *The Biblical Account of the Conquest of Palestine*, trans. M. Dagut. Jerusalem, 1953.

———. *Toledot Ha-'Emunah Ha-Yisre'elit*. Jerusalem-Tel Aviv, 8 vols. 1937–57.

———. *The Religion of Israel*, trans. M. Greenberg. Chicago, 1960.

Kennedy, J. *An Aid to the Textual Amendment of the Old Testament*. Edinburgh, 1928.

King, E. A. "The Influence of the Triennial Cycle upon the Psalter," *JTS* 5 (1904):203–13.

Kirkpatrick, A. F. *The Book of Psalms*. Cambridge, 1914.

Kitchen, K. H. *Ancient Orient and Old Testament*. Downers Grove, IL, 1975.

Knowels, M. P. " 'The Rock, His Work Is Perfect': Unusual Imagery for God in Deut. 32," *VT* 39 (1989):307–22.

Kraeling, E. G. *The Brooklyn Museum Aramaic Papyri*. New Haven, CT, 1953.

Kramer, S. N. "Sumerian Similes: A Panoramic View of Some of Man's Oldest Literary Images," *JAOS* 89 (1969):1–10.

Krauss, S. *Talmudische Archaeologie*. Frankfort am Main, 1910.

Krinetzki, L. "Zur Poetie und Exegesis von Ps. 48," *BZ* 9 (1960):70–97.

Kugel, J. L. *The Idea of Biblical Poetry*. New Haven and London, 1981.

Labuschagne, C. J. *New Light on Some Old Testament Problems*. Pretoria, 1962.

Lambert, W. G. *Babylonian Wisdom Literature*. Oxford, 1960.

Langdon, S. *Building Inscriptions of the Neo-Babylonian Empire*. Paris, 1905.

Lauha, A. *Zaphon, der Norden und die Nordvölker im Alten Testament*. Helsinki, 1963.

Lauterbach, J. Z. *Mekhilta de-Rabbi Ishmael*, 3 vols. Philadelphia, PA, 1933–49.

Leiman, S. Z. *The Canonization of Scripture*. Hamden, CT, 1976.

Levenson, J. D. *Sinai and Zion*. Minneapolis, MN, 1985.

Levine, B. A. *JPS Commentary on Leviticus*. Philadelphia, PA, 1989.

Lewin, B. M. *Otsar Hilluf Minhagim*. Jerusalem, 1942; reprint, 1973 [Hebrew].

Lewy, J. "The Old West-Semitic Sun God Hammu," *HUCA* 18 (1943/44):429–88.

Licht, J. *The Rule Scroll*. Jerusalem, 1965 [Hebrew].

Lichtheim, M. *Ancient Egyptian Literature*, 3 vols. Berkeley, CA, 1973–80.

Liddell, H. G. and R. Scott. *A Greek-English Lexicon*. Oxford, 1968.

Lieberman, S. *Tosefta Ki-fshutah (Order Zeraim)*. New York, 1955.

———. *Hellenism in Jewish Palestine*. New York, 1962.

Liebreich, L. "The Position of Chapter Six in the Book of Isaiah," *HUCA* 25 (1954):37–40.

———. "The Hymns of the Levites for the Days of the Week," *Eretz-Israel* 3 (1954):170–73 [Hebrew].

Lipschütz, L. "Mishael b. Uzziel's Treatise on Differences between Ben Asher and Ben Naphtali," *Textus* II (1962):1–58 [Hebrew].

———. "Kitab al-Khilaf. The Book of the Hillufim," *Textus* IV (1960):1–29.

Loewenstamm, "Neshekh and T/Marbit," *JBL* 88 (1969):78–80.

———. "The Lord Is My Strength and Glory," *VT* 29 (1969):464–70.

———. "The Expanded Colon in Ugaritic and Biblical Verse," *Comparative Studies in Biblical and Ancient Oriental Literatures*. Neukirchen-Vluyn, 1980:281–309, 496–502.

Lowe, W. H. *Matnita' de-Talmuda' di-Venei Ma 'arava'*. Cambridge, 1883.

Luckenbill, D. D. *The Annals of Sennacherib*. Chicago, 1924.

Luzatto, S. D. *Commentary to the Pentateuch*. Tel Aviv, 1965, reprint [Hebrew].

Magalis, E. "Nimbus," *Encyclopaedia of Religion* 10:446.

Marmorstein, A. *The Old Rabbinic Doctrine of God*. 2 parts. London, 1927.

May, H. G. "Some Cosmic Connotations of *mayim rabbim*, 'many waters,' " *JBL* 74 (1955):9–21.

Mazar, B. "The City of David and Mount Zion," in *Jerusalem Through the Ages*, ed. J. Abiram. Jerusalem, 1968:1–11 [Hebrew].

McCarter, Kyle P. "The Early Diffusion of the Alphabet," *BA* 37 (1974):54–68.

McCartney, E. S. "Notes on Reading and Praying Audibly," *Classical Philology* 43 (1948):184–87.

McKay, J. *Religion in Judah under the Assyrians*, Naperville, IL, 1973.

Meissner, B. *Babylonien und Assyrien*. Heidelberg, 1920–25.

Melammed, E. Z. "Biblical Phrases Unique to God," *Tarbiz* 19 (1948):1–18 [Hebrew].

———. "Break-up of Stereotype Phrases as an Artistic Device in Biblical Poetry," in *Studies in the Bible Presented to Professor M. H. Segal*, eds. J. M. Grintz and J. Liver. Jerusalem, 1964:188–219 [Hebrew].

———. *Bible Commentators*. 2 vols. Jerusalem, 1975 [Hebrew].

Mendenhall, G. E. *The Tenth Generation*. Baltimore and London, 1973:69–106.

Milgrom, J. *JPS Commentary to Numbers*. Philadelphia, PA, 1990.

Miller, P. D. *The Divine Warrior in Early Israel*. Cambridge, MA, 1973.

Moore, G. F. *Judaism*. 3 vols. Cambridge, MA, 1950.

Morag, S. Review of M. Wagner, *Die Lexicalischen und Grammatikalischen Aramaismen im Alttestamentlichen Hebräisch*, *JAOS* 92 (1972):298–300.

Morgenstern, J. "The Mythological Background of Psalm 82," *HUCA* 14 (1939):29–126.

Mowinckel, S. *The Psalms in Israel's Worship*, trans. D. Ap-Thomas. 2 vols. Oxford, 1962.

Mullen, E. Th. *The Assembly of the Gods: The Divine Council in Canaanite and Hebrew Literature*. Missoula, MT, 1980.

Naveh, J. "Unpublished Phoenician Inscriptions from Palestine," *IEJ* 37 (1987):25–30.

Neubauer, A. *Medieval Hebrew Chronicles*. 2 vols. Oxford, 1887; reprint, New York, 1959.

Neufeld, E. "The Prohibition Against Loans at Interest in Ancient Hebrew Laws," *HUCA* 26 (1955):355–412.

Neusner, J. *The Memorized Torah: The Mnemonic System of the Mishnah*. Providence, RI, 1985.

Noeldeke, T. *Beiträger zur Semitischen Sprachwissenschaft*. Strassburg, 1904.

Nougayrol, J. *Le Palais Royal d'Ugarit III*. Paris, 1955.

O'Callaghan, R. T. "A Note on the Canaanite Background of Psalm 82," *CBQ* 15 (1953):311–14.

Oded, B. "Judah and the Exile," in *Israelite and Judaean History*, eds. J. H. Hayes and J. M. Miller. Philadelphia, PA, 1977:435–51.

Oesterley, W. O. E. and Box, G. H. *The Religion and Worship of the Synagogue*. London, 1907.

Oppenheim, A. Leo. "Akkadian *pul(u)ḫtu* and *mellamu*," *JAOS* 63 (1943):31–34.

———. *Ancient Mesopotamia*. Chicago, 1964.

Pallis, S. A. *The Babylonian Akitu Festival*. Copenhagen, 1926.

Patai, R. *Man and Temple*. New York, 1947.

Paul, S. M. "Unrecognized Legal Idioms of Comparative Akkadian Expressions," *RB* 86 (1979):231–39.

———. *Amos*. Minneapolis, 1991.

Pedersen, J. *Israel: Its Life and Culture*. 2 vols. London-Copenhagen, 1959.

Pitard, W. T. "Amarna *ekemu* and Hebrew *naqam*," *Maarav* 3 (1982): 5–25.

Pope, M. *Job* [Anchor Bible]. Garden City, NY, 1965.

Rad von, G. *Der Heilige Krieg im Alten Israel*. Zurich, 1951.

Richardson, H. N. "Some Notes on לץ and Its Derivatives," VT 5 (1955):163–79, 434–36.

Rin, Z. "Be-'Ikvot Leshon Ugarit," *Leshonenu* 27 (1963):10–19.

Ringgren, H. *The Faith of the Psalmists*. Philadelphia, PA, 1963.

Roberts, J. J. M. "The Davidic Origin of the Zion Tradition," *JBL* 92 (1973) 329–44.

———. "Zion in the Theology of the Davidic-Solomonic Empire," in *Studies in the Period of David and Solomon and Other Essays*, ed. T. Ishida. Winona Lake, IN, 1982:93–108.

Robinson, A. "Zion and Saphon in Psalm XLVIII 3," VT 24 (1974): 118–23.

Rofé, A. *Israelite Belief in Angels in the Pre-exilic Period as Evidenced by Biblical Traditions*. Hebrew University Ph.D. dissertation, 1969 [Hebrew].

Sakenfeld, K. D. *The Meaning of Ḥesed in the Hebrew Bible*. Missoula, MT, 1978.

Sambursky, S. *The Physical World of the Greeks*, trans. M. Dagut. New York, 1962.

Sanders, J. A. *The Psalms Scroll of Qumran Cave II (IIQPsᵃ)*. Oxford, 1965.

Sarna, N. M. "The Psalm for the Sabbath Day," *JBL* 81 (1962):155–68.

———. *Understanding Genesis*. New York, 1966, 1970.

———. "Psalm XIX and the Near Eastern Sun-god Literature," in *Fourth World Congress of Jewish Studies Papers*. Jerusalem, 1967:171–75.

———. Review of J. Mann, *The Bible as Read and Preached in the Old Synagogue*, vol. 2, *JBL* 87 (1968):100–106.

———. "*Ṣaphon*" in *Encyclopaedia Mikra'it* 6:747–51.

———. Review of M. Sokoloff, *The Targum to Job from Qumran Cave XI*, *IEJ* 26 (1976):151–53.

———. "The Psalm Superscriptions and the Guilds," in *Studies in Jewish Religious and Intellectual History Presented to Alexander Altmann*, eds. S. Stein and R. Loewe. University of Alabama, 1979:281–300.

———. *Exploring Exodus*. New York, 1986.

———. *JPS Commentary on Genesis*. Philadelphia, PA, 1989.

———. *JPS Commentary on Exodus*. Philadelphia, PA, 1991.

Scharff, A. *Aegyptische Sonnenlieder*. Berlin, 1922.

Schiffman, L. "The New Halakhic Letter (4QMMT) and the Origin of the Dead Sea Sect," *BA* 53 (1990):64–73.

Schirmann, H. *Ha-Shirah Ha-'Ivrit Bi-Sefarad U-bi-Provence*. Jerusalem-Tel Aviv, 1961.

Schroeder, O. "Miscellen 2. Zu Psalm 19," ZAW 34 (1914):69–70.

Segal, M. H. *Sefer Ben Sira Ha-Shalem*. Jerusalem, 1953.

———. "El, Elohim and YHWH in the Bible," *JQR* 46 (1955):89–115.

———. *Mevo' Ha-Mikra'*. 4 vols. Jerusalem, 1956.

Silberman, L. H., ed. *Orality, Aurality, and Biblical Narration. Semeia* 39:1986.

Skehan, P. "A Fragment of the 'Song of Moses' (Deut. 32) from Qumran," *BASOR* 136 (1954):12–15.

Smith, M. "The Near Eastern Background of Solar Language for Yahweh," *JBL* 109 (1990):29–39.

Smith, W. Robertson. *The Religion of the Semites*. London, 1889; reprint, New York, 1959.

Snaith, N. H. "The Triennial Cycle and the Psalter," ZAW 51 (1933): 302–7.

———. *The Jewish New Year Festival*. London, 1947.

Spenser, A. J. *Death in Ancient Egypt*. Middlesex, England, 1986.

Strugnell, J. "The Angelic Liturgy at Qumran—4Q Serek Širot 'Olat Haššabat," *VT Sup.* 7 (1960):318–45.

Swete, H. B. *Introduction to the Old Testament in Greek*. Cambridge, 1902.

Tadmor, H. "Sennacherib's Campaign in Judah—Historical and Historiographical Considerations," *Zion* 50 (1985):65–80 [Hebrew].

Tallqvist, K. *Der Assyrische Gott*. Helsingfors, 1932.

———. *Akkadische Götterepitheta*. Helsingfors, 1938.

Tawil, H. "Hebrew, צלח הצלח Akkadian *ešēru/šūšru*: A Lexicographical Note," *JBL* 95 (1976):405–13.

Thackeray, H. St. J., trans. *Josephus, The Jewish War*. Cambridge, MA, 1961.

Thompson, S. *Motif Index of Folk Literature*. Bloomington, IN, 1975.

Thureau-Dangin, F. "La fin de la domination gutiene," *RA* 11 (1912):111–20.

Tigay, J. H. *The Evolution of the Gilgamesh Epic*. Philadelphia, PA, 1982.

———. *You Shall Have No Other Gods: Israelite Religion in the Light of Hebrew Inscriptions*. Atlanta, GA, 1986.

Torr, C. *Ancient Ships*, rev. ed. Chicago, 1964.

Tournay, R. "Le psaume VIII et la doctrine biblique du Nom," *RB* 78 (1971):18–30.

Treves, M. "The Date of Psalm XXIV," *VT* 10 (1960):428–34.

Tromp, N. J. *Primitive Conceptions of Death and the Netherworld in the Old Testament*. Rome, 1969.

Tsevat, M. *A Study of the Language of the Biblical Psalms*. Philadelphia, PA, 1955.

———. "God and the Gods in Assembly," *HUCA* 40–41 (1969–70): 123–37.

Tur-Sinai, N. H. *Thesaurus*, vol. 10. Jerusalem, 1949.

———. *Ha-Lashon Ve-Ha-Sefer II*. Jerusalem, 1950 [Hebrew].

———. *The Book of Job*. Tel Aviv, 1954 [Hebrew].

Urbach, E. E. *The Sages: Their Concepts and Beliefs*. Jerusalem, 1945 [Hebrew].

Vaux de, R. *Ancient Israel: Its Life and Institutions*. New York, 1961.

Viviano, B. T. *Study as Worship*. Leiden, 1978.

Wagner, N. E. "*Rinnah* in the Psalter," *VT* 10 (1960):435–41.

Wanke, G. "Die Zionstheologie der Korachiten," *BZAW* 97 (1966): 23–31.

Weidner, E. *Die Inschriften Tukulti-Ninurtas I*. *AfO* Beiheft 12 (1959).

Weinfeld, M. *Deuteronomy and the Deuteronomic School*. Oxford, 1972.

———. "Instructions for Visitors in the Bible and in Ancient Egypt," in *Egyptological Studies*, ed. S. Israelit-Groll. Jerusalem, 1982.

———. "Zion and Jerusalem as Religious and Political Capital: Ideology and Utopia," in *The Poet and the Historian*, ed. R. E. Friedman. Chico, CA, 1983.

———. *Justice and Righteousness in Israel and the Nations*. Jerusalem, 1985.

Weingarten, S. H. "The Ten Commandments and Their Order," *Beth Mikra* 59 (1974):549–71.

Weiss, M. *The Bible from Within*. Jerusalem, 1984.

Westermann, C. *Praise and Lament in the Psalms*. Atlanta, GA, 1965.

Widengren, G. *The King and the Tree of Life in Ancient Near Eastern Religion*. Uppsala, Finland, 1951.

Wieder, N. *The Judean Scrolls and Karaism*. London, 1962.

Wilson, J. A. *The Culture of Ancient Egypt*. Chicago, 1960.

Worrel, J. "עצה 'Counsel' or 'Council' at Qumran," *VT* 20 (1970): 65–74.

Wright, G. E. *The Old Testament Against Its Environment.* London, 1950.

Xenophon. *Memorabilia*, trans. E. C. Marchant. Cambridge, MA, 1953.

Yadin, Y. "The Expedition to the Judean Desert, 1960, Expedition D," *IEJ* 11 (1961):36–52.

———. "The Ben Sira Scroll from Masada," *Eretz-Israel* 8 (1967):1–45 [Hebrew].

Yahuda, A. S. *The Language of the Pentateuch in Its Relation to Egyptian.* Oxford, 1933.

Yalon, H. "Leshonot *y-d-', l-m-d*," *Tarbiz* 36 (1967):396–400 [Hebrew].

———. *Pirkei Lashon.* Jerusalem, 1971 [Hebrew].

Yeivin, I. "The Divisions into Sections in the Book of Psalms," *Textus* VII (1969):76–102.

Young, G. D. "UTU and Justice: A Neo-Sumerian Proverb," *JCS* 24 (1972):132.

Zlotnick, D. "Memory and the Integrity of the Oral Tradition," *JNES* 16–17 (1984–85):229–41.

———. *The Iron Pillar—Mishnah: Redaction, Form and Intent.* Jerusalem, 1988.

Zulay, M. *Piyyutei Yannai.* Berlin, 1938.

GENERAL INDEX

Abel, 9
Abimelech, 179, 181
Abraham, 19, 87, 119–20
Absalom, 120, 125, 126, 182
Adam, 19, 54, 64
Aeschylus, 13
afterlife, 45, 101, 142–43
Akkadian language, 39, 45, 55, 88,
    143, 157, 163, 183, 185
alchemists, 90
Alexander the Great, 13
Alexandria, Egypt, 12, 13, 15, 16,
    74, 121, 178
alliteration, 31
Amalekites, 104, 130, 132
"Amen," 16
Ammisaduqa, King of Babylon, 83
anadiplosis, 192
angels, divine beings, 58, 63–64,
    132, 169
  fallen, 175
  guardian, 173–74, 175
antiphonal chants, 99–100, 111,
    123–24, 126–27
Aphek, Battle of, 130
Apollo, 83

aposeopesis, 61
Arad, 21
Aramaic language, 85, 157
  script of, 14
Arameans, 172
Aranne, Zalman, 5–6
Aristophanes, 13
Ark of the Covenant, 127–31, 184
  brought to Jerusalem, 20, 22,
    109, 129, 131, 155
  cherubim on, 127–28, 133
  disappearance of, 133
  in First Temple, 127, 128–29,
    131, 133
  military function of, 128, 129–31
arrogance, 33, 35, 59, 94, 102,
    128–29, 144–45, 156, 174,
    199
Asaph, 18–19, 21, 22
Asaphites, 18–19, 21–22
Asher, 179
Ashtoreth, 72
Ashurbanipal, King of Assyria, 83
"assembly" ('edah), 46
assembly of gods, 156–57, 168–70,
    173

BIBLICAL REFERENCE INDEX

Biblical verses are in **boldface**, followed by book pages.

About the Author

Nahum M. Sarna is Dora Golding Professor Emeritus of Biblical Studies at Brandeis University. Born in England, he received his B.A. and M.A. from the University of London and received a Diploma in Rabbinics from Jews' College in London. He earned his Ph.D. in Biblical Studies and Semitic Languages at The Dropsie College in Philadelphia. For several years he was the Librarian of the Jewish Theological Seminary and a member of the Bible faculty. A past chairman of the Department of Near Eastern and Judaic Studies at Brandeis University, he has also served as Visiting Professor at Columbia University, Yale University, Dropsie College, and Andover Newton Theological School. He is also a past President of the Association for Jewish Studies. He is the recipient of honorary degrees from Gratz College in Philadelphia, the Hebrew Union College-Jewish Institute of Religion in New York, and the Hebrew College in Brookline, Massachusetts.

In 1993 Dr. Sarna received the first annual Jewish Scholarship Award from the National Foundation for Jewish Culture. In celebration of his seventieth birthday, his students and colleagues presented him with a Festschrift of scholarly studies. He is the General Editor of the Jewish Publication Society's Commentary on the Torah and author of its commentaries on Genesis and Exodus. He served as a member of the translation committee of the most recent JPS translation of the Hebrew Bible. He is also the author of *Understanding Genesis* and *Exploring Exodus* (both published by Schocken Books). He is the editor of the *Proceedings of the American Academy for Jewish Research* and has contributed major articles to the *Encyclopaedia Judaica*, the *Encyclopaedia Britannica*, the *Encyclopaedia of Religion*, the *Encyclopaedia Hebraica*, and the *Anchor Bible Dictionary*. He lives in Newton, Massachusetts.

Other Schocken Books of Related Interest